THE CREAKY TRAVELER IN IRELAND

Clare, Kerry, and West Cork

THE CREAKY TRAVELER IN IRELAND

CLARE, KERRY, AND WEST CORK

A Journey for the Mobile but Not Agile

WARREN ROVETCH

SENTIENT PUBLICATIONS, LLC

First Sentient Publications edition 2006
Copyright © 2006 by Warren Rovetch

A paperback original

Cover design by Kim Johansen, Black Dog Design
Cover photo by Gerda Rovetch
Book design by Rudy Ramos
Maps and illustrations by Michael Burrell

Library of Congress Cataloging-in-Publication Data

Rovetch, Warren.
The creaky traveler in Ireland : Clare, Kerry, and West Cork : a journey for the
mobile but not agile / by Warren Rovetch.
p. cm.
Includes bibliographical references and index.
ISBN 1-59181-027-2
1. Clare (Ireland)—Description and travel. 2. Kerry (Ireland)—Description and
travel. 3. Cork (Ireland : County)—Description and travel. 4. Rovetch, Warren—
Travel—Ireland. I. Title.
DA990.C59R68 2006
914.1904'824—dc22
2005037663

Printed in the United States of America

10 9 8 7 6 5 4 3 2 1

SENTIENT PUBLICATIONS
A Limited Liability Company
1113 Spruce Street
Boulder, CO 80302
www.sentientpublications.com

For G,
Whom I still love very much.

Contents

ACKNOWLEDGMENTS

AS A TRAVELER AND WRITER, it is my remarkable good fortune to have as a constant companion my dear wife G. Her admirable qualities include an inexhaustible supply of songs and poems that entertain and illuminate many a scene along the way, an artist's eye that helps me see much of what I would otherwise miss, and unerring good judgment and good taste that keep me out of trouble on the road and in these pages.

My three daughters, Jennifer Rovetch, Emily Whitman, and Lissa Rovetch, combine an array of remarkable talents any writer would be happy to apply to his work. It is a far better book than it would have been without their careful reading, suggestions, and corrections. Ann Guthrie, a superb potter, and Tom Woodard, teacher and writer, both good friends, were remarkably adept at nailing places where the text strayed and at correcting my casual approach to punctuation.

To Gabriel Fitzmaurice of Moyvane, Listowel, Co Kerry—Irish poet, essayist, critic, editor, and teacher—I owe a special debt. First, I have shamelessly mined his wonderful book *Kerry On My Mind—Of Poets, Pedagogues, and Place* (Salmon Publishing, 1999) for insights and poetry on writers and football, including the poem, "At the Ball Game." And then, Gabriel, ever generous, read my chapters on these subjects to catch the odd error. While on Listowel, I want to mention others who helped make our visit there the high point of our trip. Cara Trant, able and engaging Manager and Artistic Director of the Kerry Literary & Cultural Centre, including the Writers' Museum, took a day of her valuable time to introduce us to the essentials of Listowel and brought together a small group to share experiences and insights regarding North Kerry's literary tradition. I had a first-rate tutorial thanks to this group: Danny Hannon, friend to John B. Keane and other writers; Jack McKenna, a North Kerry historian who shared his family background and unique railroad experience; and Jimmy Deenihan, member of parliament and the driving force behind the creation of the Kerry Literary & Cultural Centre, which includes the phenomenal Writers' Museum. Cara also helped me with English pronunciations of Irish words. In our correspondence, John Mulvihill, principal of St. Michael's, was himself a fountain of ideas and information on the question of Listowel's literary tradition. Steve Simons of Event Ireland filled in background on the design of the Writers' Museum.

Others in Listowel helped make our experience there complete. Vincent Carmody had us into his home on our first evening to share a lifetime of experiences and his wonderful scrapbooks. Maria O'Gorman, manager of the Harvest Festival, made sure we were in the middle of festival activities. John O'Flaherty dropped off a copy of his book on the history of the Listowel Races. Brendan Daly took time out of a busy day just before the race week to share his fifty-two years of experience as secretary of the Listowel Race Committee. Armel Whyte, chef/proprietor of Allo's Bar, Bistro & Townhouse, along with Ailish Mullane and other members of the family, made sure we never lacked for comfort or sustenance. And thanks to Stephen Flynn and his quartet of Irish music makers at the Harp & Lion across the street from Allo's. Every night, through our bedroom window, their Irish tunes lulled us off to sleep.

My thanks for a successful trip and rewarding experiences go to many others. At the beginning of our trip, the warm welcome of Ita and Noel Walsh at the Rockyview Farmhouse in Fanore, Co Clare was a great launch for our Irish adventure. Suzanne Crosbie shared her personal experiences of a ten-year battle to preserve environmental wonders of the Burren. Willy Daly introduced us to matchmaking, an art of which he is a master. In Dingle, Diarmuid O Dalaigh, executive director of the Diseart Institute of Education and Celtic Culture, shared his insights on Celtic spirituality. He also introduced us to others at the institute, including Sister Dorothy Costello, whose warmth and love will remain with us always. In Kenmare, the brilliant sculptor Dick Joynt spoke to us through his masterpiece, *The Musicians.* In Castletownbere, Mary Wrigley, proprietor of The Old Presbytery, provided a room with a memorable view. Donal O'Driscoll very generously took the better part of a day to introduce me to road bowling and the intricacies of his modern fishing boat. Sue Booth Forbes shared something of her self and Anam Cara, her artists' and writers' retreat. Michael Byrne brought us up to speed on the Eircom Information Age Project. Pat and Loreto Hannon at Ardsollus Farm in Quin provided the perfect wind-up for a fine trip.

The staff of several Irish agencies and government offices were of great help with background information and essential contacts. They included Graine Travers of Shannon Development, Miles Carey and Alan Williams of Clare County Council, Kate Kennelly, Arts Officer of the Kerry County Council, Chris O'Grady of the Heritage Office, and all the folks at Tidy Towns.

I want to thank the brilliant and kind poet Seamus Heaney, who also claims to be creaky, for permission to reprint his poem "The Peninsula" (*Door into the Dark,* Faber, 1989). Thanks also to Maurice MacMahon for extracts from his father Bryan MacMahon's autobiography, *The Master* (Poolbeg, 1993); to Billy Keane for his father John B. Keane's love song *Sweet Listowel;* and to Brendan Kennelly for his poems "The Gift" and "The Learning" (*A Time for Voices,* Bloodaxe Books, 1990).

Last, but by no means least, my gratitude to Connie Shaw, Sentient Publications' patient, wise, and helpful editor and publisher, without whom there would be no book.

Thanks again to all.

WARREN ROVETCH
The Creaky Traveler
Boulder, Colorado
March 2006

INTRODUCTION

The Creaky Traveler in Ireland—Clare, Kerry, and West Cork is the second book in a series that I intend to go on for as long as I do. The first in the "series" (this may be like the Colorado Rockies being on a "winning streak" when they win two games in a row) was *The Creaky Traveler in the North West Highlands of Scotland.* Much to my delight the book did rather well. It seemed that even non-creakies found it entertaining and informative. The message of that book and this book is "get up and go." Plan well and in a way that indulges your interests and pleasures. Remember, as Confucius says, "A journey of a thousand miles begins with a single step."

MOBILE BUT NOT AGILE

FOR THE GROWING RANKS of the mobile but not agile, my wife Gerda (who prefers to be called "G") and I hope we have demonstrated in this book that independent travel is workable, even for those of us who have moved into the third quarter of our lives. G likes it known that she is 3x3x3x3. (For the arithmetically challenged, that's 81.) I am close behind. While the scope of what we can manage has diminished some over time (we walk, but not very much; we climb stairs, but not too many), our capacity to find meaning and enjoyment has grown. Now after over twenty-five trips to Europe, some of the things we have learned about travel, what you might call tricks of the trade, are outlined in a separate section at the end of the book, *On Being a Traveler.*

EXPERIENCE AND FEELINGS

ABOVE ALL, we travel by the rule of the poet William Henry Davies. It is a rule we recommend highly.

> *What is this life if, full of care,*
> *We have no time to stand and stare.*

This leads to another goal of this book. It is to share experiences and feelings of our trip and whatever insights we may have gained. Ireland, especially the west where we traveled, is a beautiful and dramatic place with interesting and welcoming people who are now at a pivotal time in their history. Three turns of speech that we heard often express an attitude to life the Irish willingly shared:

Brilliant! "I'll have poached eggs and bacon for breakfast, please." "Brilliant!" "We are going to drive over to Ballybunnion today." "Brilliant!"

It could be worse. "We got a flat tire." "It could be worse." "My wife broke her leg." "It could be worse."

I shouldn't worry. "Our flight is an hour late." "I shouldn't worry." "Tomorrow's weather doesn't look good." "I shouldn't worry."

In the midst of pouring rain, don't be surprised to be told, "Nice day." I came to understand this meant, we are both alive and good things may happen to us. The Irish are incredibly optimistic.

Irish writer Nuala O'Faolain sees Ireland as "a place all its own. The people are gifted in living. They risk themselves all the time. They live intensely. It's a way of life." Brian Bell considers Irish character to be "as elusive as the fairy gold to be found at the end of Irish rainbows and their conversation as elliptical as an incomplete jigsaw puzzle ... There's a recklessness, a tendency towards exaggeration."

In *John Bull's Other Island,* George Bernard Shaw looks at the melancholy side of Ireland. "Your wits can't thicken in that soft moist air, on those white springy roads, in those misty rushes and brown bogs, on those hillsides of granite rock and magenta heather. You've no such colors in the sky, no such lure in the distance, no such sadness in the evenings. Oh the dreaming! the dreaming! the torturing, heartscalding, dreaming, dreaming, dreaming."

G.K. Chesterton examines contradictions in his poem *Ballad of the White Horse.*

> *For the great Gaels of Ireland*
> *Are the men that god made mad,*
> *For all their wars are merry*
> *And all their songs are sad.*

It may all be true—O'Faolain, Bell, Shaw, Chesterton. But I don't think any of their words touch the economic and social transformation reshaping the country today. Ireland is both very old and very new and is becoming newer every day at a very rapid rate. Not so long ago Ireland was at war with itself. Now, in less than one generation, Ireland has put itself together in a way the rest of the world would do well to emulate. As J. P. Donleavy puts it, "In spite of all its old ways, believe it or not, Ireland is becoming by leaps and bounds a most glamorous country." Ireland's story is the story of the Celtic Tiger.

THE CELTIC TIGER

IRELAND WAS MOROSE, backward looking, and defensive. Socially, it offered a drab gray landscape. It faced declining employment and rising national debt. It had only one export: its own people. In 1987 government, employers, trade unions and farm groups said, Enough! In remarkable acts of leadership, these interests got together in a series of national programs—National Recovery (1977–1990); Economic and Social Programs (1991–1993); Competitiveness and Work (1994–1997); the €57 billion ($69.5 billion) National Development Plan (2000–2006)—and today Ireland is the richest country in the European Union after Luxembourg.

They made secondary education free, college virtually so, called women out of the kitchen into the workplace, and provided work-place training, insuring a well-trained English-speaking workforce. They slashed corporate taxes to 12 ½ percent, the lowest rate in Europe. They kept wages and government spending in check, set out to double the number of Ph.D.'s graduating in science and technol-ogy, and began pursuing brainy people from around the world to do research in Ireland. Having made themselves attractive, the Irish suc-cessfully recruited the world's top global companies including phar-maceuticals, medical devices, software design, chip production, and computer assembly. Ireland went after a tiger's share of worldwide growth in new technology.

Fifteen years ago, Canada's per capita gross domestic product was two and a half times Ireland's. Today Ireland's is 20 percent greater than Canada's.

There are four million people in Ireland and seventy million peo-ple of Irish descent worldwide. Now, as CBS's *60 Minutes* reported, "The Celtic Tiger is calling its cubs to come home."

Martin and Connie O'Brien are leaving New York after immigrat-ing to America fifteen years ago. "Everybody else is going back; there must be something good going on there."

Paul McBride is back in Ireland from Seattle where he went nine years ago to work for Microsoft. "At the time, I think most of our class emigrated. There was just no option for people." McBride runs a certification program for Microsoft, one of four such sites worldwide.

Tom Garvin, Irish historian, says he "has to make a mental effort to remember the Dublin of the 1950s, in many ways a Third World city. Horses, no motorcars, children in bare feet, dirt everywhere, people living in slums, no television, no bathroom—a really impoverished European country that really didn't seem to be going anywhere."

Conor O'Kelly left Ireland in 1983 to work on Wall Street. He now runs a financial services company in Dublin. "People are getting a lot of joy out of the success. You know I think we feel we deserve it. We've had it bad for so long."

Microsoft, Intel, and Dell, leaders in the 21st century's technological revolution, are at the head of the global parade in Ireland. Intel recently opened a $5 billion computer chip plant in Co Kildare and has plans for a $2 billion expansion. Four thousand workers are assembling Dell computers in Limerick, the town where in Frank McCourt's *Angela's Ashes* jobs were as rare as jewels. Google has built a Dublin-based European hub that looks like a California college campus. EBay opened a new European hub in Ireland. Hewlett-Packard and Intel funded a nanotechnology research center at Trinity College in Dublin.

Unemployment is down from 20 percent 15 years ago to 4 percent today. Economic growth is twice the EU rate. Latvian workers are imported to pick potatoes. *Oto Polska*, a Polish language TV program, is broadcast in Ireland. In Dublin there is a six-month wait list for $60,000 BMWs. The sale of Guinness is down and Budweiser is up. Over 50 percent of women are employed. Women were elected president of the Republic twice, Mary Robinson in 1990 and Mary McAleese in 1997. Church attendance is less than half of what it was a decade ago and the church's authority has declined even further. Divorce has been legalized; condoms are sold over the counter. Writers and poets are treated as national treasures. Along with global corporations they get special tax treatment. Ita Walsh, B&B proprietor, and her family go skiing in Switzerland every year.

This sense of a country in full flight of major social and economic changes was much on my mind as we began our trip. I wondered what impact these changes might have on our experience in Ireland.

TRANSCENDENT BEAUTY

OVER THE PERIOD of a month, G and I wandered from Ballyvaghan on Galway Bay, at the top of Co Clare, to Mizen Head, the tip of a finger of land in West Cork that reaches into the Atlantic at the bottom of Ireland. Along the way we followed roads to the ends of three other peninsulas—Dingle, Beara, and Sheep's Head—and to many a diversion that attracted our fancy along the way. We covered less than two hundred miles north to south and saw an amazing array of brilliant landscapes and spectacular seascapes. The changes in environment from gut wrenching to soul touching occurred almost one minute to the next: fractured limestone terraces, pastoral countryside, crashing seacoast, glinting lough, heathery bogland, peaceful lake, blue-granite mountains, emerald-green valleys, cliffs and coves, sounds of the sea, a quiet breeze stroking a field of flowers, ruined castles, abandoned abbeys, Neolithic remains, holy wells, ring forts, misty sun, and soft rain.

There is history. There is change. There is music and there is talk. Above all there is transcendent beauty, always there, ready for discovery. As T. S. Eliot wrote, "The journey, not the arrival matters." John Wayne's Ireland of *The Quiet Man* is long gone. Much remains of interest and excitement for any traveler. The Ireland G and I pursued on our journey of discovery is outlined in Chapter 1, "Creative Design for Travel."

So, off we amble, ready for a traveler's rewards as we stumble on one thing in pursuit of another.

CHAPTER ONE

CREATIVE DESIGN FOR TRAVEL

PLANNING A EUROPEAN TRIP of three to four weeks is for me a satisfying and creative exercise. I seek a pattern and rhythm of memorable experiences that add up to a balanced whole. I want the footprints of a trip to be our own—my wife Gerda (who prefers to be called G) and I. As I plan a trip I always have five principles in mind: (1) Nourish the soul. (2) Feed the mind. (3) Rest the body. (4) Leave time for happenings. (5) Have fun.

There is of course the "creaky" aspect to my traveling and it takes no effort to keep it in mind. The body provides a constant reminder. This leads me to a central purpose of this book, to demonstrate how creaky travelers, the growing ranks of mobile but not agile, can plan and manage successful, independent travel.

I begin planning a trip by painting pictures in my mind. I learn something of the character of the different places we might stop over—scenery, history, unique qualities, special events, interesting people, new things to learn, suitability for creaky traveling. I then choose the best scenes and assemble them in a moving picture—where we will stop and stay and ground we will cover. Each stop of three to four days becomes a setting for new experiences.

The bed and breakfasts or small hotels we choose demand a great deal of consideration. These are the rules: (1) Small, not more than six rooms. (2) Distinctive personality, run by an onsite owner and not a hired hand. (3) Beautifully situated and conveniently located near what we want to see and do. (4) En suite room (W.C. and bath or shower), not more than one flight up. Good, natural light is a must, and view is a plus. (5) Reputation for superior breakfasts. (6) Affordable, but occasional splurge permitted. (7) Finally, a place where we wouldn't mind being rained in for a day.

My planning tools are detailed maps, guidebooks, old movies, and, increasingly, the Internet. Virtually every county, town, or castle that hopes you will come and visit has a website that extols its virtues and offers photos. In addition to exaggerated claims, you have to be careful about photos. Many are taken from vantage points no ordinary human, much less a creaky one, could ever manage. (I do remember an honest claim made by the tourist board of Dorset, a county in the southwest of England. "Come to beautiful Dorset," the brochure exclaimed. "If you go to the continent and it rains, you will be sad. In Dorset, you expect rain, and sunny days are a bonus.")

Our Ireland Scenario

A SCENARIO EMERGED from my planning for *The Creaky Traveler in Ireland—Clare, Kerry, and West Cork.* Like most good travel adventures, the trip once begun became a work-in-progress.

Denver-Toronto-Shannon. Depart Denver on Air Canada at 3:45 P.M., a decent hour allowing for an easy morning at home. Stove shut off? Plants watered? Reading matter in the carry-on? The schedule also left plenty of connecting time in Toronto, seven hours in the air from Toronto to Ireland (enough time for a decent nap), and arrival in Shannon at 11:35 A.M., also a decent hour. Getting in at six or seven in the morning makes for a grouchy time, especially when your body is five or more hours behind. The website for Shannon Airport provided floor plans, showing it was a relatively small airport—not too far from plane to baggage and customs, not too many overseas flights coming in at the same time so baggage and customs would be fast, and rental cars nearby. Our car of choice was a Ford Focus, a vehicle that I could get in and out of without bumping my head. It has upright seating and a good field of vision.

Co Clare and the Burren. From Shannon to the Rockyview Farmhouse in Fanore would be about an hour's drive. It would put us in the northeastern corner of County ("Co") Clare, minutes from the rocky shore of the Atlantic and in the middle of the Burren. Being near water is always a priority; seeing ocean from a bedroom window is a bonus. My vision of the Burren was of a world apart from the usual pastoral scene of the Emerald Isle. I pictured endless and remorseless wind and rain eroding a porous hundred-square-mile limestone plateau, etching an otherworldly surface of raw beauty—stony pillows, deep fissures, cliffs, and terraces—a rare combination of light, rock, and water.

Then there was the great Battle of Mullaghmore I wanted to investigate. Twenty-five ordinary citizens of Co Clare had banded together, mortgaged their homes, and fought a ten-year battle to stop the government's plan to build a Burren visitor center that the good citizens said would be "a man-made affront to all that was holy about the gloriously eccentric symmetry of Mullaghmore." The people won and in the process forced a change in Irish planning laws. This was a war I wanted to learn more about, and I wanted to talk to the people involved.

Because of my work with public schools in the States, I was interested in talking with Irish kids to find out how they saw themselves and their futures. The headmaster at Fanore Primary thought this would be as interesting for the kids as for me. Fanore was to be the first of my visits to four primary schools and talks with sixth graders in the course of the trip. Finally, G and I were to meet Willie Daly, horse trader and a third generation Irish matchmaker of great repute.

We planned to meet with Willie during the famous Lisdoonvarna Matchmaking Festival.

The Dingle Peninsula in Co Kerry. A small car ferry would take us south over the River Shannon and then a dull drive to Lispole, a rural farm and fishing area on the Dingle Peninsula. The Dingle was the first of four peninsulas in our plan. The other three, going in steps from north to south, were Beara, Sheep's Head, and Mizen. The prospect of the Lispole stay intrigued me. G and I were to be the only guests at the Old Farmhouse. According to one guidebook, the owner, an English woman, had skippered an eleven-ton teak sloop, run a bookstore, and raised lurchers. Nearby, were the ruins of the fifteenth-century Minard Castle, a testimony to the Cromwellian purges of the seventeenth century. There was also the North Pole Inn, a pub in Annascaul opened by Tom Crean, hero of Antarctic exploration. He had been a member of both the Scott and Shackleton expeditions. It is said that Tom came home to get married and raise a family after he had grown tired of pissing into the Antarctic wind.

The Dingle Peninsula is *Gaeltacht*, meaning it is one of the few remaining Irish-speaking areas. Curious as to how this affected the way people lived and the quality of their lives, I arranged to visit with a class in Lispole Primary School, one of the schools in Ireland where all classes are taught in Gaelic. I also arranged a meeting with staff of the Diseart Institute of Education and Celtic Culture that had been established to enable people to access and understand Celtic culture. I was looking for the meaning of *spiritual,* and there was said to be a lot of this in Ireland, with retreats springing up all over. I thought the Diseart Institute might help.

The Dingle Peninsula was described in one guide as "a place of intense beauty with long beaches and staggering splinter-slatted rocks that define the extraordinary coast at Slea Head." We thought a stroll along a Dingle beach would be just the thing for a misty afternoon. If time and circumstances allowed, we would look in on some of the stone monuments, many from the early Christian period. Some articles I read warned of commercial excesses along the Dingle tourist trail, great attention to a frisky porpoise in Dingle Bay, and an addiction to an old movie, *Ryan's Daughter*, that featured romantic romps in the sand at Slea Head. I hoped we wouldn't find all this intrusive.

Kenmare. After Dingle, our plan was to head for what guide books call "neatly organized, pleasantly cosmopolitan" Kenmare in Co Kerry. This stop was on our way to the Beara Peninsula and a break in what would otherwise be a long drive. I hate long drives, especially on the wrong side of the road. It would also be time for indulgence. We planned to stay at Sallyport House—silk bedspreads, thick carpets, "mod cons," and views to Kenmare Bay. With its delicatessens and designer boutiques, Kenmare was said to feel like a "prosperous foreign enclave." Well, okay. But in addition to the necessary stop, I was curious about Kenmare's status as an award-winning Tidy Town. What, I wondered, was an official Tidy Town? It had a childlike ring to it. (Tidy your room now! Or no playtime.) I would talk with Father Patrick Murphy, parish priest and Chairman of the Kenmare Tidy Town Committee.

The Beara Peninsula. Beara was described as starting out "polite and lush" and then becoming "barren and remote with an energy of its own, bounding in great ribs of rock thirty miles out into the ocean." It held great promise. We planned to stay in Castletownbere at The Old Presbytery, a B&B perched on a bluff at water's edge. We were promised a room with a large bay window looking out over a garden to the harbor, Ireland's second largest fishing port. The business of the town involved much more than tourism, and that appealed to me. As to plans for Beara, in my reading I had come across "road bowling," a sport played only in this part of Co Cork, in Co Armagh in the north, and in parts of Germany and Holland. Two grown men compete, throwing a twenty-eight-ounce iron ball down two miles or so of curving back roads to see who can get from one end to the other in the fewest throws. Large crowds of partisans attend, betting is said to be ferocious, and a stop at a pub along the way is not unknown. My top priority was to attend a match and learn the finer points of this unique sport.

There were other Beara interests. First was Allihies, a village on Beara that was once a center of copper mining. Many miners from the area emigrated to work copper mines in Montana. There were said to be few Beara families without relatives in Butte, Montana. I wanted to learn more of this history that included ancestors of Mike Sullivan, whom I knew when he was governor of Wyoming and then U.S. ambassador to Ireland. Second was Sue Booth Forbes. She had pulled up stakes in Boston to create a new life and develop the Anam Cara Writer's and Artist's Retreat near Eyeries. It is an area advertised as having fields that are "forty shades of green." I was curious about this Boston transplant and Anam Cara's creative environment, which was said, among other things, to erase writer's block. And then there was Eyeries, a tiny, certified must-see village that wore a Joseph's coat of brightly painted houses.

Mizen and Sheep's Head Peninsulas. Our planned progression down the four peninsulas of Ireland's west coast—Dingle, Beara, and now Mizen and Sheep's Head—offered the prospect of a scenic escalation: wild, wilder, wildest. Mizen has been described as a "remote finger of land poking its way west with cliff scenery, getting wilder the further west you go." Sheep's Head was said to have "an ancient feel to it: barren land almost entirely devoid of people . . . surges of hard granite rise from sweet green fields . . . plant life, rock, and water fall together to describe some new magic ideal." Wow! Who could resist it? We planned to stay at Grove House in Schull on Mizen. I suspect the real reason for this choice was that one of my favorite playwrights, the prolific George Bernard Shaw, had stayed there in the early 1900s when he was writing *John Bull's Other Island.* I fell in love with the idea of staying in "his" room and dreamed that some of his talent might remain and rub off on me.

Listowel. Now, the final leg of our trip. It was to involve a different kind of Irish experience, one focused on town life. We were to stay in Listowel in North Kerry, not too far from the River Shannon and back near where our trip would begin and where it would end. Listowel sounded interesting because we would be there during the week of the annual Listowel Races, a horse racing tradition of more than a hundred years. It was also the time of the Harvest Festival with street dancing, buskers, and kid's parades.

The literary tradition of Listowel was another reason for stopping there. Listowel calls itself the "literary capital of Ireland" because it has produced so many important writers and has an annual writer's workshop of some note. I arranged to meet with several people involved with the literary scene to talk about the source of this creative energy. In sharp contrast to other more country places we planned to stay, our Listowel choice was Allo's Bar, Bistro & Townhouse right in the center of town. The "Townhouse" was three rooms, stacked one above the other and all above the bar and bistro. "Well," I thought, "let's give it a shot."

Quin. The end of the journey was to take us back to Co Clare with a quiet two days in Quin. That would put us less than a half hour from Shannon Airport and a 1:05 P.M. Air Canada departure. We were to stay at Ardsollus Farm, the most peaceful setting we could find. Relaxed plans included a visit to Quin Abbey, a well-preserved Franciscan friary dating back to 1433, a session with students at Quin primary school, and a drink with Michael Byrne, who headed up a project in nearby Ennis, "The Information Age town." The project was "a live experiment to see what would happen when an entire town became wired."

MEMORIES THAT GLOW

NEVER LET IT be said that we let plans stand in the way of what came naturally. Serendipity is all. In the following pages of this book, you will read what came of our plans, including a few of the strongest memories the trip produced.

On the Sheep's Head Peninsula, near Kilorohane, moss and lichen-covered low stonewalls enclosed small, geometric, neat green (yes, emerald green) fields. The fields swept down to the blue-gray waters of Dunmanus Bay, the stark hills of Knocknamaddree and Knockaphuca in the background.

In Castletownbere, from a huge bay window in our bedroom at The Old Presbytery, we looked beyond a lush garden where a crown-crested mother duck and her brood were on constant parade, to fishing boats in an ever-changing scene in the Castletownbere harbor.

In the Burren, living in the midst of a unique universe—mile after mile of limestone terraces, crisscrossed by fissures (grykes and dykes), with underground rivers and caves and a landscape dotted with megalithic tombs, Celtic crosses, and the ruins of abbeys and abandoned homes.

Sitting in the garden of St. Joseph's Convent in Dingle, talking with Sister Dorothy, one of the few remaining nuns of the order of the Presentation Sisters. We were warmly embraced by her goodness and love—a power we felt could change the world, if only the world were just a little more receptive.

On the bay in Kenmare, we shared a waterfront park with three, enigmatic, nine-foot-tall stone musicians of timeless mien.

On a farm just outside of Ennistymon, in the much-lived-in kitchen of Willie Daly, famous matchmaker, G and I were audience to a brilliant scene of cross-cultural misunderstandings. A Japanese television program crew, with a modest command of English, trying to fathom Willie's off-color Irish tales of successful coupling as they planned the visit of a "Japanese personality" to the Lisdoonvarna Matchmaking Festival.

Falling in love with sweet Listowel, the little town that can do just about anything—the delightfully eccentric oddity of the Lartigue one-wheeled Listowel & Ballybunion Railway, the Listowel Races, and the mind-blowing delight of the Writers' Museum of the Literary & Cultural Centre. There, all white replicas of famous writers sit or stand about, each in his normal surrounding of pub or classroom or study, each with his own words writ all over from head to toe.

LET THE JOURNEY BEGIN

NOW, BACK TO THE BEGINNING, the usual airport hassle in Denver, onto a spanking new Air Canada Airbus 319 (lumbar supports and seat massage if you like). It had a wonderfully cheerful and helpful cabin crew who actually seemed to like what they are doing. Announcements from the cockpit in English and French. A wonderfully smooth transfer in Toronto with kind attention to the needs of creakies, and off we flew to Shannon, feeling well cared for.

And now, let the journey begin! Off and meandering, come what may.

Let the Journey Begin

The Burren: Geologist's paradise, Botanist's enigma. Last of the great matchmakers. Mullaghmore: a preservation victory.

Atlantic Ocean

Galway Bay

A lovely cup of tea on Galway Bay.

Fanore

Ballyvaghan

Rockyview Farmhouse

Mullaghore Mountain– A 10 year preservation battle.

THE BURREN

Slieve Elva 1129 ft.

Ennistymon

CLARE

Quin Abbey

Cliffs of Moher

Ennis

Matchmaker meets his match.

Shannon

River Shannon

Road
5 Miles

N

CHAPTER TWO

ON TO FANORE, POT-BASHING, AND ROCK ARTISTRY

ONE MIRROR. NO PROBLEM.

AIR CANADA 894 into Shannon on time at 11:35 A.M., 4:35 A.M. at home. We have had a light breakfast on the flight and enough daylight so that our bodies don't protest too much as we move on. We are wheelchaired in record time from the plane, through a cursory customs check, pick up our bags, one roll-on each, move to the Hertz counter, and out into our Ford Focus, which is conveniently parked just outside the door. Airlines are happy to have you ask for a wheelchair if walking a long distance can be a strain. You just need to ask when making your reservation.

Coming off an international flight and going through an airport in a wheelchair is a fascinating experience, especially with G as a companion. First, I haven't been in an airport yet where on an international flight the route from plane to customs, to baggage was designed with wheelchair passengers in mind. The challenge for routing wheelchair passengers is how to avoid stairs other passengers have to take. The solutions are make-do and always involve a labyrinth—up and down freight elevators, through back offices, down long hallways, out a hidden door, and into the customs hall. And on the way from plane to bags, the thing I find absolutely fascinating is how G somehow manages to get the man or woman pushing her wheelchair to tell her their life story—how their marriage is going, problems their children are having, a recent operation, frustrations, hopes. It is amazing what a welcoming sympathetic style can yield. G is a natural born receptor. She would have been a brilliant spy.

With one life story in mind and a map in hand, we are off to Fanore on the Atlantic Coast in the heart of the Burren, a unique limestone universe. From Shannon to Fanore, it is about an hour's slow drive, our maximum range after an overnight flight through seven time zones. This is especially so when one's driving instincts have to flip—sit on the right, drive on the left. The tendency is to drift to the left. G is my lookout, making sure I don't get too close to curbs and ditches. As an early warning system she is perfect. She shrieks. The last time we were in Ireland, she fell asleep on the job. On the way from the airport to our first stop, I hit a curb, blew a tire, and lost a hubcap. On this trip, the first morning I was driving brilliantly until I made a wrong turn into Lisdoonvarna, a town famous for its annual matchmaking festival. The festival was in progress and the street scene distracting. People were everywhere, and cars were parked every which way on both sides of the street, leaving only a narrow passage way. Despite G's warning, I lost my concentration and lost the left side mirror of my car to a parked car. A kind soul picked the mirror up off the street, smiled, said, "No problem," and helped snap the mirror back in place. Later I began wondering, "Was it his car that met my mirror?" Looking into a cracked mirror for the rest of our trip kept the question in mind.

Out of Lisdoonvarna and minutes later, we were on R477, the Ocean Road and our first taste of the Burren, a limestone plain sweeping down to the ocean's edge. Waves gave voice as they crashed into crevices along the rocky shore and sprayed high into the sunny sky. What a grand and welcoming show this was.

Ita Plus Eleven

At the Rockyview Farmhouse, Isabelle, eighteen months and all smiles, was the first to greet us. Ita Walsh, our proprietor, was as friendly in person as she had been on the phone. Ita insisted on first things first. She sat us down for a cup of tea and cake and a bit of chat. Almost before one could say, "With milk please," G had most of Ita's life story. She had been born in this rambling farmhouse and grew up with four sisters and seven brothers. Ita qualified as a nurse in a Dublin hospital, going off in 1984 to Nigeria on a two-year nursing contract. Back in Ireland, she took over a store in Ballyvaghan from her brother who had decided to go off to San Francisco. Ita's mother had been manager of the family dairy farm and, very obviously, passed along a combination of business skills, independence, and self-esteem to her daughters. One daughter is in banking and the other four have businesses of their own.

In the early eighties, with the house empty of children and the farm leased to a relative, Ita's mother began taking in guests. This was a time when the west of Ireland was in economic decline. Farm wives were encouraged to spruce up any extra rooms, bake a few more biscuits, and get into tourism. Tourism took hold, and in 1997 Ita and her husband Noel decided to take over the farmhouse and convert it to a B&B. Their sons, Kevin, then age six, and Sean, then age eight, were in primary school in Fanore. Living and working close to school and giving new life to the family farmhouse had great appeal for them. Ita and Noel rewired, replumbed, repainted, and added a conservatory as a breakfast room. Rockyview Farmhouse is the pleasant and comfortable result. Ita said that running a B&B is not that different from growing up in a big family: "The Dutch, English, Americans, and Germans are all different in their way, and so are eleven brothers and sisters." One full house is like another.

POT-BASHING

IT DIDN'T TAKE US long to settle in. First, I made sure we had good bedside reading lamps. Next, suitcases went on luggage racks. Then a nap. We discovered many trips earlier that it was a mistake for us to try and soldier through the first day. After our nap, it was time for a leisurely amble on this soft, misty sunny day, so unlike the sharp, dry sun of Colorado. To the southeast, green, stone-littered fields rose gently for about five hundred feet. Then the scene changed abruptly to spectacular, giant-sized limestone steps rising one by one another five hundred feet. The limestone steps stretched south as far as we could see. I find not knowing what to expect allows a sense of discovery to flourish. So it's not, "So this is Slieve Elva," but another "Wow! Look at this astounding sight we have discovered right in our backyard." Then I research it.

Sliabh Eilbhe (Slieve Elva) is one of the great geologic features of the Burren. Poulnagollum, the largest cave in Ireland, is on its eastern edge. The cave is down about a hundred feet with a rippling stream at its bed. Branch passages run in several directions and can be explored for nearly seven miles. To get to the cave, you have to go down (and up on the way back) a fixed rope hand-over-hand for about seventy feet, with another thirty feet or so on rope ladders. Your reward is, grottoes, high walls polished smooth by centuries of water, marvelous formations of stalactite and stalagmite, and a water-fall sending spray into a great gallery. If you go in for this sort of adventure, you are a *potholer*, or more elegantly a *speliologist* and involved in *pot-bashing*. You treat getting wet and dirty as part of the game. We decided to skip this particular bit of new experience, however thrilling it might have been. It's not a creaky thing.

Rock Artist at Work

With Slieve Elva at our backs, we strolled down a narrow gravel road toward the Atlantic, past a drooping palm (evidence of the Gulf Stream), a few cows that took no notice, and across the very modest Murroogh River, one of the few above ground flows of water in the Burren. Most streams curl underground through limestone caverns.

The road ended at a small square pasture, rock walls on three sides, the ocean on the fourth, and a few sheep grazing contentedly. Grey rock walls, white sheep on deep green grass, blue-green water, occasional spray, and a soft blue sky—a fine combination it was. The pasture wall facing the road wall was quite remarkable. I had seen interesting dry rock walls all over Scotland and Italy, but nothing to match this. In a wall contest, this one would take first prize and carry the appellation *world class* or *museum quality*. Three- and four-inch thick slabs of Burren flagstone, two or three feet long, were balanced and stacked vertically to a height of around five feet. No mortar was used. This allowed an afternoon sun beginning to set in the west to backlight hundreds of openings of different sizes. It was a brilliant composition by a wall builder who loved rock. In a modern art gallery, people would have seen it as an inspired installation, especially if the sun could come along.

CHAPTER THREE

DRUMLINS AND RUNNELS, GRYKES AND DYKES, TURLOUGHS AND RILLS

I began to look more closely at the rocky limestone. Washed by the Atlantic rain, it was full of color, shining black, green gray, white and orange, with lichens beautiful in their depth of color and in their designs on the rocky surface—swirls, spirals, whorls so striking that they seemed to be in perpetual motion.
——Sarah Poyntz, April 2003, *Country Diary, The Guardian*

Sea, mountains and landscape, focused into a compass which the eye scans . . . such a combination of wild natural scenery, we venture to assert cannot be surpassed in any other part of the world.
——H. B. H., *Holiday Haunts on the West Coast of Clare,*
The Burren, (1891)

THE BURREN: A GEOLOGIST'S PARADISE

IRISH FOR BURREN is *Bhoireann,* "a stony place." The Burren spreads over five hundred square miles, twenty-five miles east to west and twenty miles north to south. Gentle Galway Bay is its northern boundary and raging Atlantic its western edge. Oliver Cromwell's surveyor Ludlow said of this place, "It is a savage land, yielding neither water enough to drown a man, nor a tree to hang him, nor soil enough to bury him." This lack of hospitality made the Burren one of the less-developed areas of contemporary Ireland, allowing considerable evidence of its early occupiers to remain in place. There are more than sixty Stone Age (3000–2000 B.C.) burial monuments—wedge tombs, cairns, and dolmens (four legs of upright stones, capped by a massive horizontal stone). Add to this four hundred or so Iron Age ring forts (500 B.C.-500 A.D.) plus the remains of any number of Christian monasteries, churches, round towers, and high crosses. The question now is how long all this will survive the discovery of the Burren by busloads of day-trippers streaming down from Galway and up from Limerick.

The raw face of the Burren is the outcome of a long and complex battle between forces of nature that began more than three hundred million years ago. At the beginning, the coastline lay beneath warm shallow seas, thick with sea creatures and marine plant life. As these sea creatures and plant life died, they accumulated in horizontal layers on top of a granite base. The result, millions of years later, was limestone. Massive tectonic movements in the sea bed then lifted and exposed the limestone to new elements. Rainwater seeped through this porous rock, creating fissures and underground lakes and caves. For millions of years more, organic sedimentary matter accumulated on the exposed rock surface. In several areas of the Burren, sediment mixed with mud to produce a flagstone covering of the limestone. With the flagstone above, granite deep below, and limestone in the middle, nature had created a geologic sandwich.

Nature's Work of Art

Relentless winds heavy with ocean salt, sheets of glacial ice forming and retreating, and waves beating against the coastline continued their assault, shaping this stony place, this geologist's paradise. Guidebooks tend to describe all this as lunarlike, stark, and austere.

G and I saw it differently, more as poetry and art.

Where the top layer of the sandwich was washed and beaten away, abrasive wind and great storms etched and sculpted the limestone surfaces into a variety of exotic patterns.

Listen to the geologic terms, say them aloud, and hear the geologist's song of the Burren—drumlins and runnels, grykes and dykes, turloughs, swallow holes, hollows and rills, eccentric hills and glacial erratics, karstic terrain, syncline folding, and fluted stones.

Driving slowly through the Burren, we had this feeling of being in a private outdoor museum featuring a succession of organic installations of light, rock, and water creating nature's show, "The Limestone Universe." Here's some of what we saw.

High mounds of gray-green limestone with stone tendrils reaching into fields thick with bracken. The stone is bone-white in sunshine, darkened, and metallic in rain.

A massive reach of smooth, polished flagstone (classic *karst* terrain), sectioned into a patchwork of *clints* (individual blocks of limestone paving) by *grykes* (channels weathered deep into the limestone). Some of the *grykes* widen out where *runnels* have cut deep channels into shoulders of the *clints*.

White orchids, bee orchids, fly orchids, mountain aven, saxifrages, maidenhair fern, bloody cranesbill, milkwort—the flora of the Burren has its own mystique. Mediterranean, Arctic, and Alpine plants that aren't supposed to be there prosper side-by-side in gullies and ravines of *grykes* that have become open-air greenhouses with microclimates of their own. Add to this Burren "flower pots," saucer-shaped depressions in rock surfaces where soil has collected and masses of wild flowers bloom in the spring. All in all, it is both a botanist's delight and a botanist's enigma.

Horizontal limestone beds rise in tiers of terraces on the hills in the north of the Burren that overlook Galway Bay. Below the terraces are massive smooth slopes without a crack or fracture. Above the terraces, limestone has crumbled and soil has collected to form upland pastures where grazing cattle add a living dimension to this hilly installation.

Mullaghmore Mountain, rising 627 feet, is an eccentric limestone composition of gently compressed open folds. In some folds, *anticlinal joints* expand, beds stretch out, and wind and water grind away the surfaces. In other folds, *synclinal joints* are compressed and have a squashed look. At the foot of Mullaghmore, a grassy hollow, a *turlough*, fills with water, becoming a lake in wet weather when underground systems have reached their limits. And then in drier times, these lakes drain into the same subterranean passages that had helped fill them. These passages are marked by *swallow holes* among moss-covered rocks.

An assault on the peaceful wonders of Mullaghmore Mountain inspired a citizen uprising, the War of Mullaghmore.

CHAPTER FOUR

THE WAR OF MULLAGHMORE

SOMETHING TO FIGHT FOR

THE WONDERFULLY ECCENTRIC character of Mullaghmore Mountain, its setting, and its solitude created a place with a unique spiritual quality. A passion to retain this led to the great ten-year War of Mullaghmore. The combatants, a small group of extraordinary ordinary citizens on one side and the arrogance, power, and resources of the Irish government on the other. With remarkable clarity of purpose, endurance, and a willingness to bet their homes (literally), the good guys won.

In 1991, with European Union funds for tourist development in the offing, the Irish government announced plans to build an Interpretative Center for the Burren National Park at Mullaghmore. The Office of Public Works was in charge, and charge ahead they did, without an environmental impact assessment or planning permission from Co Clare. In her essay "Ordinary People and the Mountain," Lelia Doolan writes of reactions of ordinary people and "emotions that fueled the long journey."

> First of all, there was a sense of disbelief: how could intelligent people not see their plan was daft? How could they risk polluting the very terrain they had acquired in order to protect it:

endangering the rare plant and wildlife species; risking contamination of the waters; altering the character of the area and its small country roads; providing a precedent for further building developments in an unspoilt region? Causing, in short, a man-made affront to the beneficent legacy of millennia of natural cataclysms.

Disbelief led to anger as the government refused to take seriously "this little fly." The government would not consider the argument that for environmental and economic reasons the visitor center would be better located in a nearby town or that legally, planning permission was required for the project. Bulldozers and cement trucks moved in. Work on the Interpretative Center began in earnest. Fortunately, even with bulldozers already at work, the response was to not give up. It was instead to organize the Burren Action Group (BAG), twenty citizens with one goal—save the mountain they treasured for generations to come.

A SPAGHETTI BOWL OF PEOPLE

G AND I MET with Suzanne Crosbie, one of Ita's three purposeful sisters and one of BAG's founders. Suzanne, an archeologist by training and a free spirit by inclination, lived in Holland for a period in the eighties, was then a schoolteacher in Lisdoonvarna, and is now a shop owner in Ennistymon. We crowded around a small table in the back room of Crosbie's Books and Music, a wonderfully eclectic gift shop on the main street of Ennistymon.

Suzanne recalled emotions from the times when BAG was first formed in the living room of her home in Doolin, April 1991. "We were a spaghetti bowl of people, mid thirties to mid sixties—priest, shopkeeper, farmer, college science lecturer, artist, accountant, teachers, and other like people. We knew from the beginning it had to be a legal challenge. We couldn't win with politics with the government against us. We agreed to share the financial risk, understanding that if we lost the legal case, damages could be assessed and that would be the ruin of many of us. We had guaranteed loans to cover legal costs, and some of us had mortgaged our homes."

I found this commitment even more astounding when Suzanne added, "In our heart of hearts, we didn't think we had a chance to achieve our goal, returning the site to its original magical state." In the beginning all they had were hope and belief. Most of them didn't even know how to use a fax machine. They learned fax machines, how to get on television and radio shows, and how to draw attention to their cause. One BAG team delivered an inspired performance, pushing a papier-mâché rock hundreds of miles from Ennis to Dublin, ending with a giant rally. For money, they sold tee shirts, held a monster raffle, organized concerts, and sold CDs. Some money came from green groups, but most of it came in small amounts from hundreds of people.

BAG continued to press its legal case, arguing that permission was required to build the Interpretive Center and the Office of Public Works (OPW) had not obtained it. By the eighth year of the struggle, BAG had spent £72,000 (more than $199,999) against the nearly £3 million (nearly $5 million) the government spent.

At the beginning, people called BAG members "woolheads," "hippies," and even worse, "intellectuals." Many local people saw the government's plan in terms of jobs, local business, and higher property values, and BAG was in the way. By the end, ten years on, BAG members were real pros. They had built a base of national and international support. In its way, the decade-long war became another part of family life. Life went on. Babies were born, those who were youngsters at the beginning of the effort had graduated college by the end, and there were deaths in the group. As Doolan tells the story, "There were many glum moments, many moments of hopelessness and frustration; but we were also lucky in being able to celebrate the many often unexpected sources of encouragement and good humor that came our way. Cheerfulness kept breaking through."

ROLLER COASTER TO VICTORY

SUZANNE REMEMBERS the roller coaster of ups and downs for the BAG bunch. Whenever things felt like they were going bad, one of the group would say, "Lets have a party," and they did. These ordinary people, who never in their lives had done anything like this, discovered depths of stamina, purpose, and eloquence few would ever have imagined. After talking with some of the players and reading what others had written, it seemed to me, deep down, the essential ingredients were unshakable solidarity, a boundless capacity for good times together, and friendship in a nonhierarchical group.

The court officially recognized seven BAG members as plaintiffs in the legal battle to save Mullaghmore—Frank Howard, Patrick McCormack, P.J. Curtis, Elmer Colleran, Lelia Doolan, Fionnuala McNamara, and John O'Donoghue. Following is an outline of their ten years of skirmishes and battles from April 1991, when government plans for Mullaghmore were announced, to BAG's ultimate victory and restoration of the site in May 2002.

Year 1, April 1991. Government plans announced for the Interpretive Center at Mullaghmore.

Year 2, December 1992. After being challenged, OPW says planning permission is not needed. OPW starts moving dirt and pouring concrete. Between December 1992 and February 1993, OPW rushed to complete car parks, most of the sewer system, foundation for the center and walls of the first floor. This was a cynical "we can't turn back" strategy.

Year 3, February 1993. The Burren Action Group gets an injunction to stop OPW work. The High Court rules OPW is not exempt from Planning Acts and therefore work on the site is illegal. The statutory powers OPW depended on were from the nineteenth century and deemed by the High Court as not valid for Mullaghmore or any other OPW project. *May 1993.* The government takes its case to the Supreme Court and loses again. The Supreme Court upholds the High Court.

Year 4, January 1994. OPW submits a planning application for a smaller project.

Year 5, February 1995. The government falls in a national election, and the new Culture and Heritage Minister withdraws the OPW planning application.

Year 6, October 1996. The Culture and Heritage Minister submits a revised plan for the Interpretive Center.

Years 7 and 8, September 1998. The Clare County Council (the Burren is in Co Clare) rejects the revised plan and refuses permission. *October 1998.* The Culture and Heritage Minister appeals the Clare County Council decision to *An Bord Pleanala,* the National Planning Board.

Year 9, March 2000. An Bord Pleanala says no! "Natural conservation takes precedence when conflicts arise between different objectives." The project, the Interpretive Center at Mullaghmore is dead. July 2000. BAG obtains a High Court order to have OPW restore the Mullaghmore site to its original natural condition and is awarded costs.

Year 10, May 2001. Work is completed on demolition and restoration of the wonderfully eccentric site at Mullaghmore.

Thank You BAG

AT THE END, after the final battle, Elmer Colleran of BAG put these last words to the War of Mullaghmore:

This marathon campaign is finally over and has been comprehensively won. BAG and the Plaintiffs can never repay the enduring support given by so many individuals and organizations over the past nine long years. We know that the final outcome is the reward that all of us worked for, hoped for/suffered for—we would like to think that Mullaghmore, in all its natural beauty and spiritual essence, is saying thank you to all who appreciated its value and worked for its conservation and protection.

CHAPTER FIVE

MATCHMAKER, MATCHMAKER, MAKE ME A MATCH

And there stood Dan with a pipe in hand,
Saying come away to the promised land,
For I know a dame wants a ring in her hand
And for bells in her ear to be ringing.
Oh blessed the land that simmering hour,
Blossoms bursting on every bower,
Hedgerows white with the thorn in flower,
And the whole world sweetly singing.
> —Dan Paddy Andy O'Sullivan, (1899–1966),
> the greatest matchmaker of them all: 399 marriages

SUBTLE GENTLE NUDGES

ENNISTYMON, A TOWN OF LESS than a thousand, sits comfortably in a recess among the hills at the southern edge of the Burren, two miles from the Atlantic. The road we were on coming down from Fanore in the north narrowed at the stone bridge over the Cullenagh River and then swooped gently down to the town center. Shop fronts along the way shared a common look, evidence of stonemasons skilled in their craft and painters more attuned to pastels than primary colors. A casual approach to parking was much in evidence.

Ennistymon claims a certain amount of fame for having been the birthplace and home of Caitlin McNammara, famous wife of the famous Welsh poet Dylan Thomas. Caitlin's home is now the Falls Hotel. The bar there is appropriately named the Dylan Thomas Bar. After all, he drank himself to death, mainly at the White Horse Tavern in New York's Greenwich Village.

G and I walked out of Crosbie's Books and Music onto the main street of Ennistymon, thoughts of Mullaghmore still on our minds as we began our search for Willie Daly. "Traditional Matchmaker" stands in large bold type at the head of Daly's one-page matchmaking application form. After a few questions as to age, interests, and preferences, there is at the bottom of the page, in small type, a very reasonable disclaimer: "While every effort will be made by the [matchmaking] service to find you a suitable partner, I, Willie Daly, cannot guarantee this." When we met in his kitchen that afternoon, Daly explained that he didn't need people to fill out a big, long form because his were the traditional tools of matchmaking: "Intuition, subtle gentle nudges, a little encouragement, the right atmosphere, and insightful knowledge of human nature."

DICKY MICK DICKY O'CONNOR

WHEN I WAS in the mulling and planning phase of this trip to the west of Ireland, I came across John B. Keane's *Letters of a Matchmaker*, a book of earthy correspondence between matchmaker Dicky Mick Dicky O'Connor and his clients who lived "in the midst of that wild and mountainous countryside along the borders of Cork and Kerry." Dicky Mick Dicky's concern as a matchmaker is "battling the disease" of the single life, "a curse beyond curing when it catches hold." In the course of this battle, Dicky Mick Dicky and his clients are given to trenchant observations on prospects, male and female.

"There does be any amount of anxious dames with all their possessions intact, if you follow, what thinks they have carried their burden long enough."

"A man was what she wanted and she was aisy about age as long as he had a house and a way of living and the natural faculties in fair working order."

"The nights does be lonesome. 'Tis company I want."

"There's roundy yokes called oysters what is swallowed alive out of their shells and what fills men with taspy what was only fit for the grave before."

"You say your age is a bit with the forty. What size bit if you please as my client will be anxious to know all these matters?"

"I can assure you this is one horse of a man in all departments."

"I have only one life, and the Catechism don't say nothing about courting or coupling in the hereafter."

"This was a silver-tongued lovable man with sentences that ran from one minute to ten and lovely long words like you'd hear in a poem."

"Would you be able to locate a nice firm woman for me in the regions of thirty to forty?"

THE ORIGINAL TWINKLE

I EXCHANGED PHONE CALLS and e-mails with Daly, and he was more than agreeable as to a get-together and a bit of talk about his approach to matchmaking. Finding out what others have had to say about someone you haven't met is a lot of help in preparing for an interview. Marc McCrum, in his book *The Craic*, describes Daly as a "slick professional" with longish-gray hair and "a brogue soft enough to voice over the corniest of stout ads. As for the twinkle in his eye, he was clearly the original for that expression. He had an ease of manner that would have made the awkwardest, most hopeless bachelor boy or girl feel relaxed."

To Nick Ryan, writing for *The Sunday Post* magazine, Daly explained that in addition to "traditional intuitive matchmaking," he had helped some men find an extra marital bedfellow. "The fellas I see doin' it always seem to have control of it. A legitimate affair can enhance a marriage, I believe." As to women, with what I thought was a trace of Dicky Mick Dicky, matchmaker Daly was concerned, "If they're too educated, it damages their appetite for romance and that kind of thing."

Conversation with Daly promised to be instructive. G and I headed to Daly's pub. We had been told he was very likely to be found there with a glass of Jameson's in hand. If not, the bartender could send us off in the right direction.

Daly wasn't at his pub. The bartender thought someone in Daly's restaurant just up the street, the Sugan Chair ("famous Irish and continental cuisine"), would know where he was. Famous it might be, but charming it was not. Dim lighting, well-worn oilcloth-covered tables, and a history of deep-frying in the air. A waitress thought Daly would be at his farm in Ballingaddy—sixty-three acres, thirty head of cattle, and a riding center. Go back north on the road a mile or so we were told, look for a pony trekking sign on the left, and follow that track a ways. I was to learn later that Daly traded in both horses and hearts. (If you are looking for a Little Romance or perhaps even the Perfect Partner, why not book yourself on *The Love Trail* riding holiday. *www.williedaly.com/welcome.html*).

The only livable habitat on the road was a one-story yellowish brick house that had seen better days. I knocked and rang. No one home. All I could see was a bare mattress propped up against a window in a front room. I was about to give up when Daly arrived in a weathered car with a weathered face and longish gray hair. He sorted us out, remembering that creaky fellow from Colorado, and led us down a hall past the room with the mattress in the window and into a large kitchen that had not seen the hand of a serious housekeeper for some time. Daly separated from his wife a while back. "I was off trying to make matches. It was my fault."

A Man's Kitchen Is His Castle

DALY'S STYLE WAS informal while being a bit on the royal side. He was gracious with quiet attention to G to make sure she didn't feel left out. He sat at the head of the well-worn rectangular wooden table where his seven children once ate. I sat to his left with G next to me. Daly decided he needed something to eat and plunked a whole loaf of brown bread, a pound of butter, a package of bologna, and a large butcher knife on the bare table. No need for dishes here. He held out the giant loaf of bread to us. Want some? No thanks. Daly cut off a huge, uneven hunk, smashed some butter on it, topped it with four or five slices of bologna, took a bite, and was ready to go. His effortless good social manners and informal approach to lunch were a wonderful contrast and a fine beginning to a theatrical afternoon.

Daly told us he had been matchmaking for thirty-seven years, finding wives for older men "with years of love stored up." As Daly explained it, these sons of farm families in the rural hill country of Clare, Kerry, and Cork were the ones who loved the land and stayed behind with their parents as brothers and sisters moved on to Dublin and England and America, new places, new ideas, new opportunities. For the one son who stayed on the farm, the difficulty of finding a woman to marry only increased with age. Many had to wait years for their parents to die for the inheritance of the small family farm where they could afford a wife, if they could find one, and raise a family of their own. Therefore the saying, says Daly, "Protestants marry early for love. Catholics marry late for land."

ACT ONE: NOT THE RIGHT KIND OF COURAGE

DALY WENT ON to explain the plight of the aging single farmer. Living in relative isolation, few of them developed social skills necessary for courting. At the same time, Daly explained, the number of women available for courting shrank. "There were twenty or thirty single men to every single woman in some areas. These men are poor mixers. When they have a lot of drink on them, they overdo the mixing, so again they don't appeal. All of a sudden they have the courage, but it isn't the right courage."

As Daly talked softly and wistfully, it became clear that he operated with a huge fund of empathy for the older men with love stored up who came to him for help. "I never have and never will introduce a mean man to a woman and don't help young men. They should be able to do it for themselves." He never uses photos so as to preserve "a little anticipation for the first meet."

Daly saw his task rather like that of a stage director of an improv production——choose the right actors to play opposite each other, put them in a proper setting, feed them a few opening lines, and hope they see mutual advantages of a continuing relationship. Even then, there can be problems. "There was this farmer in his seventies, a prospective match in the making, when the farmer confessed, 'She's grand, but me mother don't approve.' The mother was ninety-six."

I began to have the feeling that even with a tally of a hundred marriages and only one divorce, most of Daly's stories of matchmaking were about what had gone on some time before. "Nowadays, fewer women are willing to marry older men," Daly said rather sadly. "What a shame, because a young woman marrying an older man will take the stress out of the old fella's life."

Daly carries around a well-worn leather portfolio held together with an equally worn cord. Papers sticking out from all sides are said to be part of a stock of letters from lonely souls all over the world asking three generations of matchmakers for help——Daly's grandfather William, father Henry, and now himself. Daly is never seen in public without this prop. His daughter Marie has joined Daly, bringing a fourth generation into the matchmaking trade. A Google check for Willie Daly reveals several of his websites and indicates that the once personal one-on-one intuitive matchmaking enterprise has morphed into a modern business.

I had been saving up a question for Daly. In addition to traditional and intuitive matchmaker, publican, and restaurant operator, he is a horse trader. Put another way, Daly is a used horse dealer with a soft-spoken Clare accent and a great fund of *chairm*. I asked Daly if he could compare choosing a good wife and choosing a good horse. Without missing a beat he said, "Someone that will wear well, consistent, strong, needs to be appreciated and loved."

Act Two: Japanese Personality Meets the Matchmaker

Cast of Characters. It seemed time to leave. I got the nod from G. I pushed my chair back, and, as if on cue, a new cast of characters paraded onto the kitchen stage to act out a remarkable and unforgettable scene. I was not about to miss this one. No playwright, no matter how inventive, would ever have dreamed it up. Curtain!

In they paraded, the advance team for Tokyo Channel 10 television. At the head of the troupe was the producer——a lean, aquiline, unsmiling, carefully coiffed Japanese male in a well-cut, dark gray pin stripe. Leather-bound notebook in hand. He bowed slightly to no one in particular and marched to his seat at the head of the table. He was clearly Top Dog (TD). The rest of the cast followed, arraying themselves in a semicircle behind TD: Interpreter, a petite five-foot beauty in a gray business suit; Mr. Six-foot Leading Man; a businesslike Anglo/Asian male/female twosome from the PR firm Burton, Barton, Durstine & Osborne (BBD&O); and a second Anglo/Asian male/female team, this one from Guinness Japan, television program sponsor. (Irish Pubs, built in Ireland, crated and shipped to Japan for reassembly, have become a big thing.) And, to round out the cast, so to speak, parked on the kitchen counter, legs dangling, was Memphis-born Mark Flanagan, rotund, florid, organizer/promoter for the Lisdoonvarna Matchmaking Festival, and guide for the Channel 10 troupe.

So there we were, six standing, five sitting, on a sunny Irish afternoon in Daly's kitchen. Perfect casting in an unlikely setting for a twenty-first century Gilbert & Sullivan. Let the performance begin.

The Performance. Daly put away the remains of his loaf of bread, pound of butter, and package of bologna. With his hands he brushed the bread crumbs on to the floor, looked up, and smiled. You would think this was an every day event in his life.

It was obvious TD neither spoke nor understood much English. Slowly and seriously, pausing for the interpreter, TD outlined a television special that would introduce Irish culture to the Japanese. A Japanese woman—a "Japanese Personality," well-known to Japanese television audiences, would visit the Lisdoonvarna Matchmaking Festival. There was, TD explained, no such thing as a matchmaker in Japan, "Nothing equal to helping people meet other people. The Japanese Personality knows Willie Daly is a key person and wants to talk with you. We will take a scene where the Japanese Personality asks you 'What is your knack for matchmaking?' You are a professional, and you will give her advice on how you do it."

With this cue, Daly began to expound. "It is a gift you acquire. Getting electricity. Beauty is a funny thing. I never met a bad-looking woman. They always have beauty within."

"How has it changed?" TD wanted to know.

"Years ago, matches had to be for a reason. Good farm. Lots of cows. Dependable man. Lonely people. Now, for women there has to be 'magic,' a fast physical attraction. It has to 'ignite.' Women want the man of their dreams."

"How about men?" TD asked.

"Men are willing to let it grow. Willing to let all the parts come together—mind, body, and soul. A man wants a nice, honest, sincere woman, able to help in his business. Women are now independent and want a man to look nice. Personality is less important."

The four women in the room did not seem especially enthusiastic about Daly's description of the fairer sex and obvious preference for how the male role used to play. Daly then launched into his views on the role of drink in the art of matchmaking. "Irish people become humorous with drink. They become good entertainers, and these qualities are as good as money. With drink, the real person comes out."

As Daly's wisdom was translated, TD took it all down in his leather bound notebook—beautiful ink strokes, ideograms on unlined paper. G cast her artist's eye on TD's brilliant, perfectly aligned penmanship. Then she looked over at my scrawls, arrows, diagrams, and unfinished words and burst out laughing. The clue to my notes is that they are so disorganized that afterwards, by the time I have figured out what I was trying to record, whatever it was is fixed firmly in my mind.

TD wanted to hear stories. Daly obliged, pausing for translation. "There were two brothers, happy with mother at home, who did everything for them and lived to be ninety. The 'boys' at seventy-three and seventy-four couldn't cook, sew, or do anything for themselves. When mother died, they decided to go to Lisdoonvarna to find wives. Well, there were these two Irish girls, twenty-three and twenty-four, living in London in a ten-story apartment, 'but no one ever talked to us.' The boys met the girls at a dance and proposed. 'Would you marry us?' Yes, they said and went on a honeymoon. The older boy died in three days. 'Too bad,' said one friend to another. 'Yes, but he died with a smile on his face, and it took four days to put the lid down on the coffin.'"

The three Japanese women giggled. All the men except TD laughed. TD looked perplexed. He turned to his interpreter. She went red. He wanted to know what was so funny. Somehow, she managed to explain that the coffin lid couldn't go down was because the older boy did not suffer erectile dysfunction.

TD paused for a long moment, obviously digesting the story. He then suggested that Daly make a list of his stories and TD would choose those most appropriate for the Channel 10 audience's exposure to Irish culture. The session broke up.

Curtain. TD led his troupe out. G and I exchanged a few pleasantries with Daly, and the three of us walked down the hall to the front door. I stepped out, took a few steps toward our car, turned around, and saw G at the front door, standing close to Willie, stroking his cheek. Surprised was I, but not half so surprised as G. Turned out, Willie had said to her, "You are a lovely woman," and somehow her hand went to his cheek.

Clearly, Willie has the knack!

A Man for Every Woman and a Woman for Every Man

IN THE INTRODUCTION to his book *Letters of a Matchmaker*, Keane explains the need for Dicky Mick Dicky in "the countryside along the borders of Cork and Kerry":

In an ideal world there would be no need for such a person. Men and women would be paired off, the brave deserving the fair and, at the other extreme, every old shoe find an old stocking. There would be no surplus on either side, no leftovers, none left out in the cold. Rather there would be a man for every woman and a woman for every man. Alas and alack such an ideal climate is far beyond the hope or vision of mortal men. We must look therefore to our hero Richard Michael Richard O'Connor, otherwise known as Dicky Mick Dicky, to remedy insofar as it lies within his power this bleak and unhappy situation where men are often without women and women are often without men.

I wonder what Keane or Dicky Mick Dicky would have made of the Internet, today's matchmaker in the dating industry. The website *www.totalireland.com* lists well more than a hundred online Irish "personals and dating" websites—Maybefriends, Irish Singles Directory, SureDate, eDate, EireDate, Matchmakerireland, and on and on. While comparative data isn't available for Ireland, in the first half of 2003, Americans spent over $200 million on personals and dating sites, more than triple what they spent two years before. Forty million Americans visit dating sites each month. Yahoo Personals & Match.com have twelve million users worldwide. It seems that many Irish and American men and women share a desire to be properly paired and look to the Internet for help.

New York Times columnist David Brooks suggests that following an era of quick sex, "online dating, rather than being impersonal, puts structure back into courtship." According to Brooks, couples who meet through online dating services tend to exchange e-mail for weeks or months, progress to phone conversations for a few more weeks, then face-to-face meetings, usually in public places, and, if all goes well, only then dates, probably Dutch. With online daters able to sort through millions of possible partners and select for age, education, height, weight, politics, and religion, Brooks sees the process "at once ruthlessly transactional and strangely tender."

Members at a dating site create their own Web pages and advertise such qualities as, "I am a vivacious, intelligent, warm-hearted, attractive, cool chick, with a sharp, witty, and effervescent personality." Photos are usually included. Studies show that looks are twice as powerful as income, which may be why Daly never uses photos, so as to "preserve a little anticipation for the first meet" and give personality a chance to shine through.

For those who still crave the personal assistance of a matchmaker, Daly charges less than a hundred dollars for men, but nothing for women because in the west of Ireland women are in such short supply. At the other end of the scale, you can find Janice Spindel, owner of Serious Matchmaking, a company in New York that charges $15,000 to introduce clients, mostly men making $250,000 or more, to suitable mates. In the summer Spindel moves her whole show to the Hamptons, along with most of her clientele. Other than a few dollars difference, the lingo of Daly, "intuitive matchmaker" and Spindel is remarkably alike. She says, "It's that sixth sense that differentiates the good from the great in the matchmaking biz."

Go figure.

Like the carnival barker do say, "You pays your money and you takes your choice."

CHAPTER SIX

MOHER MADE LESS

Ah! Seaweed smells from sandy caves
And thyme and mist in whiffs,
In-coming tide, Atlantic waves
Slapping the sunny cliffs,
Lark song and sea sounds in the air
And splendour, splendour everywhere.

—John Betjeman

DESCRIPTIONS OF THE Cliffs of Moher usually begin with "majestic cliffs" or "spectacular sight." True! But . . . unfortunately, the glory of the cliffs, the creation of 320 million years of nature's artistry, has been severely diminished by a tourist-driven economy operating without environmental understanding or restraint.

The name, Cliffs of Moher, derives from the promontory fort Mothar, which was demolished during the Napoleonic wars to make room for a signal tower. While the cliffs had always attracted visitors, Cornelius O'Brien introduced tourism at the cliffs in a formal way. O'Brien was a descendant of Brian Boru, the eleventh-century high king of Ireland who vanquished the Vikings in 1014.

In 1835 O'Brien built O'Brien's Tower on this headland of the Cliffs of Moher. The tower stands today, a testament to skilled stonework in the Burren. It is a great viewpoint with sights of Galway Bay and Connemara in the north and Loop Head to the south.

There are two conflicting stories about O'Brien's reasons for building the tower. One story, according to Shannon Heritage, is that he believed the development of tourism would benefit the local economy and bring people out of poverty. The other, more popular story is that he built the tower to impress his lady friends. They were ready, whether from passion or exhaustion, to fall into his arms by the time they had climbed all the steps to the top.

G and I had heard how crowded the cliffs were. But, then, how could we be so near and not visit the certified "must see" cliffs? So we did on an overcast September day, along with 3,239 other souls, arriving in 752 cars (2.5 per car) and thirty-four buses (Forty per bus). Fourteen of these busloads, all on Burren tours from Galway and Limerick, arrive at the visitor center (parking lot, tea room, gift shop, W.C.) within minutes of each other around lunchtime. You can count the number of cars and buses competing for parking spaces or the length of lines at the restrooms to get a feel for the impact of this daily assault on the fragile ecosystem at the cliff top. Annual visitors now total 750,000. Before long, it will be a million and more. On peak days in August, there are more than a thousand cars and fifty buses.

Of course, you can get away from the crowds with a walk along the cliffs. However, you are advised to "be very careful as there are no safety barriers and sections of the cliff sometimes give way." The advice continues, "While the sure-footed will find it worthwhile following the cliff-path, it is not a good idea in windy weather, as there is little space between the path and the abyss. You're on your own so use your best judgment." Thanks a lot!

320 MILLION YEARS IN THE MAKING

THE CLIFFS OF MOHER are a line of sheer cliffs, five miles in length, reaching a height of 656 feet—the distance of two and a half football fields. Layers of siltstone, shale and sandstone, first deposited some 320 million years ago, form the cliffs. They constitute a slice through geological time, with the oldest rocks at the bottom. They are tilted slightly downward, so that layers at the bottom of the cliffs toward the south end emerge at the top of the cliffs at the north end. The layers of sandstone are more resistant to the pounding waves and winter storms of the Atlantic. Siltstone and shale layers erode and the sandstone layers stick out, forming a series of platforms. The result is a giant high rise for breeding and nesting birds—fulmars, shags, guillemots, kittiwakes, razorbills, puffins, and a variety of gulls.

The best way to experience the amazing variety of color and texture of the cliffs is at sunset from a boat. No crowds. You and a few dolphins and the cliffs. Unfortunately, there were no boats running when we were there. So ours was a more "normal" Cliffs of Moher experience.

NORMAL NEEDS IMPROVING

THE NARROW FLAGSTONE path G and I walked along, leading from the visitor center tearoom to the cliff viewpoint, was worm-eaten. The squiggly marks on the stones were impressions that soft-bodied creatures who burrowed through mud and sand in search of food left behind millions of years before. Vendors at rickety tables and kiosks lined the path, happily flogging an amazing range of tasteless objects—Celtic jewelry made in China, tea towels adorned with the clever Irish sayings. ("If you die, there are only two things to worry about: either you will go to heaven or to hell. If you go to heaven, there is nothing to worry about. But if you go to hell, you'll be so damn busy shaking hands with friends, you won't have time to worry. Why worry?") And the mother of all bad taste—little china imps, gnomes, devils, and demons from hell, all with beards and hats of red and green.

After a gauntlet of vendors, there are the cliffs—massive, breath-taking, booming waves pounding against their base with jets of spray fifty feet into the air. Howling wind gusts blasting off the sandstone and shale, a wind symphony. As G and I were beginning to take this in, there in mid-distance were a bunch of idiots prancing about at the headland's edge, some peering over, dangerously close to being swept into the sea by the next wind, and not a guide or park ranger in sight. There were none. So many people had ignored the danger signs and climbed over the sagging fence that a path had been worn to the clifftop headland.

The vendors, prancers, poorly maintained walks and railings, inad-equate trash containers, inappropriate buildings, and busloads of tourists surging in for a quick look one after another severely dimin-ished the power and meaning of the cliffs. Moher was made less, much less. I wondered how I would feel about having the *Mona Lisa* hung in a McDonald's. Perhaps the show could be titled "Mona Made Less."

FOURTEEN YEARS TO A WRONG TURN

THE CLIFFS OF MOHER visitor center was built by the Clare County Council in 1979 and operated by Shannon Development, a not-for-profit enterprise for tourism and economic growth in the region. When the visitor center was being planned in the seventies, one small voice—council member Patricia McCarthy—expressed a concern that the Cliffs of Moher were being over-commercialized. An Bord Pleanala, Ireland's planning board of final appeal, turned down a pro-posal in 1989 for a hotel on the cliff edge that aimed at exploiting the commercial value of the cliffs. The reason An Bord gave was that the proposal "would result in overdevelopment of the area, which would have a detrimental effect on the amenities of this area of special inter-est and natural beauty."

In the 1990s, with visitors to the cliffs numbering 600,000 a year and the tearoom, gift shop, and WCs clearly inadequate, the Clare County Council and Shannon Development organized a joint venture to develop a "state-of-the-art" visitor center. In 1993, they sponsored a national architectural competition for the design of a new center. The winning design by O'Riordan Staehli was for a two-story building built deep into the hillside behind the existing center. It included an audio-visual theatre, a restaurant, an exhibition area, and a grass roof designed to keep the cows and conservationists happy. But the Considine family, owner of a key clifftop parcel, of land was not happy. They wanted a piece of the commercial action. Shannon Development said no-go. They would do it alone. Shannon Development then submitted a plan that the Clare County Council turned down. Next, the council worked out a deal with the Considines, giving them a retail center in the existing parking lot.

In November 2000, having approved its own plan, the council announced its intention to proceed with an "integrated visitor facility," based largely on the winning 1993 hillside design with the Considines thrown in. In January 2002, the council detailed its plans for "demolition of the existing Cliffs of Moher Visitor Centre and the development of a new visitor's center, retail unit, public toilets, 6 casual trader's bays, waste treatment plant, revised car and coach park entrances, and a revised car and coach parking arrangement." Area business interests and bus tour operators heavily supported this.

By this time, nearly a decade on from when a new state-of-the-art visitor center was first considered, concerns about the environment and concepts of sustainability had evolved. In addition, with improvement in the economy of Ireland, a lot more people had a lot more cars. Moving with the times, Shannon Development took a new approach, "A Sustainable Management Concept" for the Cliffs of Moher. The study leaned heavily on practice at U.S. national parks, including the Grand Canyon, Yosemite, and Bryce Canyon, all having been in danger of being loved to death and turned into giant parking lots.

The sustainable concept called for three key elements that certainly spoke to the experience G and I had: (1) a booking system to control visitor numbers; (2) only essential facilities on site with retailing, food, etc. to be provided in nearby villages; and (3) a park-and-ride system from nearby villages.

In February 2002, Shannon Development announced its opposition to the Cliffs of Moher plan of its former partner, the Claire County Council, and its intention to appeal the council's plan to An Board Pleanala. John King, Director of Heritage and Tourism for Shannon Development, argued, "Best management practices at these sites recommend building tourist infrastructure away from environmentally sensitive areas. The council's proposals do not fully reflect the changes in how these important and sensitive sites are managed today. Shannon Development proposes the relocation of all visitor facilities to nearby villages and the introduction of an integrated 'park-and-ride' facility to connect the villages to the cliffs." (At Yosemite National Park, eighteen hybrid electric shuttle buses carry up to 1,050 passengers an hour from remote park-and-ride lots to the national park. The transport equivalent for 1,050 men, women, and children would be about 420 cars requiring 2.9 acres of parking space.)

Shannon Development was not alone. *An Taisce*, the National Trust for Ireland, also filed a plea in opposition to the council plan because of "the impact of the proposal on what is recognized as an internationally important landscape." *An Taisce* means "treasury" or "storehouse" of nature and is a combination Sierra Club and Nature Conservancy with government standing. *An Taisce* was established under the Planning Acts of Ireland to protect a "high quality environment [that] is central to Ireland's successful and sustainable economy, as well as a high quality of life."

An Bord Pleanala didn't get it, much less remember its 1989 decision that commercial overdevelopment at the cliffs would have a detrimental effect on the environment. Nor did *An Bord Pleanala* recall its opinion in the Mullaghmore matter, "Natural conservation takes precedence when conflicts arise between different objectives." In October 2000, after hundreds of pages of submissions and three days of oral arguments, *An Board Pleanala* gave Co Clare the go-ahead with this blessing—"The proposed development would not *seriously* [emphasis added] injure the visual or natural amenities of the area, would be in accordance with the principles of a sustainable tourism strategy for the county, and would be acceptable in terms of traffic safety and convenience." *An Taisce* described this decision as "one of the worst ever made by *An Bord Pleanala* and a breach of the European Environmental Impact Assessment Directive" and "a lost opportunity."

What began in 1993 as plans for a new visitor center at an estimated cost of €3 million ($3.7 million), had by 2005 multiplied by a factor of 9.7 to €29 million ($34.8 million).

THE AUTOMOBILE AS AN INVASIVE SPECIES

ON REFLECTION, I think the argument over development at the Cliffs of Moher lacked an understanding of the automobile as an invasive species with an insatiable appetite for more parking space. First, no parking lot at a popular facility is ever large enough. Second, economic interests will demand expansion of parking. Otherwise customers will be lost.

At the *An Board Pleanala* oral hearings, an appropriately named planner, Simon Clear, argued for a "management" solution with parking and services at a reasonable remove rather than a bricks and mortar solution at the Cliffs of Moher. This would provide "maximum flexibility and compatibility with environmental imperatives." Shannon Development, he said, had lost its faith in the "bigger and more is better" logic and was concerned about the "construction of a large, invasive, and expensive building, which might prove not to be appropriate for the needs of future generations and could not be dis-

AN INSTRUCTIVE EXAMPLE

Insatiable Appetite for Parking Space

Denver International Airport (DIA) offers an instructive example of the way parking power overwhelms planners' best intentions. DIA opened in 1995, a creative design inspired by the peaks of the Rocky Mountains that provide a backdrop to the terminal. Planning, including parking requirements, began ten years before the terminal opened. When the airport opened in 1995, it had a carefully planned and relatively unobtrusive garage with 13,160 spaces. A ground-level "economy" lot for 2,212 cars was tucked behind the garage. Total spaces: 15,398.

By 1997, economy surface lots had grown to 8,558 spaces, and a remote lot on the airport site added another 4,775 spaces. That totaled 26,519 spaces. In 1998, another remote lot was added, bringing total parking spaces to 29,793. In 2000, additions to the two remote lots raised total parking to 31,687 spaces. In 2002, the airport added nearly 3,000 spaces to one of the remote lots, for a total of 34,346 parking spaces. In addition, there are 10,780 off-site spaces in private park-and-ride lots.

While public parking was growing, an employee lot for 6,300 cars was added. A planned expansion will take employee parking to 8,000. Remote parking is to grow another 2,000 spaces and a garage module will add another 1,600 to 1,800 spaces. When the construction is done, there will be more than over 46,000 parking spaces at DIA, and that doesn't include thousands of cars filling up Hertz and other rental car lots. So what we have now is a once-beautiful terminal that a sea of cars has diminished and dominated.

mantled without leaving very significant scars upon the landscape and damage to the environment."

IF YOU CAN'T BEAT 'EM, JOIN 'EM

AFTER VISITING THE CLIFFS, the question for us was McGanns, McDermotts, or O'Connors? Which of the three pubs on waterfront Fisher Street in Doolin would we visit, me for a beer and G for a cuppa? Doolin, three miles up the road from the cliffs on the way back to Fanore, was an Irish-speaking, sleepy fishing village discovered in the twenties and thirties by artists and writers—the likes of J.M. Synge, George Bernard Shaw, Dylan Thomas, and Oliver St. John Gogarty. Their gathering place was O'Connors, the stone-front, dark-timbered bar whose first beer was served in 1832.

Sleepy no more. Doolin has been described as an international shrine to Irish traditional music. The Russell brothers, Micho, Pakie, and Gussie, put Doolin on the music map. O'Connors was their home when they were not on tour. From the sixties on, Doolin became a magnet for almost anyone who played a guitar, flute, or concertina searching for the heart and soul of "trad" music. Even now, after the death of the Russell brothers, the village continues to feast on their memory. Doolin hosts a Russell Memorial Weekend every February, and a community center is named after the brothers. As we drove into the village, an international-looking collection of young folk—knapsacks, sleeping bags, jeans, guitars, penny whistles, long hair—were hanging out, listless, sitting and lying on the low stonewall across from the pubs. There is nothing so quiet as afternoon in a music pub where the action doesn't even start warming up until after 9:00 P.M.

So G and I settled into well worn-chairs at O'Connors that we were sure had once been warmed by George, or Dylan, or J.M., or Oliver. Had they been planners for the Cliffs of Moher, we knew they would have put nature first. They would have wanted gracefully curving native stone paths that flowed with the terrain, benches carefully placed for views and contemplation of "Atlantic waves slapping the sunny cliffs," and, just possibly, discrete rolling tea carts that would be moved about the site. Above all, the natural wonders would dominate—dramatic cliffs, rolling sea, singing winds, and graceful seabirds.

Now, with millions of euros in hand and the prospect of a million or more visitors a year, the Clare County Council is forging ahead with its project. Partly tucked in a hillside, it will include a café, restaurant, exhibition center, auditorium, multimedia center, retail shops, and masses of parking. And, wonder of wonders, Shannon Development, after declaring at the *An Bord Pleanala* hearings "a fundamental objection to the nature and scale of the [proposed] development," has now agreed to market and manage the whole shebang. If you can't beat 'em, join 'em.

Perhaps, over the entrance to the visitor center, they could hang a banner with only a slight revision of Betjeman's poem:

> *Lark song and sea sounds in the air*
> *And parking, parking everywhere.*

CHAPTER SEVEN

At School in Fanore

IMAGINE A SIXTH GRADE primary school class of only seven kids. Four girls and three boys greeted me with giant smiles. There was a festive air in the classroom, most probably because time with me meant no schoolwork. Having spent a good part of my professional life working to improve the performance of schools in the States, I was interested in what students in Ireland had to say about themselves, especially sixth graders—lots of energy, a willingness to share, and not too cautious. Fanore National School (St. Patrick's) was the first of four schools I would visit. The other three were Lispole, an Irish-speaking school on the Dingle Peninsula in Co Kerry, Castletownbere on the Beara Peninsula in West Cork, and at the end of our trip, back in Co Clare, the primary school in Quin.

Small Numbers in a Large Space

The Fanore school had one story, a flat roof, yellow brick, and large windows. It looked like a smaller version of institutional-looking primary schools all over the States. (I have always wondered why school design seldom reflects educational purpose. As often as not, a school looks like it could just as well be an office building or an assembly plant.) As I drove up to the school, there seemed to be more than the usual number of tots chasing about and shrieking in the schoolyard. Brid Queally, the principal, explained the large number of small children. Primary school in Ireland is eight years, grades one through six after two preparatory years known as "junior and senior infants." I love the idea of senior infants. Two preparatory years of socialization and learning provide a head start for all students.

The National Council for Curriculum and Assessment defines the curriculum for primary schools. Priests were once managers of the national schools. Now church authorities are limited to formulating and implementing the religious curriculum. The role of the church in public education, while now less dominant, dates back to the introduction of state primary education in the mid- nineteenth century. Today, a board of management under diocesan patronage that includes a local clergyman controls each national primary school. The curriculum goal is said to encompass "spiritual, moral, cognitive, emotional, imaginative, aesthetic, social, and physical" elements of individual development.

The Fanore National School has a grand total of twenty students. This is one-fourth the number of students a century earlier. The decline in enrollment is one measure of emigration from the rural west of Ireland to the big cities and overseas. However, small numbers do not seem to limit school activities. There are whistle and fiddle classes, Irish dancing, a school choir, and watercolor instruction by a local artist. Students participate in *Slogadh*, regional and national music and dance competitions, and in student athletic leagues. Major games are soccer and hurling, an ancient Gaelic game involving *hurley* ("stick") and *sliotar* ("ball"). A year before, students made a video of *King Lear* with the rockscape of the Burren as the stage setting.

As kids talked about themselves, it was clear that they were self-reliant and used their imaginations to make the most of what the Burren had to offer. Though small in number, they commanded a lot of space. They had no fear of wandering about in the Burren or expectation that parents would be their chauffeurs, which seems to be the primary occupation of many parents in the States. The term "play date" was entirely foreign to them. While the townland (a division of land, the smallest administrative unit in Ireland) of Fanore seemed a great place to grow up, only one of the sixth graders planned to live in Fanore after finishing school. She had a pet lamb and a dog named Lassie, and she wanted to be a vet.

KEEPING PARENTS HAPPY

WHEN WE GOT down to specifics, this is what my new sixth-grade friends had to offer.

How to deal with parents? Make them laugh a lot. Tell them jokes. Clean up your room.

When you think of the U.S., what do you think about first? Disneyland. Big buildings and traffic. Warm weather.

What do you like most about living in this area? Quiet peaceful place when there are no tourist buses. Beaches and mountains. Wildlife and birds. What are the negatives? Nothing to do. No shops.

What do people need to make them happy? Get along. Be nice to each other. Family. Friends. Love. Laughter.

Watch television each day? Three kids, less than one hour. Four, two to three hours. Favorite programs? *Sheep in the Big City*, *The Simpsons*, *Nightmare Room*.

What do you want to be? Girls, one farmer/vet, one architect, and two teachers. Boys, two professional soccer players, and one accountant.

Most interesting, though it should have been no surprise, was the closeness students felt to the U.S., as if it was an extension of Ireland.

Four of the kids had been on visits to relatives in the States, and one had plans to go in a few months. Between them, the seven students had seventeen close relatives living in the States—four aunts, four uncles, eight cousins, and one brother. Those seventeen are among the 34.3 million U.S. residents of Irish ancestry, a number nine times the population of Ireland itself (3.9 million) and twelve percent of the U.S. population.

TRUE LOVE WILL FIND A WAY

SHORTLY AFTER OUR STAY in Fanore, I was to learn something of the school's history and what was once the power of the church in "public" education. The *Irish Examiner* headline read, "Sacked Teacher Case Reopened After 86 Years." The story began, "The Diocese of Galway is investigating the case of a priest who sacked a national school master for refusing to marry a colleague—86 years ago." The rest of the tale:

> The year was 1914. The setting, St. Patrick's National Primary School in Fanore. Michael O'Shea, school principal, falls in love with Kate, a Galway girl, and tells Fr. Kerin, parish priest and school manager of his intention to marry Kate. Fr. Kerin, who sounds like a character out of John B. Keane's novel *The Bodhran Makers* ("The mean spirited Canon Peter Pius Tett rules the presbytery with an iron hand and expects to rule the lives of everyone in the parish in the same way."). Fr. Kerin tells O'Shea that he won't allow him to marry Kate and that he has to marry the assistant teacher in the Fanore school so they can live, happily or not, in the official school residence. O'Shea says no way, marries Kate, and is fired by Fr. Kerin. With local support, O'Shea then starts a school of his own. Sixty of the eighty pupils in Fanore Primary are withdrawn by their parents

and sent to O'Shea's school. The Bishop of Galway, Dr O'Dea, refuses to give the children the sacrament. Then, an even greater blow, a letter is read out at Mass threatening to withdraw all sacraments from the children and their parents. This forces O'Shea to close his school and move to Cork with Kate and their five children. After a period of hard times, O'Shea starts teaching again at the city's Model School.

Two surviving O'Shea daughters, Brenda and Kay, now in their seventies, want the true story confirmed and made a matter of record. The Irish National Teachers Organization is backing them up. The Diocese of Galway is investigating.

AND A CUP OF TEA ON GALWAY BAY

It's far away I am today
From scenes I roamed a boy
And long ago the hour, I know
I first saw Illinois
But Time nor Tide, nor waters wide
Could wean my heart away
For ever true it flies to you
My own dear Galway Bay
                    —Francis A. Fahy, "My Dear Own Galway Bay"

AFTER MY SCHOOL VISIT, G and I went off on an unhurried drive up the coast to Ballyvaghan. It was a sunny afternoon. Sparkling waves of the Atlantic, quiet this day, rolled in on one side of the road, the rocky foothills of Slieve Elva guarded the other side, and a lot of blind curves slowed the sparse traffic. About three miles north of Fanore at Black Head, Galway Bay began and the view over the water fanned out to include the Aran Islands to the west and north across the bay to Galway. Black Head marks the most northerly point in Co Clare. There, the road swings sharply east and the scene changes, with the calm bay on one side and Gleninagh Mountain on the other. Along the way, remains of castles and churches and farm cottages speak for history.

Ballyvaghan, with a population of 201, is about three miles beyond Black Head. It sits at the head of the Burren beside Galway Bay and was originally an important trading post with a significant fishing industry. The village began its slide into economic decline at the end of the nineteenth century and was said to be terminal by the 1950s. At that point its revival as a tourist center began to take off. Now it has many of the "benefits" of a tourist-based economy—seasonal jobs mainly for women, a shortage of affordable housing for locals, tacky new buildings, and an overtaxed sewer system.

Along the coast between Fanore and Black Head, limestone beds form cliffs and terraces that descend to the sea. They provide breeding grounds and homes for a huge variety of plants and creatures ranging from brown seaweeds to tiny limpets, mussels, and squat lobsters. Around Black Head, limestone rock pools are rich with purple sea urchins, cockles and winkles, red and green anemones, starfish, and dog whelks. Most amazing, in the words of a naturalist, dog whelks, "marauding like wolf packs," bore tiny holes in mussel shells and inject a fluid, allowing them to suck out the mussel. Starfish are more direct. They use their suckers to pry open the shells and extend their jaws for a happy meal.

This being the fall migration time, the odd flock of birds and some stragglers enhanced the scene—auks, gannets, petrels, and terns.

A roadside sign just past Black Head announced in large letters, "BIRD HIDE." I knew perfectly well the sign indicated where to go to observe birds, but I couldn't stop myself from dwelling on the unfairness of it all. If the birds had found a place to hide, it was really bad form to tell everyone about it.

As we drove into Ballyvaghan along Galway Bay, to our good luck, *An Fhearr Gorta* ("tea and garden") beckoned us. Our memory of the tearoom resonates. Why, I wonder, did a pleasant but unremarkable place leave such an imprint? Good natural light. A table for two at the window, looking out to a small, informal garden. Tasteful crockery and silver. Excellent Earl Grey tea. Delicious pound cake. Unobtrusive service. Civilized atmosphere. It was the perfect place to linger and talk over our experiences of the last few days in Co Clare—Willy Daly and the Japanese ensemble, the war of Mullaghmore, the Cliffs of Moher, students at Fanore primary, and the rocky wonders of the Burren.

The next morning after a breakfast that would last us most of the day, it was a warm goodbye from Ita and Noel at the Rockyview Farmhouse and off to the Dingle, the first of four peninsulas we would visit—Dingle, Beara, Mizen, and Sheep's Head.

CHAPTER EIGHT

ON TO COUNTY KERRY

Oh the days of the Kerry dancing
Oh the ring of the pipers's tune
Oh, for one of those hours of gladness
Gone, alas, like our youth, too soon!
When the boys began to gather
In the glen of a summer's night
And the Kerry piper's tuning
Made us long with wild delight!
Oh, to think of it
Oh, to dream of it
Fills my heart with tears!

—James Lyman Molloy, "Kerry Dance"

THE PLACES IN BETWEEN

THERE IS A NEED for guidebooks dealing with the places in between—how to get from here to there in a reasonably efficient way and halfway enjoy it. Fanore to Lispole on the Dingle Peninsula was six hours and a mixed bag. We left Lispole at a leisurely morning hour, early enough to avoid the tour buses from Galway and Limerick. The

highway ran south, the odd ruin here and there, a peek at the ocean
now and then, past the turn-off to Willie Daly's place and memories
of the Japanese ensemble, and down Main Street of Ennistymon past
Suzanne Crosbie's shop, where we had talked of the war of
Mullaghmore.

It was near Coolraclare, round a curve and there, plain as day, an
apparition, a neat row of pink, yellow and green cottages with peaked
roofs, gingerbread trim, and ever so well-tended lawns. They looked
like an illustration from a children's easy reader pasted on to the landscape. There was nothing natural-looking about the cottages. Older
stone and stucco buildings fit. They have an organic look. These
jarred. They looked phony. We were to see a number of other new
developments of the same sort. Irish planning authorities need to
adopt a new slogan—"Modern comfort does not require bad design."

Next stop, the car ferry across the River Shannon to take us from
Kilmer in Clare to Tarbert in Kerry.

On long drives, G's job, other than map reading, is to sing a song
or two from her repertoire of 184 (I kid you not) folk songs in several
languages. As we pulled onto the ferry pier at Kilmer, G's sweet voice
was into William French's famous "Eileen Og":

> *Eileen Og, an' that the darlin's name is,*
> *Through the Barony her features they were famous.*
> *If we loved her then who was there to blame us*
> *For wasn't she the Pride of Petravore?*
> *But her beauty made us all so shy*
> *Not a man could look her in the eye*
> *Boys, Oh boys, sure that's the reason why*
> *We're in mournin' for the Pride of Petravore*
> *Eileen Og me heart is growin' grey*
> *Ever since the day you wandered far away*
> *Eileen Og there's good fish in the say*
> *But there's none of them like the Pride of Petravore*

VIRGINS ON PARADE

FROM TARBERT it was on to Tralee, capital town and administrative center of Co Kerry and the well-advertised gateway to the Dingle Peninsula. At Tralee, the highway dove into narrow back streets where row on row of small, bleak houses testified to the industrial roots of Tralee, now one of the unemployment black spots in the country. Shoes, knitwear, and plastics remain the base of the weak local economy. Tourism is the growth industry, and the Rose of Tralee Festival is a long-standing mainstay of Tralee's quest for visitors. And who doesn't know the Spencer and Glover song "The Rose of Tralee," dating back to 1845.

The pale moon was rising
Above the green mountain;
The sun was declining
Beneath the blue sea
When I strayed with my love
To the pure crystal fountain
That stands in the beautiful
Vale of Tralee.

She was lovely and fair as the rose of summer
Yet, 'Twas not her beauty alone that won me
Oh no! 'Twas the truth in her eyes ever beaming
That made me love Mary, the Rose of Tralee.

The "internationally renowned" Rose of Tralee Festival features a Miss America type contest for young ladies of Irish descent. They come from all over the world—from Boston to Cork and Dubai to Dublin—to compete for the crown of Rose Queen. The festival nearly went under in 2004. Festival promoters came up €300,000 short of the ready, but commercial sponsors saved the day. Like Miss

America, which ABC has announced it will no longer air because of lagging interest, contestants parade their assets about, perform a poem or song, and profess undying love of humanity. Press releases pronounce the Rose of Tralee Festival a "vibrant program of entertainment that is suitable for all ages." *Holidayhound Ireland* calls it a "kitsch blot on the Irish landscape."

A limiting factor for the Rose of Tralee beauty contest may be, and I quote *Holidayhound*, "All the contestants [for Rose Queen] have to be virgins. Before entering, the girls have to sign a form declaring that they have never been with anybody, in the Biblical sense."

While on the subject of Rose Queens, I feel obliged to note that the conventional wisdom has it that the true Rose of Tralee was the "papist peasant" Mary O'Connor, a maid in the service of William Mulchinock's parents, they of the Established (Protestant) Church. William fell passionately in love with Mary. It was, the story goes, unrequited love. I feel obliged to note there is also "Bessie the Rose of Tralee," written by Frank Dumont in 1875.

> *She's a gem of rare value to me*
> *The fairest and dearest of all,*
> *Is Bessie, the rose of Tralee.*
> *Her kisses are waiting for me,*
> *And soon her sweet face I will see;*
> *Without her the world is so drear,*
> *Sweet Bessie, the rose of Tralee.*

THE LADY AND THE LURCHER

OUT OF THE MAZE of back streets of Tralee, one can see a glimpse of Tralee Bay, and into Biennerville, the main port of emigration from Co Kerry during the Great Famine of 1845–1849. The huge Biennerville Windmill (This is Tuesday. It can't be Holland!) dominated the scene and looked totally out of place. Signs announced "The Largest Working Windmill in Ireland." It included a pottery, craft shops, an exhibition hall, an audio-visual presentation on Biennerville's history, a miller ready to take us on a tour to learn the four steps of flour milling, and a restaurant. We opted for the restaurant, a huge cafeteria with the ambience of a well-kept dairy barn. The tea was hot, the food was cold, it was a gray rainy day, we had been on our way for nearly six hours, and we were more than ready for our destination, twenty miles or so to the Old Farmhouse in Minard West, Lispole.

When I was planning the trip, I found the description of the Old Farmhouse and its proprietor Jill intriguing: keen sailor, skippered eleven-ton teak sloop, ran a bookshop, transformed the farmhouse into hillside oasis, breathtaking views of Dingle Bay, inviting rooms, turf fire, friendly lurcher. Finding the Old Farmhouse was another matter. Posted road names were not a priority in the area. At my third "where is the damn place" try, Patrick, a petrol station operator, said he knew the Old Farmhouse and described the way there in some detail—turn around, go past Sullivan's Bar, take a left at a disintegrating building with grazing cows across the way, and maybe there would be a sign to Minard Castle.

In Irish fashion, Patrick was expecting further chat. After talking about his relatives in Boston, his hopes to visit Colorado one day, and a discussion of Moab, Utah, and nearby Monument Valley where John Wayne movies were made, G and I were on our way, passing the South Pole Inn for the third time. (South Pole Inn in Annascaul? A reminder to check it out.) At the deserted store, turn left to Minard Castle, climb a steep hill. There were cottage ruins on left. Take a right at the new cow shed. Half mile and we were there—a single-story pink house with white stucco garden walls and black iron gates. It was late afternoon.

A sturdy, no-nonsense, tweedy, six-foot plus English woman opened the gate and told me exactly where to park. This was Jill. G looked confused, uncertain. "Well," I thought, "its been a long drive.

The poor dear is a bit weary." Turned out G, who is nothing if not imaginative, had expected to be greeted by a crusty, white-bearded sea captain who would lurch toward us with a hearty hello. Where did G get this idea? She had glanced at the description of the Old Farmhouse in *Sawdays Guide*. The description begins, "A friendly lurcher will welcome you enthusiastically . . ." and continues on about a "keen sailor" and a "teak sloop." And there, with any imagination, you have the lurching, crusty old sea captain.

Had G only known that a lurcher is a type of dog, it might have warded off her confusion. In the category of astounding things you might never have wanted to know, the Official Lurcher & Staghound website (*www.users.daelnet.co.uk/lurchers*) explains the lurcher is not a breed but a type of dog, "produced by customizing the greyhound to the specific needs of the owner. . . . The lurcher is happy at the foot of his master or the tail of a hare."

THE SMALLEST THRONE

THE FARMHOUSE HAD a small and pleasant but somewhat dark sitting room. One door from the room led to Jill's private quarters. Straight ahead, an archway opened to a sunroom facing Dingle Bay, and another door led to the guest bedrooms and bath. With coffee and cake in hand, we talked with Jill about dinner places in Dingle, my planned visit to the local school, a boat ride (plan aborted when Jill saw how creaky we were), and other things to consider during our four-day stay. G and I then went off to investigate our quarters, accurately described as simple. Bedside reading lights were inadequate, so we negotiated for additional lamps.

The "bathroom" was memorable. In a contest for a "full bath" in the smallest possible space, this one would be a clear winner. A tiny sink in one corner was of tooth-brushing and hand-washing size. The anorexic shower, about eighteen inches square, tucked into another corner, had a small curb to contain water and a curtain that pulled around two sides. Neither G nor I had the courage to try it during our stay. The throne was tucked in a closet-like alcove facing the shower. Fortunately, it had a handicap grab bar on one wall to assist in lowering and raising oneself. Rising had to be done slowly and with care, or else you could easily end up in the shower.

As we were leaving for dinner in Dingle town, I mentioned to Jill the possibility I would be getting a phone call from the States and asked if she could please take a message. For reasons we could never figure out, the use of the phone produced a certain tension. There was a sense we were not so much welcome paying guests as intruders in her home. In the end, we left a day early.

Now, it was off to dinner in Dingle town with plans for early to bed and an active day to follow.

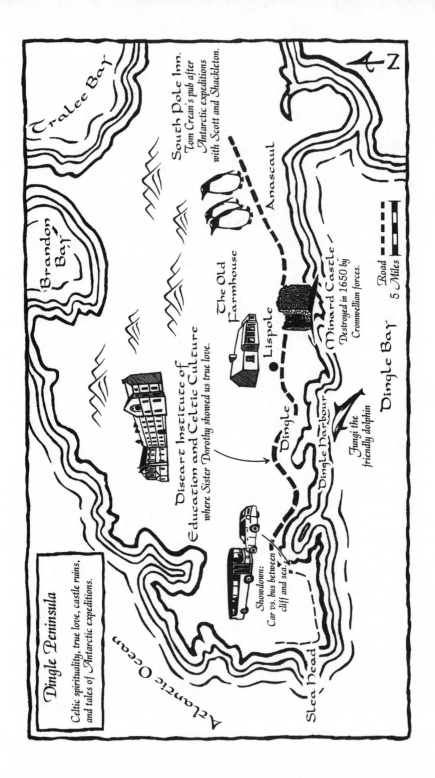

Dingle Peninsula

Celtic spirituality, true love, castle ruins, and tales of Antarctic expeditions.

Atlantic Ocean

Tralee Bay

Brandon Bay

South Pole Inn.
Tom Crean's pub after Antarctic expeditions with Scott and Shackleton.

Anascaul

Diseart Institute of Education and Celtic Culture
where Sister Dorothy showed us true love.

The Old Farmhouse

Lispole

Minard Castle –
Destroyed in 1650 by Cromwellian forces.

Dingle

Dingle Harbour

Fungi the friendly dolphin

Dingle Bay

Road
5 Miles

Showdown:
Car vs. bus between cliff and sea.

Slea Head

N

CHAPTER NINE

FROM THE STONE AGE
TO THE MOVIE AGE

THERE ARE FEW descriptions of the Dingle Peninsula that don't go over the top. "A land of blue gold hills and sandy beaches, glorious water-falls, hidden bays, wondrous rock formations, caves and arches, busy harbors and wayside pubs, a land dappled with heather, primroses, bluebells, foxgloves and fuchsia, and smiling faces to welcome you." Or this, "The Dingle Peninsula is a place of intense, shifting beauty. Spectacular mountains, long sandy beaches and the staggering splinter-slatted mass of rocks that defines the extraordinary coast at Slea Head." If that's not enough try, "Some have called it the most beautiful place on earth, this spit of land bounded on three sides by the sea, its rocky outcrops and steep cliffs the stuff of which dreams are made."

If its roots you are looking for, "There is no other landscape in Western Europe with the density and variety of archeological monu-ments as the Dingle Peninsula." But, as to the Stone Age, the Bronze Age, and other epochs that define the peninsula's change over time, there may well be none that equal the Movie Age.

THE DINGLE ON THE MOVE

I HAVE ALWAYS been interested in what conditions create readiness for change in a society, what makes for lasting change in outlook and behavior, and what artifacts of a lasting nature does a particular age produce? It took the Dingle Peninsula 4,969 years to "progress" from the Stone Age to the Movie Age and its principal product, *Ryan's Daughter.*

The Stone Age (4000 B.C.–*2500* B.C.). Stone tombs, pottery, permanent structures, shift from hunters/gatherers of the Mesolithic Period to farmers.

The Bronze Age (2500 B.C.–500 B.C.). Stone circles, standing stones, cist graves, bronze implements, weapons, and jewelry, intensive agriculture, habitation huts.

The Iron Age (500 B.C.–500 A.D.). Promontory hill forts, ogham stones (ogham is early Irish writing), holy wells, Celtic goddesses of fertility and protection, pilgrimage.

Early Christian Period (sixth to twelfth centuries). Ring forts, monastic sites—oratories, cross slabs, beehive huts, shrines, sundials—and St. Brendan, the seafaring monk who is said to have sailed to America long before Columbus.

Viking & Medieval Periods. In the ninth century, Vikings plunder monasteries, set up trade routes, and build towns. In the twelfth century, church changes to diocesan system ruled by bishops who organized parish churches; Normans arrive from the continent, build more towns, and structure Irish society on a European model. In 1585, Queen Elizabeth sanctions Dingle town (*Daingean Ui Chuis*). In the sixteenth and seventeenth centuries, rebellion and counter-rebellion.

1600s on. 1649–1650, Oliver Cromwell's army crushes Irish resistance on the Dingle peninsula with the blowing up of Minard Castle (just up the road from our B&B). From the seventeenth century to the 1920s, turbulent period of landlordism with evictions, land agitation, and the Great Famine of 1845–1849. In Ireland, 1,500,000 die of hunger and disease (five thousand die in the Dingle Poorhouse). And 1,500,00 who can afford to migrate. Ireland's population, eight million in 1830, was cut in half to four million by 1850.

The Republic. In 1870, nationalism reasserted. In 1920, separate parliaments form for northern Ireland (six counties) and southern Ireland (twenty-six counties). The year 1923 saw the beginning of the Irish Free State for the southern counties. In 1938 a new constitution declaring complete independence and renouncing British sovereignty is adopted. The Republic of Ireland is established in 1949.

And then for Dingle, the Movie Age.

THE MOVIE AGE

I KID YOU NOT. The making of the movie *Ryan's Daughter* on the Dingle Peninsula in 1969 had a tectonic impact on the culture and economy of the peninsula. It marked a new age for Ireland's western outpost. Almost every piece of Dingle tourist literature calls attention to *Ryan's Daughter.* "The peninsula has a place in film history. *Ryan's Daughter* was filmed here." Or, "Made famous by *Ryan's Daughter*, northeast Kerry offers some of the wildest natural scenery in Ireland." *Ryan's Daughter* is thrust on you at every turn. Signposts direct you to "Ryan's Daughter" beach, otherwise known as Slea Head. Or just follow the tour buses. It's been thirty-five years since the film was released and won an academy award for cinematography. It still has "legs" in Kerry.

Why the impact?

Economic stagnation and chronic emigration ruled the Dingle Peninsula and much of Ireland after the Free Staters versus Republicans civil war of the early 1920s. The depression of the 1930s followed. The Dingle Peninsula lingered on in the grip of poverty, dependent on small-scale fishing and farming. Its dramatic beauty and archeological treasures were unknown and unappreciated. In 1969, into this quiet pool, came all the people and paraphernalia and spending ways that go with the production of a major motion picture filmed on location—director, producer, cinematography, costume, make-up, sound, and, of course, the stars—Robert Mitchum, Sarah Miles, Trevor Howard, John Mills, and Leo McKern. With perfectionist David Lean directing and constantly rewriting the script, production of *Ryan's Daughter* lingered on for nearly a year. Mitchum rented a house for his family, hired cooks, maids and nannies, and partied in the Dingle pubs. All the stars, others in the cast, and production crews had to be housed, fed, driven about, and cared for. Many locals became extras in the film.

In a word, the movie was a cash cow for Dingle folk. The huge infusion of money marked the first stage in transformation of the Dingle economy and lifestyle. The second stage came after the release of the movie. *Ryan's Daughter* showed the world the beauty and adventure of Dingle at a time the global tide of tourism was rising, and Americans with Irish roots were on a search for their heritage. And so began the peninsula's boom as a tourist Mecca.

For those too young to know it or those who have forgotten it, here is the plot of *Ryan's Daughter*. The time is World War I. Young Rosy Ryan (Sarah Miles), daughter of Irish publican Tom Ryan (Leo McKern), marries passionless older schoolmaster Charles Shaughnessy (Robert Mitchum). The wedding night doesn't go well. In time, Rosy falls for Major Randolph Doryan (Christopher Jones), a wounded British officer in command of an army occupation garrison. They embark on any number of passionate trysts, always choosing locations on the beautiful and tempestuous coastline where the scenery is at its most breathtaking—Slea Head, Coumeenoole Bay, and Inch Strand. One stormy day, IRA revolutionaries are waiting at Slea Head for a shipment of arms by sea from the Germans who want the IRA to make life difficult for the British. Tom Ryan is a snitch and informs Doryan, who intercepts the shipment and arrests IRA leaders. Townspeople have learned of Rosy's love affair with Doryan, believe she was the informer, and exact revenge. Feeling himself at fault, Doryan commits suicide. Rosy and Shaughnessy reunite and leave town to rebuild their lives.

MAN VERSUS BUS

Ryan's Daughter Walk. At the very point where the scenery becomes truly breathtaking, so does the walk for all the wrong reasons. It follows narrow roads through much of Ryan's Daughter *territory to the north of Slea Head which are jammed with fume-pumping cars and coaches. And if you are expecting the landscape to look as it did when director David Lean came out here with a cast that included Robert Mitchum, Trevor Howard, Sarah Miles and John Mills, you'll be disappointed, for the glorious western tip of the Dingle Peninsula has changed markedly since then . . . scores of rectangular yellow and magnolia dwellings dotted higgledy-piggledy across the landscape.*

—Alf Anderson, *The Guardian*, May 2003

G AND I HAD PLANNED to spend our day on a tour of the peninsula with stops at archeological sites, a walk along the ocean beach and rocky cliffs, lunch at an out of the way pub, and a visit to an interesting sounding pottery. The weather was what the Irish call a "soft day." We rather like a misty drizzle, but this day the rain that began softly turned hard. It was a serious downpour. The road was full of cars and buses, all seemingly headed in our direction. The places we thought of stopping were already full of cars and people who didn't look like they were having a grand time. I was ready to be annoyed when a large sign pointing the way to Ryan's Daughter Beach filled our view. It was as if the beach was a national monument. Too damn commercial! *Ryan's Daughter*, was, after all just a movie, and Slea Head was but one of several beach locations used in the film. Perhaps they should sanctify one of the bar stools Robert Mitchum got looped on. Or maybe they have. Grumble! Grumble!

It wasn't turning out to be a good day. We may not have given the peninsula a fair shake, but we decided to cut our losses, turn around, go back to Dingle town for lunch, and make the best of the remains of the day. "Turn around" was a mistake. Two or three miles on, dead ahead, a big Mercedes tour bus, a behemoth, filled the narrow road. The driver was edging the bus very carefully around a curve to avoid a rock cliff on one side and the ocean on the other. There was no way past the bus and no pull off for me. There we were, radiator-to-radiator, *mano a mano*. The bus driver glared from his high perch.

No one had told me and no road sign indicated that traffic was supposed to move clockwise around the peninsula. And there I was, in a counterclockwise confrontation. I motioned to the bus driver to back up. He stood fast and had about twenty cars piled up behind to make his case. "Back up," he motioned to me, and smiled. Clearly, he felt he had the advantage. About a hundred yards back, there was a small pull-off but no way for me to turn around to get to it. A dent in my back left fender already indicated limited skills at backing up a right hand drive. I wasn't going to try it here between the cliff and the ocean. The solution—shut engine off. Take key, get out, and walk confidently to the bus. The driver opened the door and looked down. I looked up.

"You want the car moved, you move it," says I.

"Right mate," says he.

Back we walked to the Ford Focus. I got in the rear seat. He got in the driver's seat, turned the engine on, and put the car in reverse. And back we whizzed. With a kindly look, a twinkle, and some pity, he handed me the key, walked back to the bus, geared up, and drove by. Everyone on the bus waved, and twenty cars went by. Triumphant, we continued on our way, counterclockwise. Fortunately, the road widened some.

KITSCH CHASES CLASS

AS WE DROVE into Dingle along the quay, we saw a well-protected harbor filled with colorful fishing boats, low stone walls, and color-washed sheds and houses. We had a momentary sense of old Dingle when, as a market town and fishing port, it was a center for extensive trade with France and Spain. In 1607, when King James granted Dingle its charter, it was a walled town with only two entry gates. Thus its Gaelic name, *An Daingean*, meaning "fortress."

The sense of old Dingle passed quickly with reminders that the principal business of Dingle is now tourism. Signs advertised Dingle's most celebrated citizen, Fungi, the "world-famous" bottle-nosed dolphin. Fungi has lived and played in a small area at the mouth of Dingle Harbor since 1983. From dawn until late at night, Fungi hangs around to welcome boats, trawlers, and yachts to town. For ten dollars, you can join a bunch of other tourists and go out on a forty-five-minute tour to see and play with Fungi. Or, you can rent a wetsuit and swim out for fun and games with Fungi on your own. Locals say Fungi has been known to bring gifts to swimmers, a live fish in his mouth, but refuses anything in return.

In contrast to *Ryan's Daughter*, at least you can say Fungi is alive and real. Some people talk of their meetings with this thirteen-foot, 670-pound maritime mammal (*tursiops truncates*) in spiritual and religious terms. The critical question is what will Dingle do when Fungi passes on? As far as I know, Fungi doesn't have an understudy. Perhaps Dingle can recruit a replacement from the Dolphin Academy in Curacao. Their dolphins, Teresa, Bonnie, and Pepito, will kiss you if you ask.

Several celebrities are said to favor Dingle town as a "hideaway," including Julia Roberts, Paul Simon, and Dolly Parton. There is even a "path of stars" on Green Street to note visits by these and other luminaries. I like the idea of announcing to one and all names of stars who come to Dingle as a "hideaway." It reminds me of a flight some years ago when two minutes after takeoff my exotic seatmate introduced herself: "I'm Maxine, one of the Andrew Sisters, but I'm traveling incognito." Some incognito! Some hideaway!

As to other attributes, Dingle touts its fifty-two pubs, one for every twenty-three residents—man, woman, and child. There are growing numbers of restaurants and tee shirt, trinket, curio, and craft shops. According to Gresham's Law, dating back to 1858, "bad money drives good money out of circulation." Rovetch's law of tourist towns: "Tasteless dominates. Kitsch chases quality." I am afraid that the very aspects of Irish life that are valued most are being lost in the rush to market them. If this sounds elitist, so be it.

We did leave Dingle that day on a pleasant note. We had lunch at the Café Liteartha, a café-cum-bookshop that offers a welcome mix of literacy, good food, and conversation. It was a good send-off to our next stop, Minard Castle.

MINARD CASTLE

AS WE TRAVELED back in time, the narrow gravel road to Minard Castle wound around green hills, dipped into a shallow valley, and crossed a quiet brook. Later, I wondered if this quiet brook was the one poet and patriot Thomas Ashe had in mind. Ashe was born in Minard parish in 1885.

Brook, happy brook, that glidest through my dell;
That trippest with soft feet across the mead;
That, laughing on, a mazy course dost lead,
O'er pebble beds, and reeds, and rushy swell;
Go by that cottage where my love doth dwell.

G felt that Ashe was more patriot than poet. He took part in the Easter Rising of 1916, for which he was sentenced to death. The sentence was later commuted to hard labor for life. Released in 1917 and arrested again for agitation, he led prisoners on a hunger strike and died as a result. Thirty thousand sympathizers joined his funeral procession.

Minard Castle dates back to the sixteenth century, when it was a stronghold of the Knights of Kerry. In the Cromwellian period, Walter Hussey from Castlegregory garrisoned it, and Cromwell's forces blew it up after the defenders ran out of powder. The castle walls still stand, a foursquare fortress topping a hill that slopes to the sea. Great smooth, round boulders thrown up by the sea and piled one on another filled a natural storm beach at the foot of the hill. To the south, a series of slab cliffs jutted into the sea. G and I sat there for a while listening to the sea and watching wave after wave splash on the rocks and run up the sand. We were alone and had a sense of possession. It was ours, and we were very pleased with ourselves.

The castle and surroundings seemed not much different than the picture Samuel Lewis described in 1837 in his *Topographical Dictionary of Ireland*:

MINARD, a parish, in the barony of CORKAGUINEY, county of KERRY, and province of MUNSTER, 5 miles (E.S.E) from Dingle on the road to Tralee; containing 1474 inhabitants. It is situated on the northern side of the bay of Dingle: near the shore are the ruins of Minard Castle. The parish comprises 4927 statute acres, as apploted under the tithe act, of which 2770 acres are arable land, and the remainder consists of course mountain pasture, mostly reclaimable: good building stone is found in several places. Sea-weed and sand are in general use for manure; and the bog, being nearly exhausted, turf for fuel is brought from the coast of Iveragh on the opposite side of Dingle bay. The bay abounds with a variety of fish, but the fishery is here attended with much trouble and danger, the adjacent coast for several miles consisting of precipitous cliffs, and there is but a single narrow creek, in which only one boat can land at a time. The parish is in the diocese of Ardfert and

Aghadoe: the rectory is partly impropriate [private property] in Lord Ventry, but chiefly in the Earl of Cork, and the vicarage forms part of the union of Ballinacourty or Kilflyn.

INTRODUCTION TO A HERO

I HAVE NEVER been able to pass up a bookstore. Wandering about and picking the odd book off a shelf is never wasted time. It is rather like a lottery with pretty good odds. And so it was with Café Liteartha in Dingle and the discovery there of Michael Smith's book, *An Unsung Hero: Tom Crean—Antarctic Survivor.* Here was the answer to my lingering question. Why was there a pub called the South Pole Inn in Annascaul, Ireland? Tom Crean, proprietor of the South Pole Inn, was, according to Smith, "one of the finest characters to emerge from the Heroic Age of Polar Exploration." We know now that few men made greater contributions to the annals of polar exploration and founding the Antarctic continent. Crean played a central role in three Antarctic expeditions: Scott's *Discovery* (1901–1904), Scott's *In Terra Nova* (1910–1913), and Shackleton's *Endurance* (1914–1916).

Crean was born in 1877 on a remote hillside farm near Annascaul, one of ten children in a family struggling to eke out a meager existence on the land. Education was little more than learning to read and write. In 1893 at age fifteen, taking a boat from the bay at Minard Castle, he lied about his age and signed up with the British Navy as Boy Second Class. It was an escape from poverty. Several years later, Petty Officer Crean had a chance to volunteer on Scott's *Discovery*, the first concerted exploration of the Antarctic—the coldest, windiest, highest continent on Earth. Scott recognized Crean's unflappable qualities and asked him to join his next expedition, the *Terra Nova*. First, there were three and a half months of crossing dreadful terrain, man-hauling a sled for fifteen hundred miles in subzero temperatures. Then, to save one of his comrades who had come down with scurvy and was unable to continue, Crean, with only two sticks of chocolate and three biscuits in his pocket, no other food, and no sleeping bag or tent for protection, walked, stumbled, and crawled for eighteen straight hours and thirty-five miles to Hut Point for help. Crean's remarkable effort has been described as "the finest feat of individual heroism from the entire age of exploration."

Crean's next polar expedition was with Shackleton. After their ship the *Endurance* was crushed in the ice and sank, the crew made it to uninhabited Elephant Island in three open boats. In a search for help, Crean, Shackleton, and three others made an eight hundred mile, seventeen-day crossing of the Southern Ocean from Elephant Island to South Georgia in the twenty-two foot *James Caird.* Then Crean, Shackleton, and Worsley, the three still standing, crossed the unknown, uncharted, mountainous, snow-filled interior of South Georgia to reach the whaling station at Stromness and find help for the men left behind on Elephant Island. Adventurers today, equipped with all manner of modern gear, find the route difficult and can't understand how the "three" managed it. In Crean's words, "We had to."

In 1916, following the *Endurance* expedition, in the midst of World War I, Crean rejoined the navy. He survived the war, retired in 1920, returned to Annascaul, married Eileen Herlihy, a publican's daughter, opened the South Pole Inn, and raised a family. Other than to children, Crean never talked in public about his exploits and never gave a single interview to a writer. Words most often associated with Crean are courage, endurance, and heroism. He was said to have a "fund of wit and an even temper which nothing disturbed."

After he had gone to the end of the earth three times and bested the worst the Antarctic could throw at him, Crean, aged 61, died near his birthplace of a ruptured appendix in July 1938. Crean is buried in a Ballinacourty Graveyard in a tomb he built himself. On top of the tomb is a wreath of porcelain flowers that Teddy Evans, the man Crean saved by walking and crawling thirty-five miles for help, put there.

The South Pole Inn

IT WAS ONLY a few minutes drive from our perch on the wave-washed rocks at the foot of Minard Castle to the South Pole Inn. It seemed appropriate for us to leave for the inn from very near the spot Crean had left to join the navy nearly a hundred years before.

The Owenscaul River flows by the two-story blue-and-white South Pole Inn. The inn's road sign portrays a snowy scene with a small tent and two nearsighted penguins looking on. "Tom Crean" stands out in large gold letters on the front of the building. The pub is a personable place, with warm wood, a small bar, and a slow-burning peat fire. It is a suitable place to toast a great hero. It was easy to imagine Crean, sitting in the corner, stoking his pipe and reading the evening paper. That's the picture of him locals say they saw most often.

The wall of another room is covered with Crean memorabilia, a remarkable set of photos telling something of the story of the continent that confronted the Antarctic explorers, how they endured it, and in some cases how it subdued them. It is an impressive photographic record. The Tom Crean Society meets monthly in an upstairs room that was once Crean's bedroom.

G and I drank our toasts to the man locals called "Tom the Pole" and settled in for a pleasant dinner and a good end to the day.

CHAPTER TEN

LEARNING FROM THE LADS

JOHN THE BAPTIST

IT WAS ANOTHER soft morning, steady drizzle, a bit of fog, and peaceful green fields. I was off down Minard Castle Road to chat with sixth graders at *Scoil Eoin Baiste* (John the Baptist) primary school in Lispole, where all classes are taught in Irish. Lispole is called the gateway to the Dingle Gaeltacht, one of seven regions of Ireland where Irish is said to be the major or standard language, i.e. the vernacular. In addition to the Dingle peninsula, Gaeltacht regions include parts of Donegal, Mayo, Galway, Cork, Meath, and Waterford. Population of all Gaeltacht regions taken together totals around 86,000, only 2.4 percent of the population of Ireland.

Gaeltacht regions were recognized as distinct areas during the years of the Irish Free State beginning in 1926. Government policy aimed at restoring the Irish language as the official language of Ireland after a period of significant decline in the use of Irish. The objective of Gaeltacht policy remains "the primacy of the Irish language and its related culture in the Gaeltacht." Pronouncements of the Department of Community, Rural and Gaeltacht Affairs say this includes social, physical, and economic development and "passing the language from one generation on to the next." This language task has been dumped largely on the schools.

By the time I got to Eoin Baiste, it was raining fairly hard. Micheal O Morain, teacher and principal, greeted me warmly, "Nice day." Well, why not. Into the classroom and the usual introductions. I used the term "kids" and was told there are no kids. Both boys and girls are "lads." The lads were lively and lovely. If I hadn't known beforehand, I would never have guessed from our back and forth that I was at a school where Irish was the vernacular. I faced fourteen cheerful, self-confident, and neatly dressed eleven- and twelve-year-old sixth graders—eight girls and six boys. There was every indication English was their first language.

As in Fanore, I was the liberator, freeing the lads from their regular class work. They seemed more open and laughed more easily at my feeble jokes than the sixth graders in the Fanore school. (What did the termite ask when he walked into the pub? Where is the bar tender?) I had the lads move their desks out of neat rows and into a more conversational semicircle. Then I asked boys and girls to switch around to break up the usual division of boys on one side of the room and girls on the other. Girls tittered as they competed for the desks next to the most liked boys. Boys grumbled.

WHAT I LEARNED FROM THE LADS

THIS IS WHAT I learned from the lads.

Of the fourteen students, six lived on working farms and eight elsewhere in the county.

Career choices: girls—one psychologist, two nurses, two vets, three teachers; boys—two marine biologists, one carpenter, one builder, one disco/rock musician, one unsure. O Morain was genuinely surprised that none of the students were even thinking about farming, a traditional Dingle occupation that had declined nearly sixty percent in the past four years. I was surprised O Morain didn't know how his students felt about their futures.

How to improve school? (1) Need more art. (2) Need computer room (have only three computers). (3) Want more education on nature. (4) Want more local history projects. Families of several students reached back more than one generation. As a history project, students took photographs in every townland (smallest administrative district) to create an "in the life of" record of the Lispole area. They also recorded one unique thing about each place—where a cable car once ran, where a poet-patriot was born, where the car hit the cow.

Where do you think you will live when you finish school or college? Only three saw a future in the Gaeltacht and wanted to come back to the Dingle. All the rest planned to live away.

Number of children per family: three with two children, four with three, five with four, one with six, and one with eight. Average, 3.7 children per household.

How to have a happy family? Be kind. Share. Let people [me] live their [my] own lives. Respect others. Don't be cheeky or rude. Say, "excuse me."

Half the students have computers at home. One hundred percent play computer games, all in English, mainly Game Boy and Playstation.

Watching television: two lads less than one hour daily, eight one to two hours, and four more than two hours. Favorite programs: number one, The Simpsons; number two, Friends; number three, Jacko, number four, Fear, and number five, most things on Nickelodeon. None watched Irish television on their own. A couple watched an Irish soap opera *Roana Run* (Headland of the Secrets) on occasion with their parents.

All together, the fourteen students have eighteen close relatives in the U.S.—six in Boston, five in New York, and the rest in Florida and Chicago.

After class, O Morain and Marie Ui Grifin, another teacher, explained that the bishop is the patron of the school and provides some financing. Religious instruction is limited, and at Eoin Baiste it focuses on the spiritual content of nature and art. Catechism is long gone (said emphatically.) With deep feeling, O Morain told me that the real mission of teaching in Irish "is to preserve the language." Unfortunately, the support the school gets is not equal to the task. "Textbooks are not in Irish to an adequate degree," Grifin said. Two years after the new national primary school curriculum was introduced in 2000, it was still not available in Irish.

ANGER AND SADNESS DESCEND

QUITE APART FROM all the normal concerns about instructional resources, an interesting problem for the use of Irish in education may be that Irish works best as a language of feeling and poetry.

Feelings are expressed in a totally different way in the Gaelic (Irish) than in English and other Germanic languages. Alex Hijmans, a Dutchman who is a student of Celtic language and literature, explains, "A Gaelic speaker will never say he is angry or sad, but that anger or sadness has descended upon him. The Irish are not active possessors of feelings; they are overcome by them. That way they are able to express the finer and subtler points of their emotions, and that makes for a beautiful language and great writers and poets." It is far more lyrical to say, as the Irish do, "There's not a word of a lie in it," rather than the English equivalent, "That is true." On the other hand, Irish is not very good for teaching and learning subjects such as science and computing. It follows that English is the language of higher education.

Four Eoin Baiste students recently won the All-Ireland National Schools Credit Union Quiz after competing with six thousand other students. The contest was, not surprisingly, in English. Gaelic may be at the root of Irish culture, but English is what offers opportunity and jobs. Innis Nor offers another example. It is the largest of three Aran Islands, where tourists go to experience the "real Ireland." On the island of Innis Nor, it is hard to find an English-language sign, and the tourist office stocks booklets only in Gaelic. Yet, nearly all the youngsters speak English at home. Outside they speak Gaelic, "because the tourists like it." Their parents insist their children first learn English to be able to get on in the world. In 2002, the Commission on the Gaeltacht reported, "Even in the strongest Gaeltacht areas, the current patterns of bilingualism are yielding to the primacy of English in the life of the community."

THE RISING TIDE OF ENGLISH

IRISH HAS BEEN SPOKEN since approximately 300 B.C.–350 B.C. Writing in Irish began around the fifth century, when Ireland was first known as the "island of saints and scholars." Early Modern Irish coincides with the age of bardic poetry and a standardized literary dialect (1200–1600) when aristocratic Gaelic society was at its peak and Gaelic and Norman-Gaelic nobles had poets in their retinues. The Elizabethan conquest of Ireland (c.1600) put paid to Gaelic aristocracy and institutions that supported Gaelic law and literature. English became the language of government, education, and politics. Irish declined gradually until the Great Irish Famine (1845–1849), when its use dropped sharply and English became dominant. The Irish language was associated with the rural poor and seen as an obstacle to economic improvement. "Irish will butter no bread" and "Irish never sold a pig" were common sayings. In the Gaeltacht, in 1800, one hundred percent of Irish children learned Irish as their first language. By 1860, in just three generations, fewer than five percent of the children spoke Irish as their first language.

The Gaelic League was founded in 1893 to revive the use of Irish through promotion of historic and modern Irish literature. Hundreds of Gaelic League chapters emerged all over Ireland. This coincided with the Celtic Revival, a movement represented by W. B. Yeats, Lady

Isabelle Augusta Gregory, John Millington Synge, and other writers who saw the use of Irish as the bedrock of Irish culture and reservoir of Irish legend and folklore. The language movement became central to the political separatist movement that led to the Irish Free State (1922) and then the Republic of Ireland (1948). Even so, the use of English remained dominant.

Article 8 of the Irish Constitution recognizes the Irish versus English language dilemma. It states:

> The Irish Language as the national language is the first official language.
> The English language is recognized as a second official language.

Farming and fishing, once everyday topics in the Gaeltacht for Irish speakers, have declined, and new businesses and new jobs are more easily discussed in English. It is impossible to be a banker, lawyer, university lecturer, computer programmer, or to be effective in almost any other well-paying job or career without using English as one's working language. A newspaper headline in a recent edition of *The Kerryman* announced, "Call Center To Give 80 Jobs in Dingle." There is no requirement that any of the seventy call agents to be hired at the call center be able to speak Irish, even though the business receives a subsidy of about €15,000 ($18,000) a job for locating in the Gaeltacht. Most management jobs go to English speakers from outside the Gaeltacht, further reinforcing English as the language of opportunity.

ENGLISH FOR POCKETS: IRISH FOR HEARTS

The Celtic Tiger speaks English. The truth of the matter is that English is the common language of the global economy. Other than an educated workforce and an attractive corporate tax structure, there has been a clear connection between economic success—huge investments by Microsoft, Intel, Dell, and others in Irish operations—and the comfort to U.S. investors of having Irish opposites in middle and top management speaking something close to the same language.

So this is the equation. English made the Irish rich. Now, being rich has made them want to be more Irish, and what better way than to learn or perfect Irish language skills. As David McWilliams of the *Sunday Business Post* put it, "English for our pockets, but Irish for our hearts." In his view, the prospects for Irish haven't looked this good for a hundred years. While Irish may still not sell a pig, the attachment to it is still strong.

It is not as if Irish is dead. In the 1996 census, 1.43 million people said they could speak Irish, but two-thirds of them never spoke it or did so less frequently than weekly. Now that people have time and money, the cultural beneficiary of English may well be the revival of Irish and all that goes with it. And that is what took G and me to the Diseart Institute of Education and Celtic Culture in Dingle. It was there that we ended our time on the Dingle peninsula on a high note, sitting on a garden bench with Sister Dorothy Costello.

CHAPTER ELEVEN

FINDING LOVE AT DISEART

A QUEST FOR THE MEANING OF SPIRITUAL

IT IS HARD to read much about the west of Ireland and the Dingle peninsula in particular without getting into Celtic spirituality. There are said to be "thin places" where you are close to God, holy wells, and the odd clump of trees inhabited by "the fairies." There are pilgrimages based on "redemptive and transformational properties" and "a special kind of magic for the spiritual traveler."

Shirley Toulson, in *The Celtic Alternative*, writes of "a church without martyrs, at peace with nature and decidedly feminist, more concerned with celebrating life than recording death." Tom Davies, in The Celtic Heart, wants to "revive the values of the old Celtic heart, become passionate and proud again, [and] release the delights of music, poetry and storytelling." On a more critical note, in his recent book The Last of the Celts, Marcus Tanner argues, "Celticism has emerged as a kind of shorthand expression for almost any unorthodox or non-traditional spirituality." Tanner sees Celticism as having become "a marketing device that has attached itself like glue to the worlds of design, spirituality, music, politics, and even sport."

I wanted to get a better understanding of what the pros meant when they talked about spirituality. Here was my opportunity. The Diseart Institute of Education and Celtic Culture in Dingle was founded in 1996 "to enable people to access, understand, study, and appropriate our native Irish and Celtic culture in terms of language, literature, art, laws, folklore, values, *spirituality* [emphasis added], history, music, archeology, and custom." In a phone call from the States, I had explained my interest in spirituality to Diarmuid O Dalaigh, Diseart's executive director, and arranged an afternoon at the institute. It would include a meeting with Monsignor Pedraig O'Fiannachta (Fr Patrick Kelly), Dingle parish priest as well as founder and spiritual director of the institute.

Fr Kelly's credentials were certainly in order. Before creating the Diseart Institute, he was professor and head of faculty of Celtic studies at National University of Ireland, Maynooth. Maynooth was established in 1795 "for the better education of persons professing the popish or Roman Catholic religion" and became the largest seminary in the world. Its pattern of growth and transformation reflects Ireland's emergence as an independent nation with a modern economy. In 1896, Maynooth attained the status of a Pontifical University, in 1910 it became a part of the National University of Ireland, and in 1966 it opened its doors to lay students. Featured strengths of Maynooth are now finance, computer science, software engineering, and electronic engineering.

Fr Kelly's interest in creating a center that would focus on Irish and Celtic culture coincided with the decision of the Presentation Sisters to reduce the size of the order's presence in Dingle after nearly two centuries of aid and education for the poor. This made the order's convent available for a new life as the Diseart Institute.

There we were, G and I, strolling along the Path of Stars on Green Street in the middle of tourist-laden Dingle town looking for the institute. We peered over a wrought-iron gate into a wonderfully tranquil garden for a minute or so before we realized this was our destination—a winding path, green lawns, roses, and graceful old trees, some dating back to when the garden was first planted in 1849. The Convent of the Presentation Sisters is a beautifully proportioned, neo-Gothic three-story stone building designed by J. J. McCarthy, a student of Augustine W. Pugin, whose work included the British Houses of Parliament. McCarthy was one of Ireland's great church architects. His work includes St. Macartans Cathedral, Monaghan, St. Savior's Church, Dublin, and St. Mary's, Kilkenny. The convent chapel has a series of twelve stained glass windows by Harry Clarke depicting scenes from the life of Christ.

The wonder of Clarke's stained glass is that he brought to it his feeling as an artist and illustrator of children's and other books ranging from *Fairy Tales of Hans Christian Andersen*, to *Tales of Mystery and Imagination* by Edgar Allan Poe, and the poetry of Algernon Swinburne and Robert Graves. His pen and ink drawings include "Bluebeard," "Cinderella," "Little Red Riding Hood," and "Sleeping Beauty." The talent of an imaginative artist and stained glass craftsman came together in a glorious result, the twelve windows of the chapel.

I hope some day Dingle tourist promoters will appreciate this wonderful work of J. J. McCarthy and Harry Clarke along with the perfect garden setting and the creative purposes of the institute, just as much, if not more than, Fungi and *Ryan's Daughter*.

It was time for our chat with Diarmuid.

McNeese Instead of Me

Diarmuid O Dalaigh, executive director of the Diseart Institute, is a quiet man with a twinkle and a high regard for himself and others. O Dalaigh helped take Fr Kelly's idea for Diseart—research, courses, and cultural activities in all areas of native and Celtic culture—and, in short order produced results without building a bureaucracy to do so. The full-time staff is three. I do admire someone who understands the difference between process and product and that the road to inertia is all too often paved with good reports. I remember an executive of the Ford Foundation saying in exasperation, "I know a hundred people who can write a brilliant, incisive, analytical report. Please God, find me someone who can get something done."

Sitting in O Dalaigh's small, white-walled burnished wood office, the first thing he said, smiling, was that he was sorry he and Fr Kelly couldn't see me the day before, but Ireland's president Mary McAleese wanted to visit and they had to make a choice. I said I understood.

We talked about Ireland. He spoke of its crises of identity. "Ireland became free in 1922. It is just now learning to be a state. It is important that we as a country become more attuned to the spiritual aspect of life."

"What is that?" I asked.

"The deepest inner core of our beings. Our soul. The meaning of life within us. More than heart and intellect. It is the element that makes us human." O Dalaigh went on to explain that the spiritual tradition became synonymous with religion. But now "people are leaving religion and seeking solace somewhere else." That somewhere else is "Celtic spirituality which exists apart from religion. It is nutrition for the soul."

I wondered if the new wealth of Ireland and the ability of people to acquire material goods and comfort would allow room for spiritual growth. Or would it be a while before they started asking, "If I am rich, why am I not happy?"

We continued discussing the institute and its success. One reason for success was the diversity of outlook on the board: two artists, one archeologist, a school principal, a solicitor (lawyer), two Presentation Sisters, a Heritage Council rep, a tourist agency rep, a monk, and Fr Kelly. Another reason is an eclectic mix of arts, culture, and traditions, and a strong dose of the here and now. Courses range from Irish Spirituality and Culture to Irish Home Baking and Cooking and Web Design. Most of all, teachers are exceptionally talented, and people have a good time. The celebration of four ancient Celtic festivals tuned to the four seasons of the year: *Imblog* (spring), *Bealltaine* (summer), *Lunasa* (autumn), and *Samhain* (winter), punctuates Diseart's cultural program. Festivals bring together drama, storytelling, concerts, poetry readings, art exhibitions, liturgies, and pilgrimages.

Imblog, February 1, the festival of light, celebrating the lengthening of the day and the hope of spring.

Bealltaine, May 1, the first day of summer in Ireland, the midpoint in the sun's progress between the vernal equinox and summer solstice. Druids would create a "need-fire" and rush the village's cattle through the fire to purify them and bring luck.

Lunasa, August 1, a feast of thanksgiving, symbolizing the first fruits of the harvest and a time of contests of strength and skill.

Samhain, October 31, Halloween, marks the final harvest and a time for gathering food for the long winter ahead. Bonfires were lit, and villagers cast the bones of slaughtered cattle into the flames. Thus the term *bone fire*, from which the word "bonfire" was derived.

CELTIC SPIRITUALITY

FROM MY READING, I knew Pedraig O'Fiannachta (Fr Patrick Kelly) was a noted Irish speaker, scholar, writer, and poet. His greatest achievement was said to be *An Biobla Naofa*, the Maynooth Irish Bible, of which he was editor and translator. Fr Kelly took his vows in 1953 and was priest and teacher in Wales until 1959, when he returned to Maynooth. There, he became a professor of Modern Irish and head of faculty of Celtic Studies. When he retired from Maynooth in 1993, Fr Kelly returned to Dingle, his birthplace, became parish priest, and set about the creation of Diseart Institute.

We sat around a small table in a large room, rather like an assembly hall. G and I were on one side and O Dalaigh and Diseart's education officer, Aoife Ni Sheaghdha, on the other. Fr Kelly sat at head of the table. I am not quite sure how to put this in a positive and respectful way, which is what I wish to do, but in appearance and demeanor, slightly built, mostly bald, very soft-spoken, Fr Kelly is perfect for his role. Central casting got it right. He is best described by a beautiful phrase in Irish, *iseal uasal*. It means the natural gift of combining dignity and humility.

Fr Kelly talked about being brought up on a Dingle farm, where he learned to live without spending money. "I earned my first ten shillings in a competition at school and gave it to my mother so she could buy a sewing machine. She made me a shirt with a beautiful front and knitted a sweater to cover the rest." And then there was a blanket "so strong five boys in one bed, fighting for warmth, couldn't tear it." Fr Kelly's concern was "a lack of appreciation now for what we were." What have been lost, he believes, are the dignity and a sense of identity that came from the life-giving values of farming and fishing in an agrarian society where *Imblog* and other festivals defined a natural cycle of life. Where there were four parishes, there is now one. Where there were once six hundred farmers with dairy cows, there are now ninety and only one buyer.

As professor and head of the faculty of Celtic studies at Maynooth, Fr Kelly said, "I came to see our studies as too narrow. From this grew the idea of the Diseart Institute with a philosophy based on an Irish Christian model that welcomes enrichment from other cultures and traditions." He sees in Diseart the "champions and custodians of a deeply veined cultural heritage and of the Irish language with its reservoir of stories of the people on whose lives ours are built."

Through its university-level courses and research and its community programs, Fr Kelly sees the institute as leading a cultural rebirth extending even to cultural tourism. It was at this point that I straight out asked Fr Kelly, "How would you define Celtic spirituality?"

Long pause. O Dailaigh and Ni Sheaghdha did their best to contain smiles. Had I been seventy years younger, it could have been one of those "out of the mouths of babes" questions. Fr Kelly looked nonplussed. "I have never been asked that question that way," he responded. But he gave it a go.

"Spirituality spans all life. Dogma divides it. Theology deals with dogmatic statements. It is a system of belief. Celtic spirituality is broader. It goes beyond dogma and brings out personal truths and reactions. When I was a scholar at Maynooth, I would never want to be interrupted. Now when there is a knock at the door I say, 'could this be Christ?'"

At that point, Pedraig O Fiannachta (Fr Kelly) stood up and said he had to go to the bank.

SISTER DOROTHY COSTELLO

AFTER OUR TALK with Fr Kelly, G and I went back to the chapel for another visit with the stained glass art of Harry Clarke, and then we strolled out into the garden. There, by chance, we met Sister Dorothy Costello (*Dorothy N. Choisdealbha*). She was sitting quietly on a garden bench with a book in her lap, enjoying the sun on her face. G and I have often reflected on why, after less than an hour with her, Sister Dorothy touched us so deeply. Was it that she was so at peace? Had an inner calm? An unqualified love of humanity? Radiated warmth? All these things?

The order of Presentation Sisters was founded in 1775 in Cork to cope with hunger and provide education that would lift people out of poverty. The Presentation Sisters came to Dingle in 1829. Sister Dorothy joined the order in Dingle in 1963 when there were thirty sisters at the convent. It was an aging group, and at that time only ten of the nuns were under the age of forty. The 1960s were a time, Sister Dorothy said somewhat wistfully, "when we were ready for change in the church and missed the opportunity." John XXIII had been active in promoting social reforms. In 1962 he convened an ecumenical council to "consider measures for renewal of the church in the modern world." There was said to be "freshness in his approach to ecclesiastical affairs," and he was much loved. Paul VI succeeded John

XXIII in 1963 and stated his intention of continuing reforms. However, after five years of endless discourse within the church, a papal encyclical issued in 1968 was a disappointment to those who argued for changes the church owed the modern world. The ban on contraception stayed firmly in place, as did priestly celibacy, divorce, and the role of women in the church.

Sister Dorothy continued her work in Dingle and was for three decades a domestic science teacher and then vice principal of the Convent Secondary School. And now she was a force behind the spiritual and academic character of the institute. As she talked, it seemed that Sister Dorothy had found in the Diseart Institute much of what she had hoped for when she spoke of the church's missed opportunities in the 1960s.

"People, particularly young people, feel cut off. 'I don't belong here.' There is a different famine, a different hunger today. They are looking for more than rattled prayers. They are finding the 'church' through poetry, dance, and music. Experiences with creativity help us understand how an institution that began with famine [Presentation Sisters and their convent] is today feeding a different kind of hunger.

"We now hear happy voices. These old walls are just soaking this up, linking past and present. The ways to God are as varied as people. At the institute, people reach for a depth they will not find in an institutional church. Part of this is a spirituality that involves communing with nature."

Deeply touched, we found it time to leave Dingle and head on.

CHAPTER TWELVE

The Music Makers
of Kenmare

Rich Is Better

"I'VE BEEN RICH and I've been poor. Rich is better." So said Sophie
Tucker, last of the red hot mommas, a singer of enormous voice, still
belting out "Some of These Days" and "Aren't Women Wonderful" in
the1960s at age eighty. I couldn't stop thinking of what Sophie had
to say as Janie Arthur showed us into our luxurious room at Sallyport
House on Kenmare Bay, just outside the town center of Kenmare.

That morning, we had checked out of our very basic bedroom,
with the world's smallest bathroom at the Old Farmhouse in Lispole.
We had a leisurely drive of seventy or so long miles to Kenmare. We
began very slowly through Inch, where tourists playing Traveler filled
the road in barrel-like caravans, each one pulled by a sturdy pony
with giant hooves. Then it was through Killarney along the shores of
mystical Lough Leanne and Muckroos Lake, a test for all five gears of
the Ford Focus as we twisted through the lower passes of *Cruacha
Dubna* (Macgillycuddy's Reeks) and *An Sliabh Corca* (Purple Mountain)
behind a creeping RV. We stopped for sustenance at a viewpoint café
in Killarney National Park, and then we undertook the low-gear
downhill run to Kenmare. And there we were, delighted to be in a
richly furnished room that spoke of quality and comfort: deep carpet,
queen bed with reading lamps on bedside tables, down comforter,

down pillows, antique desk, mirrored dressing table, giant wing chair perfect for reading, daydreaming, and views of Kenmare Bay. And, glory be, a generous bathroom easily equal to a half dozen Lispole-sized bathrooms.

Sallyport House is a well-proportioned, yellow pastel, five-bedroom Edwardian house standing on the shore of Kenmare Bay near Reenagross Woodland. It was built for the Arthur family in 1932 using the stones of a nineteenth-century famine-era workhouse and has been in the family ever since. Sister and brother, Janie and John Arthur, run the five-star B&B and do so with great care.

Into the Faerie World

IT WAS GETTING on toward sunset. After a day of driving, a little rest on the divine bed, and a cup of tea, it was time for a meander. I would give the wrong impression if I called our meanders walks. We do a lot of stopping, looking, admiring, and wondering with sit-downs when we find a bench, especially one with a view and near wildlife activity. Between G's back and my knees, both of us walking with canes, we have developed our own style of ambulation. Our "walks" may not be up to physical fitness standards, but our slow pace lets us take things in and so serves our souls. What I learned at the Diseart Institute about the oneness of nature and spirituality gives me a deal of comfort in our unhurried meandering approach to the outdoor scene, especially when the setting is a rich woodland on a beautiful bay.

Off we went through an iron gate in the high stone wall along Sallyport's boundary. A narrow dirt path led through woodland of oak, beech, and ash, with holly and other shrubs growing beneath spreading branches. Ferns and wood sorrel covered patches of open ground. Ivy circled tree trunks and dripped from branches. All this added up to a feeling of mystery. A final touch to the scene was the long view across Kenmare Bay. It had just rained, and the green leaves glistened. It was getting on to sunset, a mix of mist and evening color, a time when twilight lingers. The Gaels believed lingering twilight was a time when it was possible to slip from the real world into the faerie world. On this evening in this place, the Gaels had it right. And G and I had it all to ourselves.

At the end of the forest path, we came to a paved walk leading to Reenagross, or "The Muddy Point," a private park created nearly two hundred years earlier for the Marquis of Landsdowne from sandbank and wetlands on his vast estate. Sixty years before, Reenagross was leased to the Kenmare Development Association for public enjoyment. On the right side of the walk was a mudflat. Now, at low tide it was serving as a dinner table for all manner of wading birds. A thoughtfully placed bench gave us front row seats to their performance.

On the left side of the walk, there was a five-foot rock wall where lime-loving plants—pink-flowered calamint, rusty-back fern, and penny-like wall pennywort—grew in profusion. As we walked on, we had company. A rock was missing from the wall, and in its place a Yorkshire terrier popped its head out and barked in a friendly way. We said hello, the head disappeared, and we walked on. About twenty feet on, another missing rock, again the barking terrier, we said hello, and the head disappeared. Had the wall gone on another thousand feet, I am sure the little beastie would have quite happily continued its game. We were rather disappointed not to see it on our way back.

We continued on over a stone bridge to the peninsula of Reenagross Wildlife Park, and were about ready for another sit-down. We found a bench at water's edge next to an old boathouse, under towering beeches and Irish oaks at least ninety feet high. It was the perfect place to sit and stare as twilight slid toward night.

The X Factor

KENMARE NESTLES in a semicircle of mountains, hence its Irish name *Neidín*, meaning "little nest" or "little cradle." Three rivers, Roughy, Finnihy, and Sheen, run into a long inlet of the sea known as the Kenmare River.

According to the Kenmare home page, in 1655 when the Cromwellians confiscated the lands of Kerry, "its inhabitants moved elsewhere or were shot," an approach to city planning that appears to have fallen out of favor. Sir William Petty, Cromwell's surveyor general, was a principal beneficiary of the land grab. Between confiscated land and more than a little insider trading, Petty ended up owning a quarter of all land in Co Kerry. This in addition to being a professor of medicine and of music at Oxford, a statistician, an economist, and a demographer with enough political talent to get a knighthood out of Charles II and enough additional land to surround what is now Kenmare with the Landsdowne estate. Petty founded Kenmare to serve his mining works beside the River Finnihy. He saw the village as a center of commerce and industry and imported 850 Protestant settlers from Wales, Cornwall, and the rest of England. His plan was to grow a bit of England, but the Irish birthrate tipped the balance. Petty's descendant, William Petty-Fitzmaurice, II, the Earl of Shelbourne and the first Marquis of Lansdowne, commissioned the present design of the town in 1775.

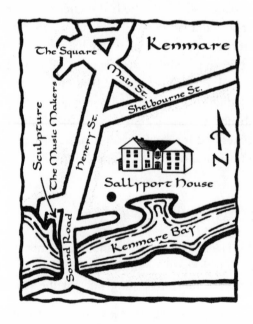

Kenmare was laid out with its main streets forming an X and a triangular park tucked in the middle. This was a dandy plan for horse and buggy. Now, anyone driving north from Cork, south to Beara, or west to the Ring of Kerry comes or goes through the X. More often than not, well-planned Kenmare functions most like a parking lot in slow motion. As to character, with any number of boutiques and trendy restaurants, Kenmare appears to be what it is, an affluent tourist town of twelve hundred in a picturesque setting.

THE KENMARE KESTRELS

KENMARE'S REPUTATION is growing in another direction. The Wikipedia encyclopedia reveals that J. K. Rowling, author of the Harry Potter books, has identified Kenmare as the home of the Kenmare Kestrels, a Quidditch team. According to *Quidditch Through the Ages* by Rowling and Kennilworthy Whisp, "Quidditch began as a simple broom-based game, with players passing a leather ball, the quaffle, which they attempted to place in goals at either ends of the pitch." In *The Journal of Hogwarts School of Witchcraft and Wizardry*, sports writer Bryon Matheson reported, "The Kenmare Kestrels have taken the lead after the first round of playoffs last night, beating the Tutshill Tornados (currently ranked sixth) 430 to 360." The Kenmare Kestrels were founded in 1291 and joined the thirteen-team British & Irish Quidditch League in 1672. The Kestrels' robes are emerald-green with two opposing yellow Ks, leprechauns are team mascots, and supporters play harps.

KENMARE—TOP TIDY TOWN

WHEN I FIRST LEARNED that Kenmare was a "tidy town" I found it hard to take seriously. Tidy, says Mr. Webster, is "neat, orderly, or trim, as in appearance or dress." Was this a plot to make Ireland into a bunch of little Switzerlands, all cleanliness, order, and efficiency where Muggles live? To my mind, tidy is sweet little girls in frilly pinafores and patent leather shoes who curtsy ever so nicely. Tidy up is what you do before guests arrive. Tidy isn't a real town, alive and in motion. But here was proof in the *Irish Examiner* that Kenmare is not only tidy but is the tidiest of "Tidy Towns":

Kenmare Celebrates on the Double with Unique First in Tidy Towns Competition

PICTURESQUE Kenmare completed a unique double yesterday, becoming the first town in the country to take the prize as both Ireland's Tidiest Town and Ireland's Best Kept Town. A record 719 towns and villages competed in the Millennium Tidy Towns Competition.

It was further reported that Mr. Noel Dempsey, minister for the environment and local government, Tidy Town organizer, and Mr. Eoin McGettigan, Chief Executive of Super Valu, Tidy Town sponsor, presented the Tidy Town Trophy and a check for €10,000 ($12,000) to Fr Michael Murphy, Kenmare parish priest and chairman of the Kenmare Tidy Towns Committee at a ceremony in St. Patrick's Hall, Dublin Castle.

Well, I thought, here was a story worth pursuing. If nothing else, "Tidy Town Trophy" had a highly alliterative quality. Janie Arthur, Sallyport House proprietor, set up a meeting for me with Fr Murphy and suggested it would not be out of order to slip Fr Murphy a little something for his time. Whether local custom or church policy, okay. I met with the tall, angular, somewhat dour Fr Murphy in what looked to me like the back entrance hall of the church. We sat at an oilcloth-covered table that had seen better days. I learned the Kenmare Tidy Town committee had forty-four members, Kenmare had scored 265 out of a possible 300 Tidy Town points, school kids were brilliant at picking up trash, and the "chimney stack" initiative—repairing and painting all the chimneys in town—was a top priority.

Tidy Town adjudicators (a committee that goes from town to town and does the scoring) offered various observations in its report on Kenmare: the corrugated roof of a vacant property on the Kilgarvan entrance needs to be refurbished, the gable wall of O'Shea's which forms the corner of New Road should be painted, a few other buildings remain to be refurbished, an open storage on the road to the stone circle could be improved upon, the charge to see the Stone Circle is questionable, Finnihy bridge could offer a greater view if the walls were lowered a little, and service cables along Main Street need to be undergrounded to leave the town center wirescape free.

On the plus side, adjudicators pointed out some buildings have been nominated for shopfront awards, landscaping is top notch, wildflowers on the river banks are a plus (Kenmare is being considered for the Waterside Award), fine stone walls throughout the town are in good repair, the pier area is well cared for and well-used, and the power hose cleaning of Our Lady's bridge was well-done.

SUSTAINING HERITAGE AND ENVIRONMENT

THE TIDY TOWN movement had its roots in the 1950s in what was called the Spring Clean Campaign, an annual effort to prepare the country for the tourist season. According to the AnCo/Bord Failte Research Project, this was a period when "Ireland displayed the symptoms of an introverted and demoralized society." There was severe unemployment and mass emigration, mainly to the U.K. The rural landscape became dotted with derelict homes, and Ireland was drained of a generation of young people. It was of this time that the poet Brendan Kennelly wrote of the flight from Ireland in his *Dublin Collection*, "Brown bag bulging with faded nothings, a ticket for three pounds one and six to Euston, London via Holyhead."

Tourism was seen as one way to boost the economy, particularly in the west of Ireland. Other larger economic forces were at work with an explosion in the technology sector. Two measures of change stand out. Over the twenty-year period, 1960–1980, car ownership grew from 170,000 to 683,000; and in one year, 1976–1977, television sets owned went from 372,671 to 593,298. With economic growth came some less-desirable changes in towns and villages. Churches tore down their iron railings and stone entrances and converted their fore-courts into car parks. Plastic fluorescent and neon fascias replaced traditional shop fronts. The most garish and largest signs of chain stores dominated main streets. Banks consolidated and covered over original signs made of stone or metal by skilled craftsmen with "modern" signs. Television dominated entertainment, people stayed home, and cinemas closed, leaving derelict buildings. New packaging—cartons, crisp bags, soft drink cans—produced new levels of litter. The Tidy Town movement fought back. The issues became those of environmental controls and standards. Adjudicator reports attacked these issues, set standards, and caused people to lobby local authorities to effect change.

Tidy Town proponents say that as a result of the movement and competition, people are viewing their towns and their whole environment differently, "seeking to manage and improve both." Three-to-five year plans, worth up to fifty out of a maximum three hundred points, are a must for competing towns. The competition has become much more than spring clean up and "make pretty." According to the Department of Environment and Local Government, to be tidy in today's Tidy Towns competition involves taking stock and looking after all of the town's assets, including "sustaining cultural heritage and environment for current and future generations."

After talking with Fr Murphy, taking a look behind Main Street facades, and reading adjudicator reports on Kenmare, I would say that while the solid qualities of Kenmare are far beyond a Potemkin's Village, there is a way to go in both what adjudicators should be looking for and what Kenmare delivers. I think they should add "reclaiming" lost heritage and lost environment and improving "quality of life" as primary concerns.

I wonder now what the Music Makers of Kenmare would have to say.

MUSIC MAKERS OF KENMARE— DREAMERS OF DREAMS

We are the music makers,
And we are the dreamers of dreams,
Wandering by lone sea-breakers,
And sitting by desolate streams;
World-losers and world-forsakers,
On whom the pale moon gleams:
Yet we are the movers and shakers
Of the world for ever, it seems.

—Arthur William Edgar O'Shaughnessy,
"The Music Makers"

THERE ARE BEAUTIFUL ways to begin a day, and this day was one of the best. A pink linen cloth on a table for two at the window of an east facing sunroom, the view across a rich garden with any number of blue tits, kestrels, and song thrush fluttering from feeder to feeder, and a chorus of cuckoo announcing themselves in the background. The green garden lawn sloped into the bay, where the sun was burning off a morning mist, slowly revealing the path on the peninsula where we had walked with pleasure at twilight the day before. After our first cup of coffee and a bowl of fresh berries, the most confounding question we faced was the choice between smoked salmon or homemade sausage with poached eggs.

We were in no hurry and had no agenda and that is often as not when the best things happen. Another cup of coffee. A few minutes with *The Irish Times.* Even the world seemed at peace that day. Into the Ford Focus and down the drive. At the T, turn right to the town center or left to the unknown? Left it was along the Kenmare River. After a few minutes, we saw what looked from the road like three stone pillars set near the riverbank. Could this be a remnant of a stone circle? Always curious, we turned in to a parking area big enough for only two or three cars. No one else was about as we walked down a sloping path that circled around to the front of the pillars. And so it was that we made our acquaintance with the Music Makers of Kenmare, a relationship that grew over the next few days. This was the first morning of our visit to Kenmare. We were to return to the Music Makers time and time again. They had a great deal to say to us.

There were three musicians, each carved strongly and simply out of his own limestone block, nine feet tall, four feet wide, and three feet deep. The button man (concertina) stood on the right, the bodhran player stood drumming on the left, and in the middle, the Boss played his bass fiddle. They were set on a gravel patch on a gentle slope. The backdrop was the perfect outdoors setting, a low stone wall around a small hill and a slightly wild grove of oak and ash trees. A simple stone bench in front of the Music Makers was just right for our visits. And we were always the only ones there.

The initial impact of the Music Makers came from their massive size. Then there was their expression. The sloe-eyed sidemen had a

G and the Music Makers of Kenmare

laid-back look. I could hear them humming just like I remembered Lionel Hampton doing when he played the vibes at the Paradise Theatre in Detroit, especially when banging away on "Cordelia, Cordelia, What Makes Your Big Head So Hard!" The Paradise was where all the greats played—Hampton, Duke Ellington, Cab Calloway, Earl "Father" Hines, and Fats Waller—and when it came to a choice between Central High School and the Paradise, the educational program at the Paradise always won hands down.

The Boss was something else. I was certain he had been through a lot in life and knew of its struggles and rewards. He was a man of no bull, a person of kindness and purpose. He was with it. Cool!

I do believe the origin of the Music Makers, one part Arthur William Edgar O'Shaughnessy's *Dreamer of Dreams* and one part sewer system, amused the Boss. The Kerry Co Council commissioned the sculpture in 1995 under the "one percent for art" program and funded it as a part of the €2.5 million ($3 million) project for the Kenmare Waste Water Treatment Plant.

DICK JOYNT—PROFILE IN COURAGE

THE MUSIC MAKERS were something of an enigma to the people of Kenmare. There was no plaque, no sign, nothing to tell us the name of the sculpture or sculptor. Janie Arthur, Sallyport proprietor, couldn't tell us anything and wasn't especially interested. Fr Murphy said that when the sculpture was first installed, some people thought it was of Celtic origin and prayed there. This brilliant sculpture wasn't on the screen for adjudicators or local Tidy Towners. We even drew a blank at the tourist office and heritage museum. After getting back to Boulder, it took several phone calls and e-mails to connect with Fiona Fitzgerald of the Arts, Culture & Heritage Office of the Kerry Co Council. Fiona began to help me fill in the blanks.

I found out that Dick Joynt was the sculptor of the Music Makers. As I learned more about him, I became sure Dick was "the Boss," and it was his voice that spoke to me on all our visits to the Music Makers. I talked to Dick by phone a couple of times. He had a small farm in Bree near Enniscorty, Co Wexford, where he had made his barn into a studio. Dick spoke of seeing his ideas in the blocks of stone and slowly chipping away with hammer and chisel to release his vision. For Dick, "The rhythm of the hammer and chisel are like a prayer." He was in later stages of cancer when we talked but still at work. His project was then *The Defiant Stallion*, a huge thirteen-ton sculpture. (Joynt never worked small.) Dick died before he finished the work. Several sculptors who respected and loved Dick completed *The Defiant Stallion*. One of them, Tom Mooney, spoke of it as "a labor of love between a small community of artists toward a fallen comrade."

Dick was known for his willingness to share his knowledge and skills and to learn from others. His struggle over several decades with a bipolar condition, sometimes very intense, also shaped his sense of life and its opportunities. During these times and at the very end, friend and artist Tadhg McSweeney said, "Dick simply refused to give up or be defeated where lesser mortals would long ago have thrown in the towel. He was the bravest of the brave." Dick's work and his life were expressions of courage and hope. I am sorry we never met.

As we drove out of Kenmare on our way to the Beara Peninsula, we stopped for a final visit with the Music Makers.

The Burren—geologist's paradise

Limestone sandwich on the Burren

Fanore Primary School—sixth grade class

Burren Atlantic shore

Perfect pasture—Dingle Peninsula

Remains of Minard Castle on the Dingle

Matchmaker Willie Daly in
his kitchen

Sister Dorothy Costello—true love

Fr Patrick Kelly, Diseart Institute
founder

Brendan Daly, Listowel Race
Committee Secretary

The Music Makers of Kenmare

Kenmare's slow moving town center

Beara Peninsula, once copper,
now cows

Family Butcher—beware

Drink, Drink, and more Drink

Beara—Castletownbere Harbor

Beara—another perspective

O'Driscoll's fishing boat: no wheel in the wheelhouse

Fish factory—after the fact

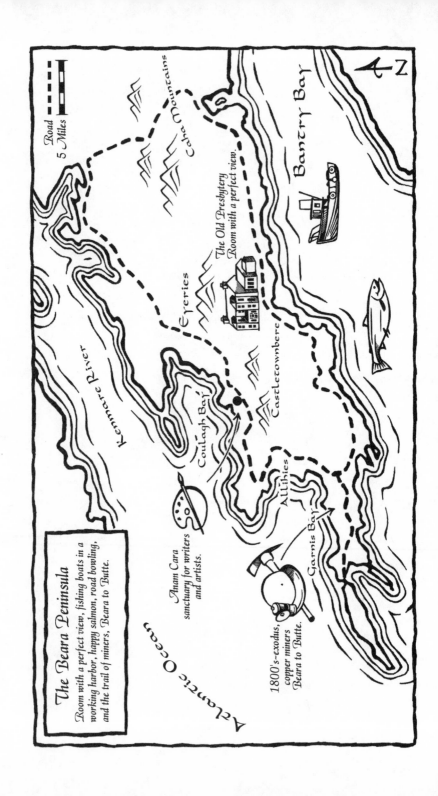

The Beara Peninsula

Room with a perfect view, fishing boats in a working harbor, happy salmon, road bowling, and the trail of miners, Beara to Butte.

Road
5 Miles

Caha Mountains

Bantry Bay

The Old Presbytery
Room with a perfect view.

Eyeries

Castletownbere

Kenmare River

Coulagh Bay

Allihies

Garnis Bay

Anam Cara
sanctuary for writers and artists.

Atlantic Ocean

1800's–exodus, copper miners Beara to Butte.

CHAPTER THIRTEEN

FROM BEARA TO BUTTE

Of 1,700 people who left the parish of Eyeries on the Beara Peninsula to emigrate to America from 1870 to 1915, 1,138 ended up in Butte. Members of 77 different families of Sullivans left Castletownbere for Butte, which explains why in 1908 there were 1,200 Sullivans in Butte.

—George Everett

BUTTE, MONTANA— IRELAND'S FIFTH PROVINCE

WE WERE AWAY from well-manicured Kenmare and soon in more adventurous country on our way to the Beara Peninsula, a less-traveled, thirty-mile-long finger of rock and moor offering Ireland's furthest reach into the Atlantic. Our road followed the meandering River Sheen. Pockets of green bordering the river merged into hillsides that rose gently and then sharply to five hundred feet or so before mountain rock took over. Close by the road, to the west, Knockeira rose fifteen hundred feet. Barrerneen to the east is a twin to Knockeira. A few sheep wandering about and derelict stone cottages completed the scene. Then Caha Mountains loomed up dead ahead, and the road rose a thousand feet or so reaching for a pass. A series of three long tunnels eased our way through to the far side of the mountain. Then a corkscrew descent in low gear down to the

Canrooska River valley into the town of Glengarriff, and schlock shock. Sign after sign advertised tours to Garinish Island and its "famed Italian Gardens."

The name Glengarriff comes from *An Gleann Garbh*—"the rugged glen"—which was derived from the rugged quality of the mountains and what used to be wooded valleys before the mighty oaks became charcoal to fuel William Petty's ore smelters.

We didn't pause in Glengarriff and drove on to the Beara Way. A light rain stopped, and sun lit the calm waters of Bantry Bay bordering Beara Way on the south while the Caha Mountains hovered over us on the north. Caha begins and other mountains continue, forming a high spine that divides the peninsula down the middle. Co Cork with Bantry Bay occupies the south side of the peninsula, and Co Kerry with the Kenmare River the north side. Two high peaks punctuate the mountain skyline, Hungry Hill (2,251 feet) and Sugar Loaf (1,187 feet). Storytellers have it that two thousand or so years ago, a medieval Spanish princess named Beara roamed these parts with her husband, an Irish clan chief, Owen the Splendid.

Speaking of splendid, I want to note again that few drivers can be as fortunate as I when it comes to a driving companion. The song and poetry G provides from her rich and seemingly endless reservoir does much to inform and entertain me along the way. Bantry Bay it is. And without a pause, "The Star of County Down," a tune that dates back to the early 1700s.

Oh, from Bantry Bay to Derry Quay,
And from Galway to Dublin Town,
No maid I've seen like the brown colleen
That I met in the County Down.

As she onward sped I shook my head,
And I gazed with a feeling quare,
And I said, says I, to a passer-by,
"Who's the maid with the nut-brown hair?"

Oh, he smiled at me, and with pride says he,
"That's the gem of Ireland's crown,
She's young Rosie McCann from the banks of the Bann,
She's the Star of the County Down."

And Road Bowling It Is

AFTER OUR SLOW and pleasant drive along the winding rocky coastal strip of Beara Way, we found ourselves in Castletownbere (the town of Beara's Castle) edging ever so slowly up a gravel drive to The Old Presbytery, the B&B that was to be home over the next few days. A white crested mother duck who had chosen the gravel drive to lead her recently hatched brood of nine ducklings on an afternoon stroll. She set our slow pace. As Mother Duck strutted and preened and the ducklings waddled along in an orderly row behind, I was reminded of *la passegiata*, the evening promenade of Italian families along the Via Mazzini in Verona.

G and I had been looking forward to a cup of tea and a bit of rest before venturing out to investigate Castletownbere. Mary Wrigley, the proprietor of The Old Presbytery, greeted us warmly and, to my surprise, told me Donal O'Driscoll would be by shortly to take me to a road bowling match. Okay? Of course!

Before our trip, when I was reading up on southwest Ireland, I came across a reference to road bowling, or "long bullets" as it is sometimes known, out of respect for the lethal quality of the sport. The more I learned, the more fascinated I became. The desire to see a road bowling match grew on me. One thing led to another and I got Donal O'Driscoll's name as someone in Castletownbere who might help me pursue my interest in road bowling from Riobard O'Dwyer of Allihes. Mike Sullivan, former U.S. Ambassador to Ireland and Governor of Wyoming had given me Riobard's name. I mentioned Donal in a phone call to the Wrigleys, and to my delight, there he was, ready to take me to a match.

Let me explain something of the sport so you can understand my interest. Road bowling, which traces back to the seventeenth century, is peculiar to West Cork in the south and Armagh in the north. A match is properly called a "score." Two contestants play it on a two-mile stretch of undulating and twisting rural road. The winner is the player with both power and control of spin who completes the course in the fewest number of throws of a twenty-eight-ounce, seven and a half inch round iron "bowl." Each player has a "road shower," a strategist who marks a target spot on the road for each throw with a "sop," a hunk of grass the bowler aims at. If the player hits the mark, he "splits the sop." The road shower also gives his player advice on velocity and the best spin, clockwise for the bowl to roll to the right, counterclockwise to the left. The amount of spin determines the amount of curve as the bowl rolls. If the road curves, the bowl had better match the curve. Each succeeding throw is taken from the "tip," the spot at which the previous throw rolls to a stop. There is a run up of about fifteen feet to the tip for each throw. There are different throwing styles, the Ulster Backswing and the Munster Windmill being the most common. The other ingredient is the crowd of passionate supporters, frequently numbering in the hundreds for a match. They line the sides of the road, cheering their man on, assessing the finer points of each throw, and being careful to stay out of the way of any errant throw.

Each side puts up a pot. The winner takes all. Side betting on each throw goes on at a furious pace. And yes, matches as often as not begin and end at a pub. According to Brian Toal, author of *Road Bowling in Ireland,* the sport has its heroes like Andy Mallon. "A natural stylist in his compact delivery of the bowl, he was a formidable opponent at the highest level of competition." And Tim Delaney, "One of the first great bowlers to bring a special art to the accepted skill of bowling."

G didn't share my interest in road bowling and decided to stay behind. So off Donal O'Driscoll and I drove. And we drove and we drove, my anticipation mounting as O'Driscoll regaled me with stories of great matches played in the past. An hour and a half later I was thoroughly lost, but we were there. No one else was. The match had been canceled. The best we could do was a stop at a pub to prepare ourselves for the return trip.

That afternoon, Donal's brother came by The Old Presbytery and dropped off a videotape of a road bowling national competition, so I did get to see road bowling at its best. I was touched by the O'Driscoll brothers' generosity in their effort to share a special bit of Ireland with a complete stranger.

Serendipity is "a desirable discovery by accident." Serendipity was with us the next morning at breakfast. We had the remarkable luck of meeting Edward O'Driscoll (no relation to Donal), a solicitor from Cork of imposing mien who G remembers for his voice—wonderfully pleasant, soothing, comforting, "the voice every child would love to hear when going to sleep." I was delighted to learn he was a top-notch road bowler and legal advisor to *Bol Chumann na hEirann*, the Irish road bowling association. O'Driscoll explained some of the finer points of the game, including legal problems when the iron bowl went astray and split the skull of a roadside fan rather than the target sop. After arranging tables and chairs to open a bowling lane, and with a hard roll in hand, O'Driscoll put on an impressive demonstration of correct run up and release, proper form for the Ulster back swing (windmill) and Munster forward swing delivery, and correct follow through. This was by far the most educational and entertaining breakfast of the entire trip.

A ROOM WITH A VIEW

I WAS SITTING in the bay window of our room at The Old Presbytery, looking out at the harbor and thoroughly enjoying this passive activity. I reflected on the elements of a perfect room. And what better place to consider the question than where I was, which came close to perfect? What were the ingredients? (1) A sweeping view, 180 degrees or better. (2) Lots of natural light. (3) Good composition, including a variety of elements to look at in the foreground, middle range, and background. (4) Activity—things happening out there. (5) Color. (6) An evolving scene, one that changes from first light to night.

The Old Presbytery traces back to the 1700s, when it was the Leahy family residence. Then it became home for parish priests, and in 1997 Mary and David Wrigley, she a nurse and he a philatelist, converted it into their home and a five-room B&B. The house is set on four acres of landscaped gardens that slope down to the quiet water of Castletownbere Harbor.

The bay window of our west-facing second floor room let in masses of light and offered a 180-degree view. Straight ahead, I could see the harbor hard at work. Tied up at the town side pier were fishing boats of varying age, color, and country of origin, all with booms, nets, and other paraphernalia making ready for extended trips to sea. I could make out the *Salamander*, bright yellow with a white pilot house; the *Resplendent*, deep red and bright white; the *San Pablo*, washed-out green and white stripe; the *Oilean Baoi*, blue with more rust than paint; and the *Golden Dawn*, orange and white. On the pier there was a stone building for the harbormaster, an auction hall, and refrigerated trailer trucks waiting to haul fish all over the U.K. and Europe. Step off the pier, and you were on Castletownbere's busy main street, a row of shops and pubs, and the Spanish Consulate, all painted in well-worn shades of beige, blue, orange, and pink. Cars were parked at random, a church tower punctuated the skyline, and the peaks of Slieve Miskish filled in the background.

On Dinish Island on the other side of the harbor, fishing boats were tied up at the island's stone quay loading up at an ice plant. A crew worked on repairing a boat out of water in a gurney. Farmed salmon in large tubs on the quay were swimming their last swim before taking a turn on the disassembly line of the fish processing plant.

Small boats scooted back and forth between Dinish Island and the town side pier. Seabirds were constantly on the hunt. A fishing boat cast its lines off and moved out to sea. And down in The Old Presbytery garden, Mother Duck was out again trailing her brood to who knows where. The harbor scene changed from a mist-filled morning to color tints of a setting sun. As twilight flowed into night, lights come on in the pilothouse of this and that fishing boat, in buildings on the quay, and in town, dotting the scene.

No Wheel in the Wheelhouse

THE CASTLETOWNBERE fishing fleet is comprised of about seventy local trawlers and thirty inshore boats working the harbor and bays. More than a hundred trawlers from other Irish ports and other countries use the harbor. Every spring, sixty or so factory ships from Eastern Europe with around five thousand crew and factory workers anchor next door in Barehaven Harbor, purchasing and processing mackerel and blue whiting. No one is surprised to hear French, Spanish, and Russian spoken in the pubs.

Make no mistake. Castletownbere works for a living. In his description of harbor facilities and services, Castletownbere's harbormaster Kris Dennisson makes this clear. "The harbor is not suitable for pleasure craft." As Ireland's premier whitefish port, Castletownbere's focus is on the bounty of the sea. While we were there, a Spanish boat, the *Aribe*, was detained for having cod on board when the Spanish quota for cod had already been fished out. With assistance from the Spanish consulate, the skipper pleaded guilty and was fined €78,500 ($94,200)——the value of the entire catch and fishing gear on board. The owner paid the fine and was then free to sell the catch and put the vessel back to work.

Donal O'Driscoll invited me to take a look at one of the fishing boats he operated with his sons. The boat, the *Carmona*, was a ninety-foot, 352-ton high-tech fishing machine. Before I saw it, I had a "heave ho, haul the nets me hardies" romantic picture in mind. Donal was delighted at my surprise when I climbed up the ladder and into the "wheelhouse." But the wheelhouse had no wheel! It had the feeling of a 747 cockpit with dials and masses of sonar, radar, and other electronic gear aimed at finding schools of fish and navigating waters that not too many years ago were inaccessible. Levers rather like joysticks on a computer game are used to operate front and rear propellers for precise maneuvering of the boat. A vacuum system sucks fish out of nets into the refrigerated hold. The captain operates all this from a black leather pedestal chair anchored to the pilot house deck. All his instruments are efficiently arrayed on a curved control panel in front of him. Looking out the windows of the wheelhouse is a reminder you are on a boat and each time you go out to sea, with good judgment and electronic gear, your catch may well be worth $100,000 or more. The *Carmona*'s average haul is a hundred tons. It can be as much as four hundred tons.

The global demand for fish is growing. Low in fat and high in protein, and the source of essential fatty acids, fish is increasingly in demand as a healthy food option. And that's the problem. Despite restrictions on the number of days for fishing, minimum landing sizes, and quotas, some species are in short supply. According to a 2002 report from the United Nations' Food and Agriculture Organization, forty-seven percent of world fish stocks are fully exploited, eighteen percent are overexploited, and ten percent are severely depleted. This means seventy-five percent of the world's fish are in trouble, with many becoming rare species.

SON OF TOWN HALL

SPEAKING OF RARE SPECIES, an amazing "craft" I am very sorry I didn't see arrive at the port of Castletownbere, 6:30 A.M., August 13, 1998, was *Son of Town Hall*. The Irish Navy escorted it into port. Calling the *Son of Town Hall* a craft or a boat would be something of a misnomer. "It looks like a garden shed patched together with nails, knots, and rope," according to Barry Roche, a Castletown local who observed the event along with hundreds of other astounded people.

Fishermen who had seen this rock-and-roll enterprise nearing the coast had alerted the navy and the citizens of Castletownbere to the approaching apparition. *Son of Town Hall* was a fifty-two-foot raft with a cabin on top. The raft was made of tree trunks, planks of plywood, foam, and tennis netting, with a sail rigged like a Chinese junk. For balance, attached on either side of the raft were sponsons. They looked like giant hotdogs. The Floating Neutrinos were a family of musicians, headed by David Pearlman, a.k.a. Popa Neutrino, 65. (*Neutrino*: in physics the most elusive of elementary particles that ordinarily passes unnoticed.) Neutrino and his wife Capt. Betsy, 46, led the *Son of Town Hall* adventure. The crew also included Ed Garry, thirty-seven, Roger Doncaster, forty-four, and two Rottweilers, Thor and Siegfried, ages unknown. The Neutrinos left their five children behind with friends.

Garry and Doncaster, who had worked on the raft in Maine, came along for the long ride powered largely by the Gulf Stream current and occasionally by a twenty-horsepower diesel.

It all began when the Provincetown, Mass., Board of Health condemned the Neutrinos' original houseboat named *Town Hall*. With stops in Manhattan, a rebuilding period in Maine, and a test run to Newfoundland, the astounding two-month voyage of the *Son of Town Hall* began. Asked to describe his emotions at the end of the trip in Castletownbere, Neutrino said, "Relieved!" Asked about the quality of the raft as an oceangoing vessel, Neutrino thought a moment and said proudly, "We broke the scrap barrier."

One "last" report had *Son of Town Hall* seeking a permanent home in France or Holland.

Another report had Popa Neutrino and Capt. Betsy at work on

another scrap-built raft, the *Vilma B.* It was to be a world-traveling orphanage, picking up orphans in Brazil and other South American countries, then Africa and India, raising and educating the orphans along the way. Yet another report in no less a source than *The New Yorker* had Popa Neutrino off on a thirty-foot scrap built raft for a solo voyage across the Pacific. Stay tuned.

YOU NEVER LOOKED LOVELIER

OF THE MANY tons of fish landed at Castletownbere every year, 120 varieties go through the Fisherman's Cooperative on Dinish Island for processing, packing in ice, and shipping. We were wandering around the island and having seen the tubs of salmon on the quay, we wondered what happened to the fish. I inquired at the processing plant, and Tadhj invited us in to have a look around. But we had to dress for the occasion to meet plant hygiene standards. Our host handed each of us a white "one size fits all" plastic ensemble to go on over our clothes—booties, pants, jackets, and a sort of garbage bag like hat with an elastic band like the ones you see on doctors and nurses in operating rooms. Our attire not so much fitted as encompassed. I thought we looked rather like a decontamination crew at a toxic spill or stand-ins for the movie *Ghostbusters*.

Tadhj led us into a large, barn-like room. Eight women, all dressed as we were except for rubber aprons, hip high rubber boots, and red elbow-length rubber gloves, stood on a raised boardwalk facing a waist-high moving belt, knives and hoses at the ready. The hoses hung down from the ceiling at each station. A lift truck hauled tubs of happily swimming fish from the quay to the beginning of the line. They must have been happy, because the water they were swimming in was pumped full of sweet-smelling nitrous oxide, otherwise known as laughing gas. Properly stunned, off each salmon went on its five-minute trip down the line to eternity. Heads off, innards out, scales scraped, fins trimmed, final wash, onto the scale, tagged, and into an ice chest with a dozen former companions. Knives flashing, blood and guts flying, hoses splashing, the women never stopped talking to each other. I looked up at the matronly woman with a blood-splashed apron at the end of the line. Says I to her, "You never looked lovelier." Says she to me with a huge smile, "Have a good one, my boy."

THE ROAD FROM BEARA TO BUTTE

Lonely I sit here in sorrow and sigh
For loved ones afar o'er the deep,
Thinking of home till the tears dim my eyes—
No comfort, alas but to weep.
At night in my dreams—how strange it all seems—
Their kindly faces I see;
Then I wake in the gloom and remember my doom—
An exile from Bere by the sea

—"An Exile from Bere," *The Eyeries Parish*

CHANCES ARE, the "exile from Bere" was in Butte, Montana. Open up a Butte telephone directory today and you will find many Sullivans, Shannons, Harringtons, O'Neills, Lynchs, Driscolls, Dolans, Duggans, and O'Briens. By 1900, when Butte's population was 47,635, one quarter, twelve thousand, were of Irish descent. More than half of the twelve thousand were emigrants from Co Cork, and of these the bulk were from Beara.

Fr Sarsfield O'Sullivan, himself from Beara, said he could count forty-two cousins living in Butte whose roots were in Beara, many in Allihies. The link that led from Beara to Butte was hard rock mining, copper in particular. The decline in the Allihies copper mines began in 1850 on the heels of the Great Famine. By the time Beara mines closed in 1884, Butte had earned its reputation as "the richest hill on earth," and the road from Beara to Butte was well-traveled.

Historian and genealogist Riobard O'Dwyer recounted the tale an Allihes miner told him of a typical emigration journey from Beara to Butte:

> With their bag of spare clothes tied with a cord, they traveled as far as Cork city with horse and cart which was bringing up the home-made butter to market in Shandon St. They had to bring their own food for a few months journey (depending on the weather) on board the sailing ship. This food consisted of a half-sack of potatoes, coarse fish and a big jar of sour milk. The men wore frieze trousers, strong hobnail boots, flannel underpants, a shirt, a gansie [wool sweater], and a cap. It cost about three or four pounds to travel across the Atlantic to Fall River, Massachusetts. Some of the men spent weeks in Fall River cutting the streets for water pipes in order to make a little money before moving across the country to places like Butte.

This may well have been the story of Mike Sullivan's great-grandfather, who, according to O'Dwyer, emigrated to the States from Allihes in 1860. Several years ago, Sullivan was in Allihes, his ancestral home, to help open the Allihes Mine Museum Project. His great-grandfather had gone from there to mine in Calumet, Michigan.

WHO IF NOT I

THE MOTTO G and I traveled by was not so much "seize the day" as "let the day happen." We were off on a slow drive around the end of the peninsula. The narrow curling road wound up and down mountain foothills and along the rugged storm-riddled coast, first to Allihes, now home to artists and craft workers, and then to Eyeries with its reputation for brightly painted houses and movie locations. It was more stopping than going with photo ops everywhere. Sheep posed nicely on stone ledges. Waves crashed against the shore, and water forced into runnels sprayed high in the air. Cows grazed on lush, green grass at shore's edge. It was a misty, soft day, and there was not a tour bus in sight. The roads are too narrow and the curves are too sharp.

In the Allihies parish, tall, chimney-shaped ruins and abandoned mineheads on hillsides are the only reminders of a mining history. The scene now was one of occasional small cultivated fields, pasture with low rock walls, white stucco cottages with smoke curling up out of their chimneys, the odd pub, mountains, and the sea meeting the sky. The population, now not more than a few hundred, is spread out along the road, sprinkled in the hills, and clustered in the small villages of Allihies and Eyeries. It was impossible for us to imagine what it was like when six thousand people lived there and copper mines employed 1,700, many of them women and children who crushed rock their husbands and fathers dug out of the pits. Even in the best of those times, miners and their families lived in incredible poverty. Three quarters were illiterate. Half the homes were no better than pigsties. An observer at the time wrote, "Never till I came to the Bere Haven mines did I witness such wretchedness of eye-revolting poverty." Diet was mainly potato. Lung-destroying mines and unhealthy homes were incubators of disease. Mine closings on top of the Great Famine of 1845—1849 defined the beginning of the end for Allihies. Fungus destroyed the potato crop two years running. Miners lost their jobs, and tenants lost their land. In one decade, a third of the people in Allihies parish died or emigrated. For more than a hundred years, Ireland lost its best people to the rest of the world. Population at eight million in 1840 shrank to a low of 2.8 million by 1961. Population is now four million.

Ignoring its mining and poverty-filled past, in a brochure aimed at tourists, Allihes speaks of itself in a romantic voice: "A beauty unspoiled and a wildness untamed and the flash of the sea at this land's end is also its beginning." According to the *Book of Invasions of Ireland* (the *Lebor Gabhala*), when the Milesians, the first invaders of

Ireland about 2,000 B.C., were about to make their landfall near where Allihes is now, it was necessary for their bard, Amergin, to chant the land into existence so they could set foot on shore.

I am wind on sea
I am wave in storm
I am sea sound
I am hawk on cliff
A word of art
A piercing point
that pours out rage
The god who fashions
fire in the head
Who if not I

On the back roads, in the hills, and in rocky bays by the sea, there remains a sense of personal discovery, of a beauty unspoiled. For those in search of ancient artifacts, there are standing stones, three holy wells, one curative well, and a haunted moor. For thrill-seekers, there is an aerial tram licensed to carry up to three people and one cow the 722 feet across Dursey Sound to Dursey Island. The trip is not recommended for the faint at heart. For history, there is Brandy Cove, so named for the brandy cargo of a schooner driven on the rocks in the great storm of 1732. Local citizens rescued each and every keg of brandy on board. For sustenance today, Allihies Village has four pubs, two cafés, and a church.

Perched above Ballydonegan Bay with mountains on three sides and the sea at its front door, this shockingly beautiful area is also home to a creative community: eight painters—one who is also a musician—two potters, one sculptor, one photographer, one graphic designer, one illustrator, one poet, and one writer. I presume in addition to the inspiring environment and summer tourist trade, all or most of the artists and writers benefit from Ireland's Taxes Consolidation Act of 1997. Section 195 of the act states, "Income earned by artists, writers, composers and sculptors from the sale of their works is exempt from tax in Ireland [if the] works are original and creative works generally recognized as having cultural or artistic merit."

ANAM CARA: SOUL FRIEND

BEYOND ALLIHIES and near Eyeries, along Coulagh Bay, a pod of dolphins leaping in the waves on an afternoon fishing expedition entertained us. G and I were on our way to visit Sue Booth Forbes, creator and maestro of Anam Cara (Soul Friend), a writers' and artists' retreat. Sue owns and conducts this enterprise, where, as she writes it, "Celtic winds clear your creative path." Sue explained that in the mid-1990s she was in a stress-filled job as communications director for a quasi-public agency in Boston. She was ready for a change in her life that would allow "a rhythm of life and nature" to nourish her writing and her soul. She wanted a place where "I could slow down inside enough to hear my own voice." A few trips to Ireland established the country of choice for Sue's new life. This cottage on a heather-covered hillside overlooking Coulagh Bay was the place. A year's work, and Anam Cara was ready. "A place to build a new life where others would find theirs."

We strolled around with Sue. The amenities were impressive. The context: five acres of patio, lawn and garden, meadow walk, hazelnut grove, old stone mill, a magnificent view over the bay, a swimming hole, and a parade of ducks, the progeny of Mary Wrigley's flock. The cottage: five studio/bedrooms, two sitting rooms, and a loft, all with turf/wood fires, a conservatory draped with grape leaves, sauna and Jacuzzi, and a gallery for the works of resident artists.

The sense of escape and the transformative quality of their experience was a recurring theme of men and women, all Americans, who attended Anam Cara workshops. I wondered how their intellectual prisons had been formed. And when they found themselves, what did they find? The bard Armergin might have asked, "Who if not you?"

Following are some of the things they wrote about their Anam

Cara experiences:

"Freedom to think and dream—hard fought goals—came abruptly, and it took a short time before I knew what to do with it."

"Making my way back from Doing to Being, reconnecting with my values."

"The place emanates healing and life force."

"An ideal place to escape from modern civilization."

"Where the soul can rest easy."

"A wonderful respite from the ongoing lunacy of life."

Workshops had this same "free at last" quality. "*Proprioceptive Writing* . . . that can free us to think, write and speak with strength and clarity. . . Writing is done to music and candlelight . . . focusing on the experience of inner hearing." "*Magic Celts* . . . adventure for your soul with other souls will deal with the mystic nature and sense of place in our lives."

And if students needed additional services, Anam Cara offered several. "Art therapist sessions for insight, personal growth, life issues and creativity." Or another art therapist and art maker who "works with people who wish to explore, develop, and perhaps unblock their creativity." Or a healer who after diagnosing a client's emotional and physical issues, "uses his own lifelong gift of healing energy, in cooperation with the client's own energy to assist in the solution of that problem." A hair stylist is also available, "priced according to treatment." Workshops are $1,000 to $1,500 a week.

EYERIES NEEDS A COLOR CONSULTANT

THE HAG OF BEARA was on my must-see list. The Hag, a weirdly shaped rock overlooking Coulagh Bay, is said to be the petrified remains of *An Cailleach Beara*, a goddess who lived through seven periods of youth and survived seven husbands. If that's not enough, she is also a symbol of sovereignty, a creator of land, and a corn goddess. If you get into a reaping contest with her at harvest time you, are bound to lose both the contest and, with a sweep of her scythe, your head. It is known that the Hag is responsible for many of the huge rocks and islands off the southwest coast of Ireland, formed when stones fell out of her apron. And she washes her clothes in the Corrynackin whirlpool near the Island of Jura.

There is little agreement on how the Hag came to her stony rest on Coulagh Bay. One story is that the Hag stole St. Catherine's mass book. St. Catherine was put out and turned the Hag into stone. Another take is that as the wife of Manaanan, god of the sea, the Hag chose that spot on Coulagh Bay to wait for his return. I'm partial to the third view—that the Hag turned herself into stone to become immortalized throughout history.

I am surprised the Hag wasn't added to the cast of *The Purple Taxi*, a movie made in Eyeries in 1977. *The Purple Taxi* painted the town red, and aquamarine, and orange, and puce, and pink, and yellow. For reasons that have been lost to history, the director decided a multicolored town was just the setting the movie needed. With a free paint job on offer and movie parts as extras to boot, the good citizens of Eyeries said fine. They liked the result, and that's how the village acquired its lasting reputation for color. Over the years, property owners have added their own touches. The result looks like something the Easter Bunny might do after a night at the pub.

While the colors live on, the movie has been long forgotten and with good reason. The cast included Fred Astaire (retired American doctor who drives a purple taxi), Peter Ustinov (a Russian exile who lives in a run-down castle), and Charlotte Rampling (love interest who smokes small cigars and bares her bosom).

The village of Eyeries is very proud of having won a silver medal in the Tidy Town competition, placing second nationally in its category. The adjudicators liked the murals at the school, the beautifully maintained church, and food sources planted in fields around Eyeries for birds and butterflies. They didn't like "motor tyres as bedding surrounds" and thought the exhibit of old farm machinery verged on "deliberate eyecatching." They liked the football clubhouse with its "smart red and white paint" and the green post office looking "as fresh as a new pod of peas." I do sincerely suggest that next time round the Tidy Town adjudicators take a closer look at the shock effect of an ultramarine blue house next to one of fiery red. It's just possible one of their recommendations will be for a color consultant.

From Castletownbere to Allihies to Eyeries, we had driven west on the south side of the peninsula along Bantry Bay, then around the western tip, the most westerly point of Ireland, and then up the north side of Beara along the Kenmare River. Rather than retrace our way, we decided to go up and over the Caha Mountains, crossing the Beara divide at Healy Pass. It was a wild, winding road with clear evidence of landscaping by the Hag of Beara. Huge boulders were everywhere. We snaked up to the summit pass at eleven hundred feet on grades much steeper than current engineering standards allow.

At Healy Pass, the 360-degree view was spectacular—Bantry Bay to the south, Glenmore Lake to the west, Kenmare River to the north, and Mcgillycuddy's Reeks in the distance. Looking down, we were able to make out Allihies, Eyeries, and other places we had been earlier that day. It was exciting to see a large piece of the world all at once as the sun penetrated the late day mist. We were at that moment, king and queen of the mountain.

And the colors of Eyeries do blend some and look better from a distance.

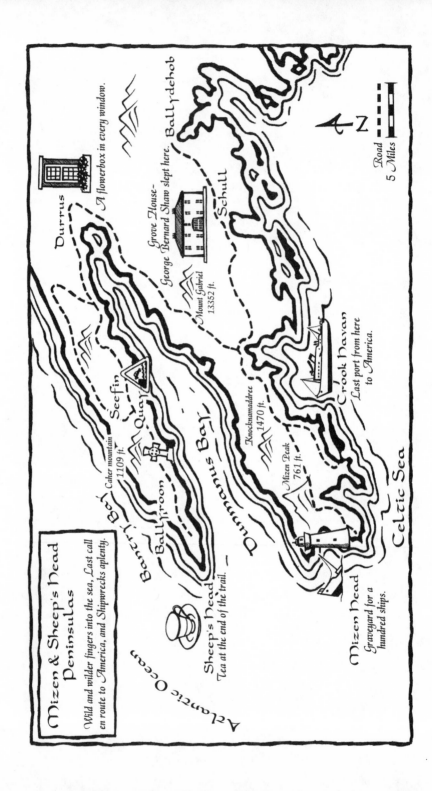

Mizen & Sheep's Head
Peninsulas

Wild and wilder fingers into the sea, Last call
en route to America, and Shipwrecks aplenty.

Atlantic Ocean

Sheep's Head
Tea at the end of the trail.

Bantry Bay

Caher mountain
1109 ft.

Ballydroon

Seefin

Quay

A flowerbox in every window.

Durrus

Dunmanus Bay

Grove House—
George Bernard Shaw slept here.

Ballydehob

Schull

Mount Gabriel
13352 ft.

Knocknamaddree
1470 ft.

Mizen Peak
761 ft.

Crook Navan
Last port from here
to America.

Mizen Head
Graveyard for a
hundred ships.

Celtic Sea

N

Road
5 Miles

CHAPTER FOURTEEN

The Last Peninsula

People are always blaming their circumstances for what they are. I don't believe in circumstances. The people who get on in the world are the people who get up and look for the circumstances they want, and if they can't find them, make them.
—George Bernard Shaw, *Mrs. Warren's Profession* (1893), Act II

MIZEN AND SHEEP'S HEAD in southwest Ireland were our last two peninsulas. At its tip, Mizen Head marks the most southwesterly point of the Irish mainland. Nearly nine miles beyond Mizen Head, Fastness Rock Lighthouse rises 147 feet from the sea. It became known as "the Teardrop of Ireland," being the last bit of Ireland countless thousands of emigrants saw as they left for America.

We were on our way to the Mizen, moving along the N71 at a good clip. The N71 is one of the newer highways built with European Union (EU) funds at a time the rest of Europe was helping its poor cousin rise out of poverty. I wonder if this help might not have had an element of payback for those times several EU countries invaded the Emerald Isle. As Laurence Doyle so aptly puts it in Shaw's play *John Bull's Other Island*, "I am a genuine typical Irishman of the Danish, Norman, Cromwellian and (of course) Scotch invasions."

Speaking of people looking for the circumstances they want, G says the reason I wanted to stay at Grove House in the village of Schull on the Mizen was because that was where Shaw stayed when he was writing *John Bull's Other Island*. The play became famous after a command performance at the Court Theatre in London in 1905. The King laughed so hard he broke his chair. "Well," I thought, "maybe some of Shaw's huge creative spirit lingers on at Grove House, and a small bit might rub off on me."

WHICH WAY IS DOWN?

BACK TO THE N71. We passed through Bantry and headed to the Mizen Peninsula. While the EU may have been concerned with improving highways, their interest seemed to end at the village gate. As we entered Bantry, the wide N71 changed character and deteriorated into a wild mélange of narrow lanes. All signage disappeared. I was lost. It was then I discovered the Irish inclination to please, even at the cost of truth. Three times I stopped to ask locals if I was headed south where I would hook up again with the N71. "Of course." "Oh yes." "Most certainly, Yank." Two of the three had relatives in the States, and one had been to Florida. The truth was, I was headed in the wrong direction, back from where I had come. I realized this when I got a glimpse of Bantry Bay on my left. Since I intended to go south, down the coast to the Mizen, the water needed to be on my right. I think my new Irish friends didn't want to be the bearers of bad news, leaving it to someone else to tell me that any fool should know he was headed wrong. Clearly, I didn't know down from up.

I turned around (no small task on a road barely adequate for a goat cart), finally got to where I could keep the water in sight on my right, and then popped right out from the narrow lane into a modern roundabout at the tip of Bantry Bay. We went round and round and round to a symphony of angry car horns, trying to figure out which of four roads running out of the roundabout would take us on our proper way. I identified with captains in an armada of forty-six French naval vessels caught in Bantry Bay in 1796. Loaded with French troops, they were on their way to overthrow the British. Their ships got hung up in Bantry Bay in a ferocious storm and went round and round looking for a place to land. They couldn't make shore for six days, giving the Brits time to mount a defense and force the French to retreat.

We escaped the roundabout shaken but unharmed. We continued south to Ballydehob, a colorful small town nestled against a fold of hills at the neck of the Mizen Peninsula. As to exterior decoration, Ballydehob could give a lesson in color coordination to Allihies. It was certainly more subdued and had no jarring clashes. Ballydehob got its color back in the 1960s, when it emerged as hippie capital of the west of Ireland. "Blow-ins" from Germany, the Netherlands, and the U.S. colonized the place, and, for a time, outnumbered the locals. As far as we could make out, the only remaining testimonials to this hippie past were a few health-food stores, an array of craft shops, and Deborah, "Clairvoyant & Energy Therapist," available by appointment.

Ordinarily we might have stopped in Ballydehob for a look-around since we are not addicted to getting-there-itis. Though Turn-off signs to Foilnamuck, Cappaghnacallee, and Ballycummisk tempted me along the way, Shaw called.

As George Said

SCHULL IS A CHEERY seaside market town with restaurants, shops, and other amenities aimed at holidaying families and the yachting fraternity. Unlike Castletownbere harbor where pleasure boats were not especially welcome, Schull was more than ready for the better-dressed sporting crowd with pleasant places for tea, upscale pubs, and tony restaurants. Every which way, parking reduced Main Street to a single narrow lane. This produced a form of vehicular Main Street etiquette. Cars come at each other from opposite directions on course for head-on collision. Both drivers slow. Each searches for some small open space at the curb or even a place to pull up on the sidewalk. The first driver to find an opening pulls into it and stops. As the cars come abreast, both drivers wave, smile, pass, and move on. Depending on traffic, the accommodating driver may wait for five or six cars to pass. The real test is truck versus car.

Billy O'Shea greeted us at Grove House with a fine cup of tea and scones. Our second-floor corner room in the carefully restored period house looked out over horseshoe-shaped Schull harbor. The house sat on a low hill, so we had a good view from our room of nearby harbor activity and a long view over the harbor. I wanted to believe our room was the one Shaw had slept in. So I did and I do!

Shaw was born in Dublin in 1856, moved to London when he was twenty-one, and let his mother support him until he was thirty and started making serious money from his plays. At age forty-two, after a life of successful philandering, Shaw married Charlotte Payne Townsend, a wealthy Irish woman. In his proposal, he offered her the prospect of widowhood since Shaw was sure he would die early. He was very wrong. Shaw wrote fifty-three plays in his lifetime and was working on the last of them, *Why She Would Not*, when he died in 1950 at age ninety-four. Shaw's plays that I remember best are *Mrs. Warren's Profession* (1893), *Arms and the Man* (1894), *Pygmalion* (1912), and *Heartbreak House* (1917).

Shaw was many things—dramatist, literary critic, socialist spokesman, freethinker, supporter of women's rights, advocate of equality of income, opponent of private property, and proponent for the simplification of spelling and reform of the English alphabet. When awarded the Nobel Prize for Literature in 1925, he accepted the honor and refused the money. In his life and in his plays, Shaw had a great deal to say. I appreciated the following observations in particular:

"Democracy is a device that ensures we shall be governed no better than we deserve."

"England and America are two countries separated by a common language."

"I often quote myself. It adds spice to my conversation."

"If all economists were laid end to end, they would not reach a conclusion."

"Martyrdom is the only way in which a man can become famous without ability."

"Patriotism is your conviction that this country is superior to all other countries because you were born in it."

"The reasonable man adapts himself to the world; the unreasonable one persists in trying to adapt the world to himself. Therefore, all progress depends on the unreasonable man."

"When a thing is funny, search it carefully for a hidden truth."

"You see things; and you say, 'Why?' But I dream things that never were; and I say, 'Why not?'"

"The more things a man is ashamed of, the more respectable he is."

"The worst sin toward our fellow creatures is not to hate them, but to be indifferent to them: that's the essence of inhumanity."

"Silence is the most perfect expression of scorn."

"He who has never hoped can never despair."

"A government that robs Peter to pay Paul can always depend on the support of Paul."

SHIPWRECKS AT MIZEN HEAD

Night and a starless sky,
Ship on wild billows tost,
With tattered sails and opening seams,

And deck bestrewn with falling beams,
Swift plunging to her doom. . .

Some ships go out to sea
That never more return,
Souls that from heaven in infancy come,
Tarnished and ruined by sin may become,
Like the Dove to the Ark they never return,
But sink as ship to doom.

—Mary Weston Fordham, "Shipwreck"

HAVING SPENT HOURS under bed covers reading C. S. Forester's Horatio Hornblower books by flashlight ("A captain of steel who used his brains to defeat his enemies."), Mizen meant adventure of the sea to me. So while we ordinarily would have begun our time on the peninsula by investigating Schull, G indulged me, and off we went to the peninsula tip, Mizen Head. On our drive, I recounted for G what I could of Forester's wonderful series, with, just possibly, a bit of Gregory Peck thrown in. Peck played Captain Horatio Hornblower to a fare-thee-well in a 1951 Hornblower movie.

Forester's first book in the Hornblower series, *Beat to Quarters*, was published in 1937. I was eleven. The last, *Admiral Hornblower in the West Indies*, came out in 1958. Throughout the series, Hornblower remains cynical, compassionate, courageous, quick thinking, decisive, and above all, a consummate seaman who remains loyal to his men. He starts out a midshipman and ends up an admiral. Along the way, he earns a living as a card shark, fights innumerable sea battles, recovers sunken treasure, suppresses an uprising in Nicaragua, is taken captive by the French, escapes the French, recaptures a British ship, sails back to England, marries his true love Lady Barbara, carries out a delicate mission to Russia, quells a mutiny, and helps defeat Napoleon. G said Hornblower sounded just like me. Well, now!

The drive from Schull to Mizen Head took us through progressively more remote country but without much of a view of the sea.

There was little to prepare us for the sheer tortured red sandstone cliffs at the very end of the peninsula. The vertiginous cliffs rose seven hundred feet from where the roaring Celtic Sea met the raging Atlantic. I have looked down from mountain heights with steep drops but never had the dizzying sensation Mizen Head produced. I think it was looking down into the riled sea at the bottom of the cliff that made me feel I was on tilt. With winds blowing hard, it didn't take much to imagine sailors struggling to secure mizenmast sails in raging storms or, peering through a fog, listening for the sound of waves smashing against the rocky cliffs. The days of sail were a time when men were constantly stretched to their limits and beyond.

In a little more than a century, more than eighty major ships and many smaller boats struck rocks or ran aground, meeting their ends in the Mizen graveyard. Here is a roll call of several of those eighty ships:

(1796) *L'Impatiente*, frigate bombardier of the French fleet. Of 250 soldiers and 300 seamen, 7 survived.

(1822) S.S. *Bohemian*, bound Boston for Liverpool, cotton, bacon, and passengers. 35 of 57 crew lost.

(1889) S.S. *Queensmore*, bound Baltimore for Liverpool, cotton, wheat, 900 cattle, 23 cattlemen, and 2 stowaways. Cargo abandoned, all on board rescued.

(1896) S.S. *Memphis*, bound Montreal for Avonmouth, timber, butter, bacon, flour, cattle, and coal. 9 crew lost.

(1906) S.F.V. *Ribble*, stream trawler, fish. Captain R. Collinson, crew of 8 and 2 passengers, all rescued.

A fog signal station at Mizen Head did not go into operation until 1909. It sits on Cloghane Island, little more than a big rock in the sea a bit beyond the end of the peninsula. An arched bridge 150 feet above sea level and 172 feet in length connects the mainland cliff to the island and signal station. If G and I were fifty years or so younger, we might have tried the ninety-nine steep steps down to the bridge. Though even then, thinking of ninety-nine steps back up, we might have had second thoughts.

Originally, the fog warning signal was a big bang, an explosive charge set off at three-minute intervals to warn ships they were nearing danger. In 1934, a brilliant flash was added, and in 1959 a white occulting light, a beacon flashing at regular intervals, was installed atop the signal station at a height of 180 feet. The beacon had a range of thirteen miles. Warning systems continued to evolve. A radio transponder beacon was installed in 1968 and then a global positioning system in the 1970s. In 1993, the signal station operation went fully automatic, and the light keepers were retired. Their residence has become a visitor center. While it displays artifacts of interest, it lacks the drama of the sea.

A Sweet Spot

ON THE WAY BACK to Schull from Mizen Head, I had the good fortune to miss the turnoff at Dough, which would have taken us directly to Crookhaven. Instead I turned at Ballyvoge Beg, a bit southwest of Ballyvoge More. We got to Crookhaven later in the afternoon. It is tucked in on the sheltered side of a curving neck of land creating a deep inlet, the "crooked haven." Today, it is hard to imagine the haven when it was the first and last port of call for ships going between Northern European ports and America. It was where ships stocked up with provisions and took on fuel before heading across the Atlantic. When they came back, ships anchored at Crookhaven to learn in which port their cargo had been sold. According to tales told of the time, the harbor was often so full of ships you could cross from one side to the other hopping from deck to deck and never touch water.

At the end of the nineteenth century, seven hundred people lived and worked in Crookhaven. Today, there are twenty-nine permanent residents. Off-season when we were there, Crookhaven had the feel of an abandoned movie set. Pastel-colored cottages sat silent. No smoke curling from their chimneys. A couple of small boats were tied up at the stone quay, with drying fishing nets along side. Tables and chairs spilled out of the quayside pub. And there wasn't a live body in sight.

My mistaken turnoff had taken us down a narrow lane to a low hill with front-row seats to a magical view over a tide lake, a narrow mile-long arc of water at the head of Barley Cove. At high tide, the lake filled with spill from Barley Cove, water running over a shallow beach and through a neck of land connecting lake and cove. At low tide, much of that water runs back to the sea, leaving a shallow, smooth, green-gray surface where swans nest among the rushes. That's the time we came to the scene. Water birds scrounged their fill along the muddy shoreline flats. Soft breezes bent the rushes and rippled the surface of the water in odd patterns. It was late afternoon, and the sun made an appearance and delivered an array of tints for this painterly scene. It was a sweet spot and all our own.

CHAPTER FIFTEEN

SHEEP'S HEAD—A WORLD APART

A POET'S PICTURE OF SHEEP'S HEAD

THE IRISH POET Seamus Heaney was awarded the Nobel Prize for Literature in 1995 "for works of lyrical beauty and ethical depth, which exalt everyday miracles and the living past." Among a people renowned for its great gift in language, Heaney is an outstanding practitioner of, as he terms it, "an art that is earnest and devoted to things as they are."

Heaney wrote this poem of the everyday miracle that is Sheep's Head Peninsula.

The Peninsula

When you have nothing more to say, just drive
For a day all round the peninsula.
The sky is tall as over a runway,
The land without marks so you will not arrive
But pass through, though always skirting landfall.
At dusk, horizons drink down sea and hill,
The ploughed field swallows the whitewashed gable
And you're in the dark again. Now recall
The glazed foreshore and silhouetted log,
That rock where breakers shredded into rags,

The leggy birds stilted on their own legs,
Islands riding themselves out into the fog
And drive back home, still with nothing to say
Except that now you will uncode all landscapes
By this: things founded clean on their own shapes,
Water and ground in their extremity.

THE COUNCIL'S PERSPECTIVE

THE SHEEP'S HEAD Community Council defined the geography, population, and other characteristics of their peninsula in the following words:

Our Geographical Situation. The peninsula is the smallest of the West Cork peninsulas. It is fifteen (15) miles long and two (2) to three (3) miles wide. It is bounded by Bantry Bay on the north and Dunmanus Bay on the south. Its eastern boundary is the village of Durrus. The northern side is mostly rocky with high cliffs and rugged rough ground. There are no villages or any large farms on this side of the peninsula. The southern side has the area's only village, Kilcrohane. To the east of Kilcrohane is Ahakista, the only other area in the Peninsula which has a concentration of population. The few larger farms in the area lie on the southern side of the peninsula.

Our Population. The total population is five hundred and fifty-five (555). There are 143 children. 53% of the adults are over 50 years of age. There are four hundred and fifty two (452) households in the peninsula. Of these one hundred and fifty four (154) or 34% are "Holiday Homes."

Local Employment. The area is entirely rural and the principal occupation is farming. Tourism is increasing but is still not a big source of income. The vast majority of those not engaged in either farming or tourism travel (35 miles round trip) to work outside the area. There is very little unemployment.

Our Local Facilities and Deficiencies. There is bus service to Bantry on one day a week, Friday. The Medical Center is serviced one day a week. Cork County Council provides a library service once a fortnight. There are no hotel, bank or police barracks or public toilets in the area. A once thriving potato growing Co-op has ceased trading. An associated daffodil growing Co-Op has become defunct. The road network consists of badly surfaced unclassified roads.

PERSONAL FEELINGS

G WITH HER artist's eye said it was the light. It was high noon, and for G it had a brilliantly fresh luminous quality. Everything bright and light—rocks, flowers, fields, sky, and sea. For me, it was more the way things I observed came together of a piece. Every curve or dip in the road, every new bay along the undulating coast created a new composition of lush green fields, some spotted with sheep, low stone walls, white cottages, honeysuckle, and heather, all changing color ever so subtly from one minute to the next as moving clouds hid and then revealed the sun. Everything fit naturally. There was nothing false or forced. And, as Sean O'Faolain observed, there is always "the cup of blue sea on the horizon."

Spectacular, unspoilt, timeless, serene, ancient, tranquil—all the words apply. Kieran O'Reilly of *The New York Times* writes of "rolling patchworks of green fields, stretching over hills and valleys, herds of brown-and-white cows framed against the sky . . . the heathland, bristling with gorse and purpled with heather." Patrick Whitehurst in *Forgotten Ireland* describes "wild fuchsia hedges [that] dangle delicate crimson ballerinas over the roads. Hedges heavy with wild cherries, sloes, damsons and strawberries line the byways."

Whether it is Heaney's sense of "things founded clean on their own shapes" O'Reilly's "rolling patchwork of green fields," or the scenic compositions that touched me, little remains to remind one of time past, before the 1845–1849 Great Famine. At that time, more than 8,300 people lived on the peninsula. Now, 555 live there. In 1846, there were sixty-nine marriages and 344 baptisms. In 1847, there were only nineteen marriages and fifty-six baptisms. Families that could afford it left for the States, many on boats from nearby Crookhaven on the Mizen. Sheep's Head was emptied, and that is the feeling that defines it today.

EXPLORING SHEEP'S HEAD

OUR EXPLORATION OF Sheep's Head began at Durrus. It is where Four Mile Water flows into Dunmanus Bay on the south side of the peninsula. Houses, shops, and pubs in the village were painted bright sherbet colors, and there were few windows without baskets or boxes of billowing flowers. The Gulf Stream warms Sheep's Head, and daffodils bloom in January.

The road from Durrus to Ahakista at Kitchen Cove hugs the bay, moving in and out with every curve of the shoreline. The Mizen Peninsula seems close. It is less than a mile away across the bay, with Mt. Gabriel dominant against the sky. The lovely thing about less-traveled roads like the one we were on was no one crawling up our tails anxious to get by. We could stop, gaze, and take pictures wherever we wanted, for as long as we wanted. Had it been Sunday, we might well have encountered a road-bowling score (contest) between Ahakista and Kilcrohane, the small village just down the road.

Beyond Ahakista, we drove down a narrow track to the Goleen Strand and discovered a touching and very old cemetery. A herd of brown and white cows grazed contentedly in a neighboring pasture. Remains of a stone chapel stood in the center of the cemetery. While the roof and large sections of the four walls had collapsed long before, those sturdy stone parts that formed the entry or a window remained in place, and the sun from the southeast poured through each opening. We walked around reading headstones—some simple, others elegant—many from the 1800s and some relatively current—Daly, Hegarty, O'Brien, O'Donavan, O'Mahonbey, Tobin, McCarthy—family groups of young and old. Inscriptions spoke of love. The grass was cut. Flowers grew. The sun shone. And we moved on.

MELANCHOLY DANES

NEAR KILCROHANE, a small sign pointed to a quay, a place built for loading and unloading small boats. So down the narrow track we drove, honeysuckle and bramble whisking the sides of the car. A few hundred yards on, we came upon one of the most arresting warning signs I have ever seen. It showed a car tilting off the end of a cliff, its nose headed straight to the waves below. After a moment's consideration, I realized this was visual shorthand for "don't be a damn fool and drive off the end of the quay." As it turned out, the sign should have added, "and beware of melancholy Danes."

There was no place to turn around, so we continued down the grade toward the bay. Around a final curve there was the stone quay. And smack in the middle of the small quay was a car with Danish license plates. And sitting on the grass next to their car were two very melancholy Danes munching away on sandwiches. At least we presumed they were Danes. Not a sign of recognition from them. Not a slight smile. Not a feeble wave. They just went on eating and looking at their feet. Any fool could see that with their car parked in the middle of the quay, it would take very artful maneuvering for us to turn around without fulfilling the prophecy of the warning sign and landing in the drink. Maybe that's what the Danes hoped to see. Damned if I would ask them for help. G guided. Back and forth I inched the sturdy Focus. After some minutes, we made it around. G got in. I moved off the quay and onto where the rear wheels sat on the dirt and gravel track. And with spinning wheels in a Detroit start, I left a high spray of dirt and gravel flying behind.

A Cup of Tea at Land's End

WE WERE BACK on Sheep's Head Way, now climbing Ballyroon Mountain and headed to the very end of the trail at the tip of the peninsula. The road wound this way and that. Paved surface gave way to gravel, and the trail narrowed as we twisted, turned, and rose higher and higher, penetrating ever wilder and more threatening rock formations of strange character and color. At times, the hood of the car pointed nearly straight up, tending to create some wonder of what came next. We had this sense of being explorers going where few had gone before.

We crested the last rise out on to a high plateau, where we surveyed the world around us. To our right was a magnificent panoramic view of Bantry Bay, and beyond it was Beara Peninsula with the Shehy Mountains to the east, the Caha Mountains in the center, and the Slieve Miskish Mountains at the western end. To our left was another all encompassing view. This one of Dunmanus Bay, the Atlantic, and Mizen Head Peninsula.

And there, right in the middle of this "undiscovered" wilderness, was Benie Tobin and her tea wagon, a six-foot by eight-foot cabin on wheels. Benie told me she had set it up eight years earlier and had always served apple rhubarb pie, scone and jam, cake, coffee, and tea. Ordinarily, this "intrusion in the wilds" might have offended me. But Benie was very sweet, she and her cart fit right in, and the pie was damn good.

Add to the wilderness scene a large, white RTE television recording van (Irish National Broadcasting) parked next to Mrs. Tobin's tea emporium. Sarah and Emmet were there from RTE interviewing James O'Mahoney and Tom Whittey, local farmers, for *Ear to the Ground*, a program, said Sarah, that "put you in the know." For many years, the government had provided small annual subsidies of €500 ($600) to €1,000 ($1,200) to farmers who allowed public access to holy wells, burial grounds, and other historic monuments on their private land. O'Mahoney and Whittey were concerned about ending the subsidy, leading farmers to close off access, and the number of new people buying property and putting up "No Trespassing" signs. There were also negative implications for the Sheep's Head Way, a fifty-five-mile walking trail of growing repute. The trail is discretely marked with simple Irish oak posts, each with a small hiker stenciled in yellow pointing out the right way to go. O'Mahoney helped organize the cooperative effort throughout the peninsula that made the walking route a reality. As we talked about Sheep's Head, it was clear he had that love and feeling for place that comes from deep roots. He spoke of three generations. He, his father, and grandfather had all been born on the O'Mahoney dairy farm.

As I was talking with O'Mahoney and Whittey, G strolled among the mossy rocks and mountain flowers. She will always remember the remarkable light that afternoon, a light that gave a special bloom to all things along Sheep's Head Way.

FINN MACCOOL

ON OUR WAY back to Schull, we drove from the north shore to the south shore of Sheep's Head over the thousand-foot Seefin Pass. The way is called The Goat's Path, appropriately so. The way up is somewhat gradual and slow, all in first and second gear, rather like the slow crawl of a roller coaster ride as you grind up toward the first peak. Then whoosh, it was sharply down at what seemed like a forty-five-degree angle. It was a drive taken with great concentration.

Seefin means "the seat of Finn," named for Finn MacCool, one of Ireland's legendary heroes who lived in the third century A.D. He ate a salmon of knowledge and became very wise. He swallowed water from a magic well and acquired the powers of a sorcerer. He led a famous band of warriors, the Fianna. In his youth, Finn could outrun deer and speed through forests without disturbing a twig. His massive wolfhounds, Bran and Sceolaing, stood high as his shoulders and helped him. Finn made a wishing chair at Seefin Pass, a place to rest on his great hunts for wild boar. Legend has it that wishes made there will come true. Finn's chair has been kept in good order. The *Guide to Sheep's Head Way* tells us, "We thought it appropriate to have a seat ready for Finn when he returns to us to hunt again. In the meantime, you are more than welcome to use it."

It was goodbye to Finn and to Sheep's Head and as fine an end as you could wish for on our journey of the peninsulas—Dingle, Beara, Mizen, and Sheep's Head. The next morning we began our return travels north to Listowel.

CHAPTER SIXTEEN

CREAKY TRAVELER'S GOOD FAIRY

RV VIRUS IN THE BLACK VALLEY

ORIGINALLY, WE HAD PLANNED a one-day, morning-to-evening drive from Schull in the southwest corner of West Cork to Listowel, near the River Shannon in North Kerry. But this being the third week of our trip and having been thoroughly tested by Irish roads and drivers, wisdom prevailed and we decided it would be prudent to break the drive and spend a night in Killarney. This would get us into Listowel before noon the next day. How wise we were.

Our first stop on the way was in Glengarriff, gateway to the Beara Peninsula. We took tea at the Eccles Hotel, a period establishment on Bantry Bay that carries its 250 years magnificently. It was a sunny morning, and we were served on the porch that sweeps across the entire front of the hotel and faces the bay. According to hotel literature, the Eccles had been "graced with the presence of Queen Victoria" when she toured the area in 1861. The Eccles was also where Shaw wrote part of his play *St. Joan,* sitting at a table in the hotel dining room. G and I were sure both the Queen and GBS had also had tea in this very spot, possibly at the same table, and enjoyed the view, as did we.

I wasn't able to find out why Shaw chose to write in the dining room or which part of *St. Joan* he completed there. In any case, the view was grand, the tea was lovely, and another creaky traveler axiom was confirmed. It seldom costs that much more for tea and biscuits at a lovely place than it does at a grubby one.

When you are in Glengarriff, Garinish Island (*Ilnacullin* in Gaelic) in Bantry Bay is one of those certified "must see" places. For me, Garinish Island is simply one more example of man's triumph over nature. G and I decided to avoid such horticultural wonders after our visit several years earlier to Glenveagh Castle Gardens in Co Donegal, certified by the Irish Tourist Board as "an oasis in a desert of bogs and moorland." Garinish Island is noted as yet another "oasis" of exotic plant life. It was created in the 1920s. Here's the trick. Ship tons of topsoil to a thirty-seven-acre pile of barren rock in the middle of Bantry Bay, hire a celebrated architect and garden designer (Harold Pito) to create an Italian garden, a "veritable paradise" including a whole range of nonnative exotic species such as New Zealand privet, sacred bamboo, magnolias, and rare conifers. Then add stone balustrades and Grecian pillars and dot the place with little classical buildings. And there you have it, the perfect tourist attraction.

With so much natural beauty all around on the Beara Peninsula, a tricked up exotic garden seems all wrong. If you go, the tariff is €6.35 ($7.62) for a ten-minute boat ride to the island plus an entry fee of €3.18 ($3.82). And thousands go. And every guidebook says you should.

Continuing north from Glengarriff, winding up through the Caha Mountains (*An Cheacfha*), we stopped round nearly every bend for just one more shot of peaks, clouds, and sea. Near Caha Pass was the ultimate picture—a huge ram posed on a mountain outcrop against a raw sky, Bantry Bay in the distance, clusters of sheep grazing on patches of green grass in the foreground. The ram cooperated, remaining fixed in place, seeming to survey his world. Between us, G and I must have shot two rolls of film, and none of the results equal the recollection.

Some distance on, past Kenmare, after Moll's Gap, we descended into the isolated and appropriately named Black Valley, the last valley in all Ireland to get electricity. As one blind curve blended into another, we caught the RV virus. There, looming in front of us was an RV, lumbering along a road barely sufficient for a small car. The back end of the behemoth seemed to grow larger by the minute. There was no way to pass, unless you were immortal (an article of faith for many Irish drivers). After five minutes, it became clear the RV driver had no intention of pulling up on a verge to let cars stacked up behind get by. The only cure for the RV virus, and one I recommend for stroke avoidance, is to pull off, stop, shut off your motor, admire the scenery, read, nap, or whatever. After a half hour or so, start up again, and more often than not, the RV will have disappeared.

LADIES VIEW AND QUEEN VICTORIA

AS IF TO COMPENSATE for the RV virus, we next entered Killarney National Park, a remarkable Ice Age composition of glacial sculpted limestone valleys, deep lakes, eerily balanced boulders on rugged mountain crags, and circling three lakes, virgin forests of oak, bilberry, woodrush, and arbutus, the bright red "strawberry tree." Mosses, liverwort, greater purple-flowered butterwort, saxifrages, and lichens completed the horticultural display. We stopped on a sweeping bend high above the *Loch Uacharach* (Upper Lake) at the same spot Queen Victoria and her ladies-in-waiting, "climbed out of their carriages to admire the view"—a gray, cool lake set in a deep mountain valley with the Gap of Dunloe and the peaks of *Na Cruacha Dubha* (Macgillycuddy's Reeks) beyond. Queen Victoria made known the joy and pleasure this scene provided that day in September 1861, and so the name, Ladies View. (In her book, *Ladies in Waiting*, Dulcie Ashdown explains that ladies-in-waiting, Mistress of the Robes and Ladies of the Bedchamber, serve as companions to the Queen, "a handsome appendage on State occasions, a confiding gossip in private, a subsidiary hostess to visitors, and the penman of innumerable notes and memoranda on the Queen's behalf.")

There is now a nicely designed café at Ladies View offering various delicacies, including whiskey-laced Irish coffee, a questionable specialty on a twisting mountain road. There is also a gift shop and a large parking area for tour buses. It being late afternoon when we arrived, most of the busses had gone home, reminding us it was time to head for Killarney, where we would stop for the night. On the way into Killarney, we passed two more National Park lakes, *Lough Mhucrois* (Muckross), the middle lake, and *Lough Lein* (Leane), the lower lake. I made a mental note to come back for a closer look if we could.

CREAKY TRAVELER'S GOOD FAIRY

THE *ROUGH GUIDE TO IRELAND* notes, "Killarney has been commercialized to a saturation point." This is an understatement. As we drove along Muckross Road toward the town center, it was clear that Killarney's sole reason for being is as an access point for tourists to Killarney National Park and a departure point for up to a hundred tour buses a day that head for the Ring of Kerry. Tourism as Killarney's business began in the 1750s and took off after Queen Victoria's visit in 1861. As we drove into Killarney, we passed block after block of somber brick row houses, best described as being unlucky in their architect. The houses were built out to the sidewalk, each with a B&B sign hanging out front. Here and there, souvenir shops, cafés, pubs, and occasionally a larger hotel interrupted the wall of B&Bs.

If, over the previous three weeks, we had not stayed at peaceful and attractive farmhouses and B&Bs with wonderful views, we might have been less depressed by Killarney's offerings. But then, when all seemed lost, the Good Fairy of Creaky Travelers worked her magic, tapping into the recesses of my mind. As we were leaving Killarney National Park, hadn't I glimpsed a large Georgian house set on a hill?

Back we went and there it was—a sign at the road, a long, sweeping tree-lined drive. Set in a garden at the top of the hill was Carriglea House. Yes, said proprietor John Beazley, there had been a cancellation and a large upstairs corner room was ours. We settled in, gazed out past a bed of roses to Lake Leane, and out came the flask for a toast to the Good Fairy. Then we were off for an amble along the shore of Lake Leane.

The Muckross gate, the main entrance to Killarney National Park, was five minutes down the road. As we parked our Focus, two jarveys (drivers) of Killarney's famous legion of jaunting-cars (two-wheeled, horse-drawn carts) were leaving the park and swinging shut iron entry gates, the kind you see in movies, set at the head of a drive leading to "the grand mansion." There, the drive led to Muckross House, a nineteenth-century, sixty-five-room Elizabethan mansion. Now part of the park, it has become the Kerry Folk Centre with potters, weavers, and other craftspeople demonstrating their trade and selling their wares. One of the jaunting-car drivers tried to sell us a twenty-dollar ride, the evening discount rate for American tourists, he said. The horse seemed happy to pack it in, and we wanted to amble on alone. The driver assured us that a small side gate next to the big gate was always open.

As a movie script, our next few minutes in the park could read this way:

PLACE: Muckross Estate entrance to Killarney National Park.
TIME: Early moments of dusk on a warm September day.
SCENE: Couple in their mid seventies, alert but somewhat creaky, contented smiles, both walking slowly with canes. They exchange a few friendly words with a heavy-set jaunting-car driver (he with a stage Irish brogue). She pats the horse's neck. The driver gets down from his cart, shuts the huge gate, mounts his cart, and with a flick of his whip rolls off, waving a friendly goodbye. The couple pass through the side gate. Holding hands, they amble down the drive, both in sync with a slight

right leg limp. It is dusk and the scene is an artist's dream—mist rising from the still lake softens the light, an orange sun sinks slowly, backlighting clouds, painting each with a silver edge. A perfect emerald-green lawn sweeps down to the scalloped shore of Lough Lein. The couple looks out to rocky islands and across the lake to shelving hills that rise green from the water's edge. Mountain peaks loom in the background. Only the whisper of the wind across the water and a few songbirds are heard. She turns to him with a wistful look. They hug. They kiss.

Cut. It's a wrap.

LAKE OF LEARNING

Sweet Innisfallen, fare thee well
And long may light around thee smile,
As soft as on that evening fell
When first I saw thy fairy isle.

—Thomas Moore, from *Irish Melodies*

"SERENE, PEACEFUL, and very holy," Innisfallen is the largest of the islands we saw in Lough Lein. Remains of a Romanesque church and a twelfth-century Augustinian Priory suggest something of the island's past. In the sixth century, Inisfallen was at "the very edge of the known world. . . . Europe was awash with barbarians [and] Innisfallen was the place to get away from it all, the perfect place for prayer, reflection and study." It was a sanctuary and became the first new university in Europe in more than eight hundred years. Princes from all over came to study, leading to the name *Leough Lein*, "Lake of Learning."

A succession of monks on the island between 1015 and 1320 wrote the famous *Annals of Innisfallen*. These monks were of a special group known as Annalists. Their task was to "record, with the utmost accuracy, all remarkable events simply and briefly, without any ornament of language, without exaggeration, and without fictitious embellishment." As a general rule, the Annalists "admitted nothing into their records except what occurred during their lifetime, and was of their own personal knowledge, or what they found recorded in the compilations of previous Annalists, who had themselves followed the same plan." It was this discipline that gave integrity to the work of annalists who continued their chronicle from age to age for some three hundred years.

Written in Gaelic mixed with Latin, the *Annals* gave a history of the world to the time of St. Patrick, then concentrated mainly on Irish affairs. The *Annals* were taken to England in 1686 and are now at the Bodlian Library in Oxford. The Irish wonder when the *Annals of Innisfallen* will come home.

ON TO LISTOWEL

THE SUNSET MIST of the evening before had given way to a bright sunny day at Carriglea House—glistening morning dew, sparkling lake, and emerald hills. Our hosts, the Beazley family, were more relaxed than many B&B proprietors and were happy to serve breakfast when slower paced folk like G and I got to it. This gave us time to have a wake-up cup of tea in our room (the equipment and makings were at hand), admire the view, and feel a bit smug about our working relationship with the good fairy.

Carriglea House is nearly two hundred years old and has the comfort and feel of an old family home, which makes sense because John Beazley's grandfather bought the farm in 1922. Sitting in the kitchen for another cup of coffee, John told me his father had been born on the farm in 1923 and he in 1966. Carriglea has been a guesthouse since 1932 and has always been part of a working farm.

After friendly goodbyes, we were on our way to Listowel.

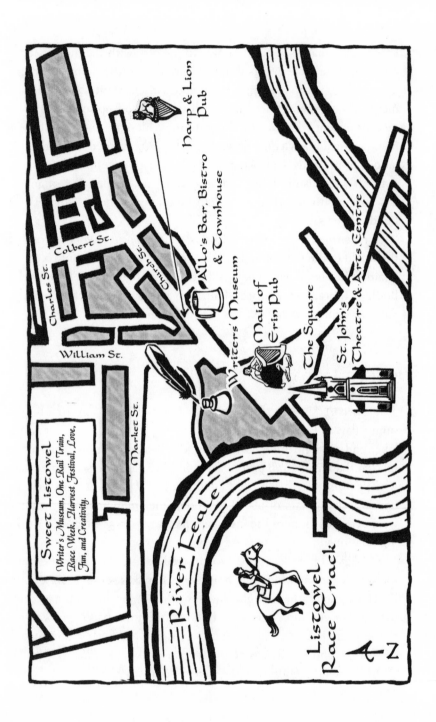

Sweet Listowel
Writer's Museum, One Rail Train, Race Week, Harvest Festival, Love, Fun, and Creativity.

Charles St.

Colbert St.

Church St.

William St.

Market St.

Allo's Bar, Bistro & Townhouse

Harp & Lion Pub

Writers' Museum

Maid of Erin Pub

The Square

St. John's Theatre & Arts Centre

River Feale

Listowel Race Track

N

CHAPTER SEVENTEEN

SWEET LISTOWEL

Beautiful Listowel, serenaded night and day
By the gentle waters of the River Feale.
Listowel where it is easier to write than not to write,
Where first love never dies, and the tall streets hide the loveliness,
The heartbreak and the moods, great and small,
Of all the gentle souls of a great and good community.
Sweet, incomparable hometown that shaped and made me.

—John B. Keane

Oh, Puck may be famous and Galway be grand,
And the praise of Tramore echo down through the land,
But I'll sing you a ballad and beauty extol,
As I found long ago in the town of Listowel

—Bryan MacMahon

Listowel, a workaday Irish town . . .

—*The Rough Guide to Ireland*

LISTOWEL IS A MARKET TOWN of 3,393 in North Kerry, with the
slow, meandering River Feale winding through it. Going to Listowel
was my choice, and G said okay. I liked the idea of going to the
Listowel Races, an annual race week dating back to 1858. It was said

to be a time of "legend and folklore" when exiles scattered to the ends of the earth came home. During Race Week, there is also a Harvest Festival with parades, buskers, and street parties. And then I was really curious about Listowel's reputation for sprouting writers, poets, and playwrights.

Looking back, of all our Irish memories, those of the people we met and things we did in Listowel, remain the most vivid. There were prettier places and any number of memorable experiences. So what was it about this "workaday" town that made such a deep and lasting impression? Three things. First, Listowel is authentic, as Webster says, "not false or copied, genuine, real." Next, it is a community where class knows no class. Listowel refuses to set boundaries for itself. Like the little engine that could, the good people of Listowel believe "we can, we can, we can." And finally, like John B. Keane and Bryan MacMahon, they love the place, and we all know what love can do for you.

HAIL TO THE GREEN AND GOLD ABOVE

WE ARRIVED IN LISTOWEL (**Lis**-toe-el) on a busy Saturday morning to a mix of new sights, close encounters with other cars, and a search for clues that would lead us to Allo's Bar, Bistro & Townhouse on Church Street. Green and gold banners and pennants were every-where—every building, every car, and it seemed, in the hands of hundreds of pennant waving kids. It didn't take long to learn that green and gold were the colors of Co Kerry's Gaelic football team. (And colors of my junior high school in Detroit some sixty years before: "Hail to the green and gold above, hail to the green and gold we love, hail to Durfee Junior High.")

Kerry was to play Armagh in the All-Ireland Football Finals the next day in Dublin. "Passionate" is an inadequate adjective when applied to the feelings that men, women, and children of Co Kerry have for their football teams. The parish priest had scheduled a special Saturday evening mass so local folk could put in a word for their team and get an early Sunday start on the five-hour drive to Dublin to see the match.

SPIRITUAL VERSUS TEMPORAL

THE ROAD INTO LISTOWEL took us over the River Feale on a stone bridge of five graceful arches and directly into The Square, Listowel's social, cultural, religious, and business center. The sight of two towering early nineteenth-century Gothic spires elevated our spirits. On our right was the once Protestant St. John's, now a theatre and arts centre, and on our left was St. Mary's, the Catholic Church. A more temporal dimension of the urban streetscape lay directly ahead. Staring us full in the face was the very colorful and richly endowed bare-breasted *Maid of Erin*, a giant-sized bas-relief covering much of the upper front above a pub, appropriately named "The Maid of Erin."

This ornamental creation was the work of Pat McAuliffe (1846–1921), a builder and plasterer who, according to historian Rev. J. Anthony Gaughan, "demanded a free hand." The *Maid* depicts "a Romantic image of Mother Ireland surrounded by a harp, a wolfhound and other symbols of Eire." A crisis occurred in 1999, when a new owner of the pub said the *Maid* was "unseemly" and decided to "rescue her dignity." He painted on a dress covering her famous bosom. An outcry followed. Good sense prevailed, and the *Maid* was returned to her natural state. (This reminded me of former Attorney General John Ashcroft's decision to have the buxom, twelve and a half foot Art Deco statue the *Spirit of Justice* curtained off. Ashcroft was moved to this action after seeing a newspaper photo showing *Spirit's* breast hovering over his head as he announced the Department of Justice's anti-terror plan to reporters. The succeeding attorney general, Alberto Gonzales, undraped the *Minnie Lou*, as the

statue in the lobby of the Department of Justice building is affection-
ately known to the press corps.)

Knowing that both church spires and the *Maid* deserved a return
visit we moved on. The road bisecting the Square fed into a system
of one-way streets—after a left, right, and right again, we were heading back to The Square on Church Street. And there, with a very discrete sign out front was our destination, Allo's at 41 Church Street,
just where it has been since 1859. To my delight, across the street
from Allo's was the *Harp & Lion*, another of Pat McAuliffe's large plas-
terworks celebrating Celtic spirituality while decorating the front of
a pub. (The lion represents courage, bravery, and strength. The nine-
string harp represents both hope and the nine baronies that first
defined the boundaries of Kerry.) Following Irish rules of the road—
wherever, whenever, and however—we parked in a no-parking zone
in front of the pub. The police station (gardia) was just down the
road, but the law never seemed to mind.

BAR ME NOT

IT WAS LATE MORNING when we opened the door to Allo's Bar, Bistro
& Townhouse. (The townhouse had three rooms, one per floor on the
second, third, and fourth floors above the first-floor bar and bistro.)
First came the "snug," an intimate wood-paneled section of the bar
with only three stools. Then we walked through another door sepa-
rating the snug from the full bar and into a room of nine or ten tables
in an unpretentious, café-like setting. G looked a bit uncertain, and I
must confess for a moment memories of a sleepless night in a very
noisy room above a bar in Bern, Switzerland, flashed by. But, there,
behind the bar was Ailish Mullane, blond, full of smiles, an old friend
of two telephone calls and two faxes. She was one of a staff full of
nieces, nephews, cousins, and mothers, all cheerful and helpful. Ailish
had our bags fetched from the car and led us through an arch at the
back of the room and up a narrow flight of stairs to our room. It had

a four-poster bed, writing desk, a couple of easy chairs, paintings, mirrors, and a marble bathroom, all as advertised. Ailish asked us to come down for a cup of tea whenever we were ready.

Settling in didn't take us long since we never unpack very much. G and I have carry-on bags with wheels plus small tote bags. My tote is a student-sized backpack with wheels and the shoulder straps cut off. We checked out the reading lamps, set our suitcases on luggage racks, and rearranged the room slightly so chairs sat around a small table where we would have tea in the morning. Then I pulled down the top section on each of the two double-hung windows facing Church Street to let in some air. Surprise! The elderly windows stuck on open. The windows wouldn't go down again during our stay. For three nights, we had the pleasure of drifting off to sleep to fiddle, button box, and piccolo music floating over from the *Harp & Lion*—"Blind Mary," "Noble Emerald Land," "The Teetotaler," and other cheerful tunes.

KINDNESS COMES NATURALLY

THEN, GENTLE READER, as John B. Keane would address you, there began a series of encounters with the unforced and helpful ways of the people of Listowel. Small acts of kindness seemed to come naturally. Now, when G and I think of Listowel, a halo of warmth surrounds our memories.

When we were into our second cup of strong Irish tea, Armel Whyte, chef/proprietor of Allo's, left a pot of seafood chowder to simmer and came out of the kitchen to see how we were faring. I can't recall how it entered into the conversation, but when Armel learned my cell phone wasn't working, he said a friend in a radio shop down the street was a wonder and could fix it in a minute. I would have expected Armel to tell me where the shop was and get back to his kitchen. But, no. He grabbed the phone, dashed off, and was back in ten minutes with a working phone. The speaker had gone bad.

Then Ailish handed me John O'Flaherty's book *Listowel Races—1858–1991, A History* with a note from John. He had learned (jungle drums beat loudly) I was interested in the races and planned to meet with Brendan Daly, secretary of the Listowel Race Committee. John said he was sorry he would be away the days I was in Listowel, but he wanted me to have a properly inscribed copy of his book. He wrote, "To Warren Rovetch With the Compliments of John O'Flaherty. Welcome to Listowel and I hope you enjoy reading about the Listowel Races."

After the cell phone and the book, for the Listowel kindness trifecta (a high-odds racing bet, picking win, place, and show horses in a race, the first, second, and third finishers), there was our visit with Vincent Carmody. Cara Trant, director of the Kerry Literary & Cultural Centre, had suggested I get in touch with Vincent, who was said to be Listowel's walking encyclopedia. Cara was getting several people together to discuss the roots of Listowel's literary character and creativity, but Vincent couldn't be there. Now, with my working cell phone, I called Vincent. "Come right over," he said, as if there was nothing more in the world he wanted to do than meet G and me on short notice. He gave me instructions on navigating the few blocks to his house, but no street number, assuring me, "Everyone knows where I live, and my name is on the house."

I had visions of peering at little brass nameplates up and down William Street. Not to worry. No missing Vincent's house. Running the full width of his house, above the first floor windows, "CAR-MODY" was etched in foot-high letters in a strip of stone. This was the house Vincent's grandfather built nearly a century earlier in a row of nearly identical houses. He was a horse trader, and it was clear he wanted people to know where to find him.

Vincent, on the phone and in person, was equally warm. We became friends in no time.

He is a self-confessed magpie. He searches out old sales receipts, letterheads, and "cut sheets," topical ballads and poems printed on leftover "cuts" of paper and sold in pubs and at fairs by their authors for drinking money. What began as a hobby for Vincent grew into a passion for acquiring what he calls documentary history. "I feel these personal items give me a special reminiscence to lives gone by," he said. "As records of day to day activity, these receipts and letterheads bring people back to life." G and I saw an exhibit of items from Vincent's collection at the Literary & Cultural Centre, and Vincent was right. These written, scrawled, and printed credit slips and bills of sale, recording horses traded, fish bought, and shoes mended, form an intimate history of life in and around Listowel. Vincent's hoard includes photographs he has assembled as a documentary history in a fascinating book, *North Kerry Camera*.

Vincent is a rural postman, driving a seventy-mile circuit each day. There are few deliveries that don't also involve a word or two. Whatever there is to know, Vincent knows first. Some years earlier, Vincent learned of a great hoard of receipts at a big house. "People living in little houses usually dealt with only one or two stores, ran up accounts on credit, and paid only one or two bills. Big houses dealt with the lot of merchants and had a lovely lot of different bills." With the first hoard in hand, Vincent never looked back.

We talked a bit about the literary tradition of Listowel and John B. Keane, much-loved writer and pub keeper. We began to learn that the knowledge of and devotion to writers and writing was classless and near universal. Love of "the word" was broadly shared. Vincent thought it had much to do with classical education having been the rule up to a generation ago.

Talk turned to football, and Vincent revealed that both he and Keane had at one time and another been secretary of the Listowel Emmets, the local Gaelic football club. Vincent's time was 1975–1989. I mentioned the green-and-gold banners and pennants all over town, and Vincent was off. He recited the three Fs of Kerry— family, friends, and football. Vincent is far from alone in his feelings about football. Gabriel Fitzmaurice, a Kerry poet, offered his own trinity, with football first. "Three elements which largely constitute the mystical body of Kerry are football, politics, and religion." This central role of football is reflected in Keane's short story "Waiting for Tuesday." Keane writes of a man meeting a schoolmate he hadn't seen for a number of years. "We spoke of many things, dead teachers, departed colleagues, local and national scandals and, of course, Kerry football."

Vincent predicted that on the following day, Sunday, if we were on the street at three o'clock, we would be very lonely. "Everyone from Listowel will either be in Dublin or in front of a TV." It was Kerry versus Armagh in the All-Ireland Final, the super bowl of Gaelic football. Just as Vincent was really getting wound up on football, his wife came in and gently reminded him that it was time to go to church because they would be leaving very early the next morning for the match in Dublin. There was a hug and kiss on the cheek for G, a firm handshake for me, and a warm goodbye.

There was more to learn about the Listowel Emmets, the local Gaelic football team, formed on June 27, 1885.

THE LISTOWEL EMMETS

Bold Robert Emmet, the darling of Ireland,
Bold Robert Emmet will die with a smile,
Farewell companions both loyal and daring,
I'll lay down my life for the Emerald Isle.

—Thomas More

CAN YOU IMAGINE an American football team named after Robert Emmet, a failed reformer who was convicted of treason, hanged, and beheaded (but not disemboweled out of deference for his aristocratic background)? Jets, Giants, Raiders, Broncos, Titans. Yes. But a team named the Listowel Emmets? William Faulkner could have been thinking of Ireland and the memory of Robert Emmet when he wrote, "The past is never dead. It's not even past."

Emmet's short life came to an end in 1803 at age twenty-five. The insurrection he hoped to lead failed, French help never came, and, in a chance encounter, his followers pulled the lord chief justice and his young nephew from a carriage and "piked" (pickaxed) them to death. Emmet had hoped to escape to America with his true love Sarah Curran, "she" of Thomas Moore's song, "She is far from the land where her young hero sleeps." Emmet was captured when he left his hiding place in the mountains of Wicklow to be near Sarah. His failed effort to free Ireland left a mythic mark on Irish history. The words Emmet spoke from the dock, after being convicted and condemned to death at his treason trial, resonated through the land and made him an icon of national faith:

> I have but one request to ask at my departure from this world—it is the charity of its silence. Let no man write my epitaph. No man can write my epitaph, for as no man who knows my motives and character dares now to vindicate them, let not prejudice or ignorance asperse them. Let them rest in obscurity and peace until other times and other men can do justice to them. When my country takes her place among the nations of the earth, then shall my character be vindicated, then may my epitaph be written.

Michael Whitty, editor of the *London & Dublin Magazine* in the early 1800s and a contributor to the Emmett legend admitted: "His rebellion was an abortion, his preparations for it boyish. But his youth and obvious love for Ireland, his ardent love for Sarah Curran, had about them all the elements which in all ages have sufficed to constitute personal heroism."

THE BEST THAT A MORTAL CAN DO

I AM DELIGHTED to report that the Listowel Emmets won their football division title the year of our visit. They were among the best.

It's a Kerryman's clear understanding,
That when to those colors he's true,
He's wearing a mantle demanding,
The best that a mortal can do.

—Joseph Smyth, "The Secret of Kerry"

As I looked out the window of our townhouse room on the bright Sunday afternoon, just as Vincent Carmody had predicted, not a person was stirring, not even a mouse. With twenty thousand or so Kerry fans at Croke Park in Dublin cheering on their team, I wondered how many of the other 124,000 Kerry folk were anywhere but in front of a television. Kerry won its first All-Ireland Final in 1903 and had won another thirty-one finals since. This was going to be the double three, the thirty-third time the Sam Maguire Cup came back to Kerry. Armagh had never won. With a Guinness in hand, I settled down in front of the television for my initiation into Gaelic football, a nonstop affair that emphasizes skill and tactics rather than strength and aggression—no timeouts, no commercials.

The pitch (field) is 150 x 90 yards with American football-type goalposts at either end. There are fifteen position players per side—corner-back, full-back, half-back, right-forward, and so on. The round ball is a little smaller than a soccer ball. Now here is the tricky part. The ball can be carried by hand for three running steps and then kicked or "hand-passed," hitting the ball with the palm or fist. If not kicked or passed, the ball must be bounced or "solo-ed." While running, you drop the ball to your foot and kick it back into your own hand. You may not bounce the ball twice in a row. To score, you kick or "fist" the ball over the cross bar of the goal post (one point) or into the net below the bar which is protected by a goalkeeper (three points). Everything is done on a dead run. There is a maximum of five substitutions a game.

To this novice viewer, the first half looked like a walk in the park for Kerry. Then, apparently, Kerry's overconfidence and Armagh's new determination turned the tide in the second half. As Kerry football guru Willie O'Connor put it, "When they [Armagh] began the second half they found that extra power, energy and self-belief that began to overwhelm us [Kerry] as the half progressed. . . . We must give them credit for their tenacity and concentration . . . that ultimately deprived us of our thirty-third title." O'Connor added what was to become the loser's mantra: "We accept our defeat graciously and congratulate Armagh on winning their first-ever All-Ireland Senior Football Title. After all, we have already won thirty-two times." One local wag found solace in the words of that old Irish sage and coach of the Green Bay Packers, Vince Lombardi. "The greatest accomplishment is not in never failing, but in rising again after you fail." Wasn't it also Vince who said, "Show me a good loser and I'll show you a loser"?

Football Feelings Run Deep

As far as I can make out, there are several reasons for the deep feelings Kerry people share for Gaelic football. Like most things Irish, the sport is rooted in history. Michael Cusack became disillusioned with the "social exclusiveness" of English games—cricket and rugby—and founded the Gaelic Athletic Association (GAA) in 1884. The GAA was a nationalist but not revolutionary movement. In the early 1900s, it rode the waves of new nationalism and a growth in spectator sports. Then, the building in Dublin of Croke Park in 1913 provided a national focus for the growing addiction to Gaelic football. Teams and competitions were organized at every age level. Today, reading Willie O'Connor's weekly e-mail reports on the Kerry GAA website of who is playing whom and then who beat whom and how and why, makes you wonder if anything but football is happening.

Perhaps most importantly, the players are genuine amateurs. They are "one of us." Heroes are local; they live and work next door. They are not itinerant gladiators for sale to the highest bidder. This, says Brendan Kennelly, the distinguished Kerry-born poet who played minor, junior, and senior football on top countywide Kerry teams, is why football feelings run deep. "It is about eternal things: style, courage, speed, cunning, defeat, and renewal." Gabriel Fitzmaurice, another important Kerry literary figure, writes in his essay "No Man Is An Island," of football as an incarnation of community. "The boys and girls, the men and women who make up these teams lose, as it were, their individual identity as they become a team—the visible expression of their community. And that is why we get so passionate about the game: because it is ourselves we see out there on the field. Our team wearing our colours are not just individuals: they are in a mystical way, the physical expression of their community." Fitzmaurice also expresses this in his poem "At the Ball Game."

Everything out there you see
is a version of reality
As heroes triumph over doubt
And bring their kind of truth about.

Each, according to his way,
Engages on the field of play,
And, urging on, the faithful crowd
Are cheering, praising, cursing loud
For beauty only will suffice,
Beauty to infuse our lives:
No cup, no trophy will redeem
Victory by ignoble means.

And so we take the field today
To find ourselves in how we play,
Out there on the field to be
Ourselves, a team, where all can see;
For nothing is but revealed
And tested on the football field.

GAA rules enforce the local aspect of the game. To play for a county you must have been born there, raised there, and work there. For many a footballer, it is not unusual to play for the same club as his father and grandfather did. Kerry's All-Ireland Final Senior Panel (team) that I watched on television consisted of thirty-one top players drawn from twenty different senior Gaelic football clubs from all over Kerry. These thirty-one players included nine students, four teachers, three policemen, two insurance agents, an engineer, a fitter, a block layer, a lawyer, two bank officials, an actuary, a radio announcer, and five men working for different businesses.

Altogether, there are sixty senior A-level clubs all over Kerry, including the Listowel Emmets. Together, these clubs have about 1,800 players. With Kerry's population of 132,500, there is one A-level club for every 2,200 men, women, and children. Looked at another way, one of every seventy-four living bodies in Kerry plays for an A-level club. In addition to the A-level clubs, there are other club teams at B and C levels and minor and junior clubs for younger players.

So it's not hard to see why feelings run so deep and football is so much an everyday part of life in Co Kerry.

CHAPTER EIGHTEEN

WHAT WAY ARE YOU PADDY?

AFTER WE LEFT the CARMODY house, G and I ambled down William Street, taking in the scene. It was late afternoon and seemed a good time for a closer look at the *Maid of Erin*, so we aimed for The Square. Listowel has the feel of a place going about its business. There aren't a lot of people looking as like they are searching for something to do. Listowel is happy to see tourists and aims for more, but it has a life of its own. Rowhouses, pubs, and shops line Main, Charles, William, and Church streets—the four streets that make up the town center of Listowel and carry traffic north to the River Shannon and south to Tralee.

Listowel dates back to 1303/1304, when it first appeared in recordings of legal actions on parchment Plea Rolls. With The Square as its front yard, fifteenth-century Listowel Castle was the Anglo-Norman stronghold of the Fitzmaurices and one of the last fortresses to hold out during the early seventeenth-century Elizabethan conquest of Ireland. All that remains of the castle are two square towers connected by an arch and a sculpted face, said to be that of the builder McElligott. Beginning some two hundred years ago, the good citizens of Listowel initiated a recycling program. Using the abandoned castle as an urban quarry, they carted off precut castle stones to build new homes. Now, Listowel Castle is a heritage project, and they are trying to put the pieces back together again.

EGG AND FEATHER, FISH AND FRUIT

LISTOWEL PROSPERED as a market center for farms and townlands all around. The 1901 census of "urban Listowel" of the "Iraghticonner Barony, Listowel Parish, Listowel Poor Law Union, in the North Kerry Parliamentary Division" lists the activities of each property. By my tabulation of the 1901 data, properties listed No.1 to No.125 in the four blocks that still constitute Church Street included these functions: twenty-seven public houses, twenty-seven private dwellings, thirty shops (including egg and feather, fish and fruit, bacon, stationery and flour, bookshop, three tailors, two harness makers, five victuallers (purveyors of provisions and licensed to sell liquor), three shoemakers, six grocery stores, a bookmaker, a confectioner, a carpenter, four drapers (including one draper's shop that was also the town hall), two eating houses, one restaurant (the eating house/restaurant distinction is not explained), a medical hall, the Royal Irish Constabulary Barracks, and National School #42. With twenty-seven pubs, one wonders what an active evening was like on Church Street a century ago.

Writing in a 1939 issue of *The Saturday Evening Post*, Maurice Walsh, author of *The Quiet Man*, describes market day on The Square in Listowel:

> From the earliest dawn the old square—with its ivied Protestant church in the middle—had been close crowded with clumps of cattle each guarded by two or three country lads. . . . The public houses—and there are four score in that town—were reaping their brief harvest; for the breeders having been paid for their cattle, were in soothing long throats strained from hard bargaining, and no farmer would care to leave Listowel with, as they say, the curse of the town on him. Before each and every public house was a row of red-painted springless country carts harnessed to donkeys or jennets or short-coupled horses with remarkable clean legs; and the hum of high-pitched Kerry voices came out of the bars like the song of bees swarming.

Today on Church Street leading into The Square, there are the ACC Bank, Chic Boutique, Cut and Curl, The Lingerie Room, Spotless Dry Cleaners, one grocery, a solicitor, Maguire's Pharmacy, Finesse Bridal Wear, P.J. Broderick Taxis, newsagent, antiques, twenty-five other shops, Allo's, and seven pubs. Since 1901, there has been a seventy-five percent decline in drinking options on Church Street, and the number of private dwellings has about doubled.

As G and I strolled by the open area known as The Market just off The Square, carnival workers were busy assembling a merry-go-round and harmless "thrill rides," most of them in need of a little paint. Ring toss and other "winner guaranteed every time" skill booths were also going up. Sidewalk superintendents of all ages were in attendance and free with their advice. The carnival is part of the Harvest Festival, a staple of Listowel Race week for forty years. The festival program includes street dances, a kid's fancy dress parade (all participants get free carnival rides), races (egg and spoon, barman and barmaid, wheelie bin), and, the high point, selection of the Harvest Festival Queen. Norma Carmody, Vincent's daughter, was crowned queen in 1990.

STUMBLING ALONG BETWEEN THE IMMENSITIES

BRYAN MACMAHON had this vivid recollection of The Market when he was a boy in the early 1900s.

> My grandfather was "weighmaster and marketkeeper," in charge of the market yard and its environment. To me the place onto which our back gate opened was like an eastern bazaar. It seemed always thronged with farmers, buyers, labourers, roustabouts, peddlers, politicians, quack doctors, old-clothes sellers, showmen, and conmen. All kinds of farm animals and farm produce were offered for sale. There were also seasonal visits from circuses and bazaars, and even dancing bears. And I can recall the recruiting sergeant in scarlet uniform and tall black bearskin hat moving through the throng.

The Market remained important to MacMahon. He regularly took evening walks through Listowel "in search of high talk and tall tales," nuggets he would fashion into literature. MacMahon notes this litany of answers in reply to his question, "How are you?" he put to older folk idling in The Market.

"What way are you, Paddy?"
In sepulchral tones, "Perpendicular, no more."

"What way are you, Jack?'"
"Keepin' the best side out like the broken bowl in the dresser."

"Jim, what way are you?"
"If I felt any better I'd see a doctor."

"What way are you, Vincent?"
"Stumbling along between the immensities."
"What immensities?"
"The immensities of birth and death."

Other responses MacMahon noted: "My day is sound when I'm overground." "Endeavoring to squeeze the last drop of my endowments." "That's a question that demands several considerations—mental, moral, physical, and spiritual." "Are you sure you have the leisure to wait for a comprehensive reply?"

MacMahon felt the individual replies were, in each man's way, an attempt to mute or cancel the thought of impending death. "The half jocular poetic answer provided them with a moment or two of ease from this burden." MacMahon also heard in the vernacular a linguistic fusion between Gaelic and English. "The grandiose element derives from English and the poetic, humorous, and spry from the Gaelic."

Like the "football heroes" of Kerry, the Listowel writers are "writer heroes" who live and work in the midst of the people whose lives are the guts of their literature. It is a wonderful reciprocal relationship, and it is why writers like MacMahon, the schoolmaster, and John B. Keane, the publican, are so widely read, loved, and appreciated. In his essay "The Singular Achievement of John B. Keane," Gabriel

Fitzmaurice explains Keane's appeal. "He is widely read among his people, he reaches out to ordinary people, touching them with magic and mystery, transforming the ordinary to the extra-ordinary, giving back the people their own lives, but with a difference—their lives are now examined lives: the only lives worth living." It is said that there is a John B. Keane book in every household in Ireland. Fitzmaurice believes that's not far off the mark.

We strolled by Keane's, the pub that John B. established. His son Billy now runs it. It sits at the junction of William and Market, just half a block from where MacMahon lived and where his back gate opened on to The Market. Then, a block further, where Church Street joins Main Street, a short jog left to The Square and, glory be, there is the *Maid of Erin*. The late afternoon sun burnished her not so hidden charms. After some study of the subject, it was on to the Listowel Arms, tucked away in a corner of The Square, where it had been since the late 1700s.

The hotel advertises as famous guests Daniel O'Connel (1775–1847), Charles Stewart Parnell (1846–1891), and William Makepeace Thackeray (1811–1863). O'Connel, a hero of moderate nationalists, was a master of political theatre whose contributions included a new style of mass agitation, the "politicization of issues." He would have been right at home today. Parnell was a force in land reform and led the formation of an Irish Parliamentary Party, which brought home rule to center stage. His famous affair with Mrs. O'Shea, of which the Listowel Arms can lay no claim, contributed to the end of his political career. Thackeray, long famed as the author of *Vanity Fair*, observed in his *Irish Sketch Book, 1842* that the Listowel Arms "is a great Jeremy-Diddler-kind of hotel . . . swaggering and out at the elbows." Diddler, a character in *Raising the Wind* by dramatist James Kenney (1780–1849) was "adept at raising money in false pretenses."

We settled into The Writers' Bar—peat fire, stuffed couches, and wing chairs. Portraits of Listowel's literary giants—Keane, MacMahon, Kennelly, Walsh, and Fitzmaurice—looked down on us from the walls. I had a Guinness, sherry for G. The bar began filling up with the race crowd—owners, trainers, and bookmakers. They reminded us of a similar racing crowd we mixed with several years before in Goresbridge on the River Barrow. But that's another story.

ANOTHER TIME, ANOTHER PLACE, ANOTHER STORY

Running a forty-five-foot barge on the River Barrow in Co Wexford, G and I started off at Athay, near where the River Barrow ties into the Grand Union Canal. Our plan for the week was to cover about six miles a day, traveling slowly forty-two miles down river through Carlow, Leighlenbridge, Bagonelston, and Goresbridge, ending up at Graiguenarnanagh. Things started out well enough. But then, on day three, it began to rain, and it rained and it rained. The intrepid bargeman, I stood outside on the rear deck, tiller in hand, getting wetter and wetter and colder and colder. Rain-swollen streams flooded into the Barrow. The river rose higher and higher and ran faster and faster in its rush to the Irish Sea.

With both our lives and the barge at risk, we pulled into safe harbor, the quay at Goresbridge. And there we stayed, warm, dry, comfortable, and happy to watch the river rush by without us. A nearby swan tended her eight signets. It wasn't long before G shared maternal duties, contributing to the diet of the signets at regular intervals.

At the quay, we were only a few steps from pubs and shops in the town center. On a stroll the first evening I saw a poster that read, "GORESBRIDGE HORSE SALES: Ireland's Leading and Largest Auctioneers of Sport Horses." We had lucked on to the annual three-day auction: showjumpers, hunters, eventers, dressage horses, and broken and unbroken four-year-olds and five-year-olds. We went the next day, and it was wonderful.

Walking through the gates to the auction yard was like entering a movie set—the hum of a milling crowd; air of anticipation;

breeders, trainers, farmers, traders, and buyers; rumpled macs and bespoke hacking jackets; fresh-faced, young girls in blue jeans; reserved, botoxed, carefully made-up women in tailored country dress; a mix of Irish, English, French, American, and Middle Eastern accents; small clusters of people engaged in animated conversation; and big hellos to old friends. In the background, carefully groomed horses were being put through their paces, jumping fences in a show ring, before being led inside for their turns in the small auction ring.

As each horse was led around the auction ring, some well-shined, elegant, and lively, others well past their prime, the auctioneer's assistant announced the horse's number as listed in the program, and offered a few of its credentials, whatever would hype the bidding. Then the auctioneer took over with an impenetrable sing-song chant, interrupted now and then with an encouraging word: "I have . . ." "Do I have . . ." and, finally, "Sold to." Bidders and visitors sat in a semicircle of bleachers close to the ring. G and I tried to identify the bidders by their sly nods, shrugs, and other hidden signals. Not much luck. I asked a knowledgeable-looking man next to me what influences buyers. "The Irish," he said, "buy for performance. The English buy for appearance. They want to look good sitting up there."

G and I decided for our horses we would want to combine good looks and names to be proud of. Here are a few we chose from the auction list: Merry Sue out of Merry Mate by Prince Regent; Lucky Strike out of Golden Woman by Stan the Man; The Mortgage Man out of Political Merger by Clover Hill; Bizet out of Carmen by Prince of Thieves; Cavalier out of Buttercup Lady by Welsh Captain; and Achy Breaky Heart out of Derrycoole Beauty by Hello Gorgeous.

And there in the Writer's Bar of the Listowel Arms were many of the faces, sounds, and styles we had heard and seen in Goresbridge several years before.

FITTING END TO DAY ONE IN LISTOWEL

BACK TO ALLO'S and a "tastings" dinner that served to confirm Armel Whyte's reputation as a top chef. Here is what G and I shared:

Sautéed Lamb Kidneys in a Crispy Pastry with a Grain Mustard Sauce
Fenit Bay Crab Meat wrapped in Oak Smoked Salmon
with a Lemon & Chive Dressing

~

Oven Roasted Crispy Half Duckling on a Nut Stuffing
with a Port & Berry Sauce
Baked Fillet of Hake with a Pesto & Mozzarella Crust,
With essence of Ratatouille

~

Warm Apple & Cinnamon Crumble with Whipped Cream
Ginger & Orange Crème Brulee with a
Chewy Chocolate Biscuit

~

Irish Farmhouse Cheeses
Cashel Blue, Carrigbyrne, Cooleeney & Millens
With a glass of Tawny Port

Then, after dinner, we walked just a few steps across Church Street to the *Harp & Lion* for a nightcap, a bit of *craic* ("banter") at the bar, and a little music. Then it was back across the street to Allo's and to bed, looking forward to another day in Listowel.

CHAPTER NINETEEN

A Day at the Races

I've been to Bundoran, I've rambled to Bray,
I've footed it to Bantry with its beautiful Bay,
But I'd barter their charms, I would pon my soul,
For the week of the Races in lovely Listowel
                              —Bryan MacMahon, "Lovely Listowel"

There is we understand, an intention of setting up a first class race meeting
near Listowel. The proposed course is one of the best in the United Kingdom.
It is to be on a low lying piece of land called the Island.
                              —*Tralee Chronicle*, August 20, 1858

THE LISTOWEL RACES, held late every September are historic, local, personal, much loved, and easy to be a part of. The track is a ten-minute walk from The Square. Schools are closed for the week. A Ladies Day, Best Dressed Man's Day and a "Little Miss" competition are features of the event. There are seven days of flat, steeplechase, and hurdle racing on the left handed track of a little over a mile. Each day, when the horse racing ends, contests and games and good times of the Harvest Festival take over in The Square and The Market. Brendan Daly, race secretary and course manager, explained the festive air to us. "It's the last big outing before Christmas. The harvest is in and farmers are free to come. The summer crowd is gone, there is less trade and it's time for fun." Bryan MacMahon, in his introduction to John O'Flaherty's book, *Listowel Races,* recalls the races as an annual event that "long since entered the realm of legend and folklore . . . one of our beloved gatherings" and, "above all a time for meeting of old friends . . . renewing the comradely events of shared childhood and, inevitably, music and song."

AND THE WINNER IS G

THE CLOSEST G and I had ever been to a horse race before the Listowel Races was the 1937 Marx brothers movie, *A Day at the Races.* Our day at the Listowel Races was a new experience. For G it was a winning one. Shortly after arriving at the track, we headed for the parade ring to check out horses entered in the second race. I thought the horses looked a lot more alert than the grooms who led them around the ring. G thought Peru Genie (by Paragino, out of High Concept) looked "pretty and strong." She liked the maroon and white striped colors. She reasoned that an Arab name was connected with the syndicate owning Peru Genie and that Arabs know a great deal about horses, *ergo,* the horse had to be good. G bet on Peru Genie. G won. And that was the end of G's betting for the day. Then, when people asked, she could in all honesty say it was a winning day at the races for her.

I, on the other hand, decided to bet a system. We had met Brendan Daly the day before. He has managed the Listowel Races since 1951. It turned out Brendan and G were born in the same year and same month (May), on a day in May with a "four." He was born on the fourth and she on the fourteenth. "An omen," I says to myself. So I bet Turn Back Time, the number four horse in the third race, Drunken Wisdom, number ten (the spread between four and fourteen) in the fourth race, and number fourteen, Proud Bishop, in the fifth. None won and one ran last. So much for omens and systems. It was also a day on which G learned that a "withdrawn horse" was not one with psychological problems, but a horse listed to run that was pulled before the race.

No Small Task

WIN OR LOSE, it is a fine setting and a brilliant spectacle. The River Feale curves around three sides of the track. All the buildings, railings, and stands are a bright white. The grass is deep-green, and sixty or seventy bookmakers provide a sea of colors with each standing on a small box-like platform under a giant umbrella of some exotic hue. Bookmakers give forth a line of patter as they chalk up odds for horses in the next race. The good-natured crowd, ten to fifteen thousand each day, moves in waves—study the racing form, stroll to the Parade Ring to check out the horses in the next race, move along to a bookmaker, back to the stands, cheer their horses, stop at the bar, and then start over again.

Brendan is a pixie with a twinkle if I ever met one. At the time, he was in his fifty-second year as secretary of the Listowel Race Company, a purely local not-for-profit enterprise. In 1951, Brendan was a law clerk in solicitor Jack McKenna's office, without, Brendan says, "an excess of knowledge about horses or racing." And here he was more than half a century later seeing to an enterprise involving all the comings and goings before, during, and after race week—fifty-six races; seven hundred horses, with their owners and trainers; a hundred jockeys (eight of them women); seventy-five bookmakers (one of them a woman); any number of stable hands, bartenders, waitresses, parking lot attendants, and vets; and eighty-five thousand or so race-goers—and not a policeman in sight. Brendan does this with one assistant. How?

IT'S A TRIBAL THING

I HAD TO REMIND myself that Listowel is a town of only 3,393 men, women, and children. It is not just the Listowel Races that they manage. There is Writers' Week, Ireland's oldest literary festival, with workshops on every aspect of the printed word and a worldwide reputation. St. John's Theatre and Arts Centre puts on an array of plays, dance, and music that would command attention in Dublin, London, or New York. The *Fleadh Cheoil*, festival of traditional Irish music in Listowel, boasted more than four thousand competitors for awards and prizes, another six thousand musicians who just came for informal gigs, and another two hundred thousand visitors who came to watch and listen. And then there is the astounding Literary & Cultural Centre with the Writers' Museum, a new and brilliant expression of five great writers of North Kerry. How does Listowel do it?

One reason is that Brendan Daly (Listowel Races), Mary Kennelly (Writers' Week), Maria O'Gorman (Harvest Festival and *Fleadh Cheoil*), Joe Murphy (St. John's Theatre), and Cara Trant (Literary & Cultural Centre) are talented, hardworking managers with little need for self-aggrandizement. They operate in a self-administering, homogeneous, Irish-only tribal culture where people grow up sharing memories, pleasures, standards of behavior, and common goals. Volunteer efforts go toward a common good. The elders are there for the young to emulate. One generation passes tasks on to another. For example, members of the Fitzmaurice family have been accountants to the Race Company for fifty-five years, three generations of the Hannon family have kept the race stands in repair, the Flahertys have seen to plumbing at the track, and the Coppinger family has laundered saddle cloths and white coats since 1928. There isn't much evidence of a rich/poor gap in Listowel, or of people who feel they are better than others. Traditions are rooted in history and experience—Listowel Races began in 1858, Harvest Festival in 1894, and Writers' Week in 1971—and centuries of love for literature, poetry and "the word."

What this adds up to is that not much energy has to go into rules and regulations. People do a good job of taking care of themselves. And when it comes to events, the folk of Listowel fall naturally into place, helping and participating. It's their town. Keane speaks for most in his love song "Sweet Listowel."

Oh Sweet Listowel I've loved you all my days
Your towering spires and shining streets and squares
Where sings the Feale its everlasting lays
And whispers to you in its evening prayers

Of all fair towns few have so sweet a soul
Or gentle folk compassionate and true
Where'er I go I'll love you sweet Listowel
And doff my distant cap each day to you

Down by the Feale the willows dip their wands
From magic bowers where soft the night wind sighs
How oft I've roved along your moonlit lands
Where late love blooms and first love never dies

Of all fair towns few have so sweet a soul
Or gentle folk compassionate and true
Where'er I go I'll love you sweet Listowel
And doff my distant cap each day to you

BILLIE ROVETCH

THE HARVEST FESTIVAL picks up during race week each day when the horse races leave off. The festival is a literal cornucopia of entertainment. The Egg and Spoon Race, Donkey Derby, street dancing, and a lot of music carry through the week. Choice of the Festival Queen is a high point. Festival manager Maria O'Gorman invited G and me to the competition and crowning ceremony.

The ballroom was packed and the bar very busy pulling pint after pint for the well-oiled crowd. Maria told me I would be introduced at the beginning of the ceremony along with other dignitaries. I protested, "I haven't done anything to deserve it."

"They'll never know," she said. As the emcee started down his list of dignitaries, it was clear he had had a few and was feeling no pain. Even so, it was something of a surprise when he got to "that distinguished American writer who elevates us by his presence. Let's have a round of applause for *Billie* Rovetch." I rose, nodding regally this way and that, wondering if the emcee had never heard of a "Warren" before and figured "Billie" would do just fine. G thought "Billie" was just fine. After one Billie too many, I told G if she didn't stop calling me Billie, I would divorce her.

The competitors for queen came in a wonderful variety of sizes and shapes, each one cheered lustily by supporters. One sang a pop hit and another recited a poem in Italian. There was step dancing and acrobatics. Miss America it was not. Electrifying it was, and a lot more fun.

A Pre-Teen "Traveler"

IN THE AFTERNOON between the races and the queening festivities, Maria invited us to the children's costume Harvest parade. Kids get all dressed up, faces painted, and parade from school grounds to a reviewing stand at the Market. Parents cheer and applaud, winners are chosen, and all the kids get free passes for carnival rides as their pay-off—mini coaster, merry-go-round, tilt-a-whirl, and all the usual carnival stuff.

At the school playground, Maria and other women tried to get the kids into some sort of parade order. G and I noticed a very pretty, neatly dressed ten-year-old standing to one side looking hopeful and expectant. She had put on lipstick and rouge, trying for a dress-up parade look. One of the women spoke to the girl sharply, telling her to wait where she was and mind, even though as far as we could see she hadn't done anything wrong. The woman told us the girl was a *Traveler*, saying "Traveler" as if it was a communicable disease. "She wants to get into the parade just to get free passes to the carnival rides."

"Well, why not," we wondered? And we will always remember the girl looking at us appealingly, as if we had some sort of authority able to grant her wishes.

This was as close as we got to the Travelers. There are twenty-five thousand in Ireland, fifteen thousand in Britain, and ten thousand in the States. In Ireland, they form a separate social group outside the mainstream of Irish society. About a third live in official caravan camps set up by local authorities, another third live in permanent homes, and the rest live nomadic lives, stopping where they choose to.

Little is known about the origin of Travelers who are said to go back in history to 200 A.D., or even as early as 600 A.D. Various sources say they were any or all of the following—tinsmiths (tinkers, *tinceir* in Irish) who wandered about repairing pots, traveling musicians, Druid priests forced out of their villages when Christianity defeated Druidism, tenant farmers who lost their land, and wandering poets. They once spoke Shelta, a language of pre-Celtic origin and now mostly speak English with their own variations. They are a distinct ethnic group within Irish society with needs, wants, and values different in ways from the settled community. They are ostracized, despised, disadvantaged, undereducated, and discriminated against and live on the margins of Irish society. Travelers are stereotyped as dishonest or criminal.

They are also young, median age eighteen for Travelers versus thirty-two for all Irish; age fifteen and under, forty percent of Travelers versus twenty of Irish; sixty-five and older, 3.3% of Travelers versus. 11.1% of Irish. Age expectancy of Travelers versus "settled population," twelve years less for women and ten years less for men. Mortality in the first year of life is three times greater for Travelers than for the settled population.

And for a ten-year-old Traveler, it's not easy to get into the parade.

CHAPTER TWENTY

One Rail Train and a St. John's Full House

IT'S HARD TO THINK of a day beginning well with a traffic ticket. But many things are possible in Listowel that don't happen elsewhere. Cara Trant, the engaging, bright, and energetic manager of the Kerry Literary & Cultural Centre, had offered to take us around to the Lartigue and St. John's Theatre & Arts Centre. She had also arranged an evening meeting with a few of Listowel's prime movers. What a day it was.

Cara picked us up at Allo's in the late morning, and we had no sooner set off than a policeman waved the car over. G, sitting in the back seat, was not wearing her seat belt. He would have to ticket the driver. Damn! I told the policeman it was unfair because I was distracting the driver with questions, and as American visitors, we didn't know all the rules. After some thought, he came up with an Irish solution. He had to write a ticket (to make quota?). So why didn't he think of me as the driver (or the cause of the ticket) and give me the ticket, since I wouldn't pay it anyway. I handed over my driver's license, he filled out ticket NW0571784 with all the particulars for "an offence involving the use of a mechanically propelled vehicle," handed me the ticket, told me he had cousins living in New York, Florida, and Montana, and wished us a pleasant visit.

FOUR-YEAR-OLD ENGINE DRIVER

I BELIEVE I can say, with reasonable certainty that J. G. (Jack) McKenna is the only four-year-old who ever drove a steam locomotive on his own. I am sure I can say with absolute certainty he is the only four-year-old who ever drove a double boiler monorail locomotive. As Jack tells it:

> My father lived over the shop in Listowel during the week and used to travel the ten miles out to Ballybunion at weekends to join the family at the ocean shore, and we would all go to the station to meet him. Being an inquisitive four year old (1922) I plagued him with questions concerning the Lartigue. "Daddy this and Daddy that" so that on one occasion when we were walking past the engine my father called to the Engine Driver: "Jackie (Reidy), like a good man will you show this young fellow how the engine works."
>
> Saying to my father, "Jack will drive," Jackie took me up in his arms and into the cab. "There now boy" he said, "pull that lever" and I gave a heave to this black handle and with a CHUFF CHUFF the engine moved to the end of the platform. I will never forget the thrill of the moment. Jackie handed me back to my father. "Here's the engine driver," he said.
>
> What I did not appreciate at the time was that this was a singular railway—a Monorail with its extraordinary system of rail switches, drawbridge-type crossover bridges at farm entrances, unique double boiler engine and carriages where passengers sat back-to-back.

Nearly eighty years later, in 2000, McKenna made a significant contribution of land and equipment to help bring the Lartigue back to life. Jack was the third generation of McKennas to own and manage McKenna Hardware, located in the heart of Listowel. He is part of a story, as Jack explained, that tracks back to 1798. Thomas McKenna, who came from Co Monaghan, is described on his tombstone as "A Leader in the Rebellion of 1798." He fought against the Captain of the Yeomen, a man named Foulkes in the Battle of Vinegar Hill. Foulkes' daughter Jane donned a man's clothing and fought beside her true love, Thomas McKenna, against her father. When the Irish suffered defeat at Vinegar Hill in 1798, Thomas and Jane fled for their lives and escaped to the hills outside Listowel. Years passed, and in 1870 their great grandson Jeremiah and his wife Johanna came into Listowel and started McKenna Hardware. In time, their son Jack took it over. Jack's son Simon is now the fourth generation of the family to run the hardware store. And so goes the remarkable continuity of family and life in Listowel. Now, back to the Lartigue.

The Lartigue began operation March 5, 1888. After thirty-six glorious years of operation it went bust in 1924, and Jack's father bought a sizeable portion of the station site for future development. Development never materialized, and Jack inherited the site, including many remnants of the original Lartigue track system. "It was always my hope," Jack reminisced, "that restoration of this legendary railway would miraculously come about, and when the national Millennium Committee offered very substantial financial support, I gladly handed over this site to the Lartigue Monorailway Restoration Project." I do hope, on the day the recreated Lartigue is inaugurated, that Jack McKenna will be the first to pull the lever and be Engine Driver No. 1.

THE LISTOWEL & BALLYBUNION RAILWAY

There's only one wheel on the line,
And the track like the story is single,
Sure there isn't a railway so fine,
Not excepting the Tralee and Dingle.

Of railways let anyone speak,
Of the Grand Trunk or Western Union,
Sure there isn't one like the Lartigue,
That runs into famed Ballybunion.

The old train's held together with rope,
And the tackling they say won't endure, Sir,
Sure they balance the people with soap
And sometimes with bags of manure, Sir.

—James Leslie, "The Song of Lartigue"

THE RECREATED Lartigue locomotive was a wonderful sight, and all the more wonderful because G and I were so unprepared for it. If Willy Wonka had designed a train for his candy factory, this would have been it. If Thomas the Tank had a makeover with an eye to character and class, the Lartigue engine could have been the result. If Marc Chagall had painted a train, this would have been it—red and green and brass, self-assertive but not aggressive, and ready to fly. G said it reminded her of our emerald green and red trimmed longboat on the Oxford Canal and that she could imagine it at a fair surrounded by happy, laughing children.

In his book *Transport in Ireland, 1889–1910,* P. Flanagan explains the workings of the Lartigue. "Technically [the locomotives] were 0-3-0 tender engines with twin horizontal boilers on each side of the running rail. The chimneys, steam domes, safety valves and fire boxes were all in duplicate but there was only one headlamp—a massive acetylene-fueled affair mounted in front over the running rail and between the chimneys. In full cry these engines were an awe inspiring sight."

Balanced passenger load on the "One Rail Train"

The running rail, a single railroad track, three feet and three inches from the ground, was mounted on A frames positioned three feet apart. The engine, carriages, and freight wagons were divided into two sections like an upside down U, each side hanging over the central running rail. This rolling stock and the flanged center wheels were mounted on axles. Lighter guide rails were mounted on either side of the A frames, and side wheels attached to carriages running against the guide rails helped maintain balance. But the real key to balance was the even distribution of weight. Passengers sat back to back, looking out at the slowly passing scene. So, if there were ten passengers, they were placed five on each side. According to Rev. J. Anthony Gaughin, "As its appearance gave the impression of two hampers of turf strung across a donkey's back, [the Lartigue] was frequently referred to as *the ass and panniers railway.*"

There is a story of the woman who shipped an upright piano from Listowel to Ballybunion. After much thought, the piano was put on one side of a wagon and balanced with two calves on the other side. When the train reached Ballybunion and the piano was unloaded, one of the two calves was moved to the piano side, and the train, again in balance, returned to Listowel. Then there was the time driver Jack Reidy stopped the train so a boy could recover his new hat. In fact, the train was given to stopping wherever a passenger wanted to get on or off. On occasion, more than one passenger had to get off and walk a bit to lighten the load on an uphill climb.

Another story reflects the casual and personalized approach to schedule. About two miles from Listowel, the line passed close to a thatched cottage, from which the lady of the house, Mamie, often took the train to town. One day when the train passed the house, Mamie was outside harnessing her little donkey to his cart. The engine driver of the Lartigue, Jack Reidy, hailed her and said, "Aren't you coming with us today Mamie?"

To which she replied, "Yerra no Jackie. I'm in a bit of a hurry today!"

Cliff Thomas, in *The Railway Magazine* writes of the Listowel & Ballybunion as "a delightfully eccentric oddity . . . which has entered the realms of railway folklore." Bryan MacMahon spoke of the Lartigue as "the queerest railway in the world [and] the people loved every wheel of it." All in all, it does seem appropriate that the inventor, a Frenchman, Charles Francois Marie-Therese Lartigue, got his inspiration while in Algeria. It came from a camel, which is after all an animal said to have been assembled by a committee. Writing in 1886, George Petit, a civil engineer, and F. B. Behr, managing director of the Lartigue Railway Company Limited, explained the origin of Lartigue's idea for this "queerest railway."

> Mons. Lartigue conceived the idea of his Railway . . . in a very curious manner. It was the appearance of a caravan of camels on the horizon which furnished the starting point. The sight of these animals following one another in a long string and laden with thellis, a kind of wallet which hangs down on each side of them, and which he had sketched, brought to his mind's eye an elevated rail. To his mental view the legs of the camels became trestles, their humps were transformed into wheels, and the thellis took shape as a car. The idea once conceived was rapidly matured.

When the Lartigue comes back to life, G and I plan to return for a ride, sitting back-to-back.

PLAYING TO A FULL HOUSE

ST. JOHN'S, with its conical tower reaching heavenward, was one of our first sights when we drove into Listowel. It dominates The Square and the cultural scene in North Kerry.

For performers, chances of playing to a full house at St. John's Theatre & Arts Centre are pretty good. Rows of comfortable seats can be easily removed and stored out of sight. Smaller ticket sale for a play or concert? Take out the last four or five rows. This approach to full-house seating and a diverse array of concerts, plays, dance programs, and summer workshops is the product of the frenetic mind and energy of Joe Murphy. Murphy is usually dressed in black, had been a teacher for fourteen years, and likes to portray himself as a farmer. In our chat, it became clear he combines the creative energy of a persuasive impresario with the talent of a standalone performer. I could see cows on his farm dancing to his tune.

In a little more than a decade, the theatre has taken its place as one more of this small community's remarkable achievements. As a Church of Ireland, St. John's served as a place of worship from 1819 until its deconsecrating in 1988, by which time North Kerry had pretty much run out of Protestants. The remaining Church of Ireland community and the people of Listowel were anxious to preserve both the building and its tower clock, a landmark feature of The Square since the clock was installed in 1860. A brass plaque documents the origin of the clock and makes clear it was not a frivolous expenditure, being paid for out of "surplus funds."

> With the sanction of the
> ECCLESIASTICAL COMMISSIONERS
> and under the authority of a vestry called by the
> Vicar and Church Wardens of the Parish of Listowel
> and held on the 26 day of November, 1860.
> THIS CLOCK
> was erected in the tower of the Parish Church of
> Listowel, for the benefit of the public by the
> LISTOWEL RELIEF COMMITTEE of the WINTER 1846–47
> and paid for out of their surplus funds.

Fortunately, preservation was seen in active rather than passive terms, and the St. John's Theatre & Arts Centre was the result. While the character of the church with its stained-glass windows remains, St. John's has become a first-rate performance center with great acoustics. Murphy has managed to make it into a regional center, drawing enthusiastic audiences from all over North Kerry, and an attractive venue able to draw performers from all over the world. A typical year's events and activities include 134 adult theater, music, and dance presentations, performances by at least a dozen touring theater companies, twenty-four children's theater presentations, eight film programs, and 265 workshops for primary and secondary students in music, dance, and theater. Here, for example is the St. John's Theatre & Art Center program for August 2002:

St. John's Theatre & Arts Centre
The Square, Listowel, Co Kerry
AUGUST

2nd-18th   **EXHIBITION OF PAINTINGS.** A solo exhibition by Michele O Donnel, Lisselton. Landscapes and portraits in oils and watercolors.

7th Wed   **SONGS OF JOYCE.** A musical odyssey through the life and works of James Joyce. Aidan Coleman & Family, voice, piano, guitar and percussion. "An artistic triumph," Prof David Norris.

8th Thur   **THE BEST OF TRADITIONAL WITH KEVIN BURKE.** An evening of magnificent fiddle playing from Kevin (ex Bothy Band) and friends.

9th Fri   **CAULDRON OF THE BRONTES.** A play based on the fateful struggle of the three novelist sisters, Charlotte, Emily, and Anne to find freedom and meaning through their art set against the moral and physical disintegration of their beloved brother Branwell. Praxis Theatre Company.

11th Sun   **FEVER—PEGGY LEE TRIBUTE.** Susanah De Wrixton takes you through Peggy's extraordinary career from her early days with Benny Goodman to her death last January. With Cian Boylan—piano, Dave Flemming—double bass, and Tim Dunne—drums.

13th Tues **THE SAN FRANCISCO BAY STREET BAND.** Mix of blues, folk, Celtic rhythms.

14th Wed **JULIET TURNER IN CONCERT**

18th Sun **MARTIN HAYES AND DENNIS CAHILL.** An evening of beautiful and rousing music drawn from the lyrical traditions of East Clare.

19th-25th **TAISPEANTAIS EALAINE.** In Ionad Na Gaeilge— Naomh Eoin lci rith na Fleidhe, aiseanna foghlama teangan, iarsmai an tseansaol, is logaimmeacha na Gaeilge freisin.

19th Mon **TEADA—THE BEST OF TRADITIONAL.** With Sligo fiddle player, Oisin Mac Diarmada, Tristan Rosenstock—bodhran, John Blake—flute and guitar.

20th Tues **THE SPIRIT OF IRELAND.** A stage spectacle of Irish music and dance by Ceol Chiarrai.

21st Wed **LIAM O MAONLAI. A TRADITIONAL** Irish gig in keeping with the spirit Fleadh.

22ndThur **CAIPINL.** Brendan Begley's stage presentation of his unique TG4 performers.

23rd Fri **SEO CHONAMARA.** Le Martin Daibhi O Coistealbha.

26th Mon **EILIS KENNEDY IN CONCERT.** Eilis from Dingle is a traditional singer in both Irish and English, with guitarist William Coulter

29th Thur **NATTI WAILER & THE REGGAE VIBES.** An evening of explosive Jamaican sounds with members of the original Bob Marley band.

30th Fri **GLAN LEAT.** A St. John's August Summer School presentation directed by Jo Jordan.

31st Sat   **KATE PURCELL.** Clare singer songwriter, native of Feakle, lives in Tulla. Traditional material and original songs, with Ted Ponsonby—guitar and Rod Patterson—bass.

**SUMMER SCHOOL—Drama/ Music/ Dance Workshops,
Mon–Fri, 10–1 pm.
For First and Second Level Students.
Director: Ms. Jo Jordan.**

PRIME MOVERS

G AND I PLANNED to visit the Literary & Cultural Centre the next day, and Cara had invited a few people to talk with us in advance about Listowel's literary tradition. And there we were that evening of a fine day sitting around a table at the Listowel Arms. Besides Cara there were:

Danny Hannon, who G remembers as the embodiment of courtly Irish charm. I remember his quick wit. Hannon is cofounder and director of the Lartigue Theatre Company, an innovative group that has performed all over Ireland and in the States, including stops in New York, Boston, and San Francisco. And then there are Hannon's Bookstore and Daniel Hannon & Sons, Realtors ("Listowel for relaxed living and better quality of life"). Hannon, a friend to many authors, is an authority on the literary tradition of Listowel and North Kerry.

Jack McKenna, hardware store owner, is president of the Lartigue Restoration Committee, a noted North Kerry historian, and the best guide you could find for walking heritage trails of Listowel.

Jimmy Deenihan, Kerry football great, is now a member of the Irish parliament. He combines the force of a winner-take-all personality that I associate with football, sharp intellect, and a clear sense of purpose. He is a man I wouldn't want to get crosswise with. Deenihan's focus is on the link of heritage and economic growth through tourism—keep one and grow the other. It can be a neat balancing act.

We talked about classical education being at the root of literary prowess, the poetic and literary quality of the Irish language, and the significance of great writers being an integral part of the community. One thing became clear in our discussion. Everyone loves Listowel.

CHAPTER TWENTY-ONE

THE WONDER OF IT ALL— THE WRITERS' MUSEUM

A NEW EXPERIENCE

IMAGINE THIS. Open the door to a dazzling white room, a regular door, nothing to announce anything special. There in the room is *John B. Keane*, playwright, novelist, poet, and publican, sitting on a stool in his natural space at the bar in his pub on William Street in Listowel, a pint of Guinness in hand, ready to exchange pleasantries of the day. But here in the Writers' Museum, this replica of John B. is plaster-white, his body covered from head to toe with his own words, lines from his books and plays—*Durango, The Bodhran Makers, Letters of a Matchmaker, The Field, Sive.* You survey the room, all white. There is a window that is not a window, and a closet door partly open to reveal more of John B.'s words written on the closet walls. There, at one of the pub tables, is a man, also plaster-white, with a bucket covering his head. They say he was a patron, too shy to sing facing the public. And just as you have begun to wonder what this is all about, John B.'s own words fill the room.

I was born on the 21st of July 1928, in the town of Listowel, in County Kerry. Apart from my birth it was an uneventful year, free of plague, war and famine . . .In Ireland tobacco was one and fourpence a quarter pound and whisky was ten pence a half glass. Television was unknown, radio was a luxury and gramophones with indecent appendages were the order of the day.

I was the fourth member of a family of five boys and four girls, I was christened plain John but assumed the 'B.' legitimately at confirmation as a mark of respect to the late Brendan the Navigator, patron saint of the diocese of Kerry.

My father introduced me to Sam Weller, Micawber, and other distinguished notables. It was years before I discovered that they weren't his personal friends at all . . .

I never missed the summer holidays in the Stacks Mountains. Those were wonderful days and it was there, for the first time, that I met characters who mattered and people who left a real impression.

These were lively and vital people, composed of infinite merriment and a little sadness. They lived according to their means and if you didn't like them you could leave them . . .

Dan Paddy Andy O'Sullivan was the last matchmaker to operate in Kerry. From his modest home in Renagown, Lyreacropane he conducted a flourishing trade and was responsible for directing four hundred couples to the altar of God . . .

On the 6th day of January 1952, I set out to make my fortune. I chose England. It was nearer for one thing, and many of my friends were already settled there. In Dublin I met Eamon.

We celebrated the beginning of my exile in style . . . I remember as I walked up the gangplank, I heard Eamon shouting after me. "Write!" he yelled. "Write something every day. Write . . . Write . . . Write . . ."

Open the door to another room, and there, standing in a classroom, plaster white, covered with his words, is Bryan MacMahon, "Ireland's most eminent schoolmaster," and ballad maker, playwright, novelist, translator, lecturer, and storyteller. On a blackboard McMahon has written, "*Mol an oige agus tiocfaidh si; cain an oige agus crion-*

faidh sí"—"praise youth and it will come; disparage youth and it will wither." His spoken words fill the room, Irish music in the background.

> I come from a small country town in the south of Ireland. I'm a local schoolteacher. The place is only a speck on the map. We cherish our characters, our heroes, our people of significance. Would you care to hear about them?
>
> Teaching was in my blood. Three of my mother's sisters had been teachers, So was my brother Jack; two of my own sons are now teachers in different levels of education.
>
> There are three great hungers in the human being: the hunger of the body, the hunger of the spirit, and the hunger of the mind. The hunger of the body is appeased by food and physical activity. While the hunger of the spirit is appeased to some extent by the endeavor to solve the mystery of human existence and to probe what lies beyond. The hunger of the mind, of the imagination, is so ethereal as to almost defy definition, but it commonly indicates its presence in the story. The common cry of children is "Tell us a story."

In another room, *Brendan Kennelly*, poet and professor of English literature at Trinity College, Dublin, is leaning over the railing of a small arched footbridge, watching his words flow by on the stream below and speaking aloud his poetry and the meaning of being a poet. Open another door and *Maurice Walsh* is writing at his desk in the garden shed of his summerhouse in Scotland. And in the last room is a forlorn scene, playwright *George Fitzmaurice*, a contemporary of W. B. Yeats and J. M. Synge, looks out the window of his rented bed-sit in Dublin, where he spent the last isolated years of his life.

No other experience in Ireland, nothing at all, came close to the impact of the Writers' Museum of the Literary & Cultural Centre on The Square in Listowel. G and I shared the thrill of being involved in something wholly new to us. The impact on us was profound and remains so to this day. In this writer's search for descriptive words, *pow!* and *bam!* come to mind. G, the artist for whom light and color are paramount, was stunned by the whiteness of the setting. For me, it was the brilliant execution of a simple concept—"to exhibit words, not objects." Simplicity transformed these installations into art.

I asked Steve Simons of Event Ireland, the designer of the project, how the core concept originated—an author in his setting and his words both written on him and spoken? Simons—"Where does any concept originate—the bath, the bed, the country walk, the bar! The concept to me was obvious. Writers write words—people read words—in a writers' museum, you have to exhibit words not objects. 'What other way could it be done,' I asked myself! The environments [the rooms] were in fact installations not galleries. What marks the men apart? John B. Keane—communicator, barfly—his conversation was his word. Brendan Kennelly, his poetry flowing on a stream. Maurice Walsh. Hunter, fisherman, gardener—living in Scotland, creating amongst the things that were his life. A writer from a garden shed, albeit a smart one. Bryan MacMahon, the schoolmaster in his classroom."

Beatrix, William, and Jimmy Did It

While Simons and his associates executed their commission brilliantly, I wondered where the idea for the centre originated and what force brought it to life. Turns out it was a combination of a country walk, Beatrix Potter, writer of children's stories, William Wordsworth, romantic poet, and Jimmy Deenihan.

Jimmy Deenihan is a football great, famous in Ireland for having captained Kerry to a historic four-in-a-row All-Ireland wins in the 1980s. He is now the North Kerry *Teachta Dala* (T.D.), member of *Dail Eireann*, the Irish National Parliament. In 1992, Deenihan was on a walking tour in the English lake country. This is where Beatrix Potter lived at Hill Top, near Hawkshead. There, a century earlier, she wrote about the adventures of Peter Rabbit, Squirrel Nutkin, Jemima Puddle-Duck, and Mrs. Tiggywinkle, all staples of the Rovetch household and millions of other homes. On his walking tour, Deenihan visited the Beatrix Potter Gallery, a National Trust Museum that displays original illustrations from Potter's famous children's storybooks. Deenihan also visited The Wordsworth Museum in Grasmere, which houses exhibits showing the way the poet worked and original manuscripts of *Home at Grasmere* and other of his celebrated poems.

The light went on. "Why not," said Deenihan to himself, "a museum in Listowel featuring Kerry literary greats?" He came home, organized the Literary Task Force with Billy Keane, John B.'s son, as chairperson. Its task was to "develop a centre of literary and cultural excellence . . . to acknowledge and honor the literary greats that have made Listowel the literary capital of Ireland." Deenihan took on the pivotal job as chairman of the fundraising committee, and the Task Force of Listowel, the little town that could, was off and running. The Task For consisted of a publican, a TD, four teachers, two solicitors, a retired farmer, a retired printer, two members of the Kerry County Council, and four other locals.

Asked how it went from concept to completion, Simons said the concept came easily. The task force "loved it and sped into the night waving concept sketches at bankers and other interested parties. John B.'s son Billy moved mountains and then had another pint! There was a will in the village, but it moved at a pace that only the West Coast of Ireland would refer to as rapid!"

Maybe not rapid, but certainly effective. In 1995, a three-story Georgian period residence at 24 The Square, Listowel was optioned. By 1997, Deenihan's committee had raised €261,566 ($313,879) and the building was purchased. All told, over seven years, 1995 to 2002, €1,604,602 ($1,925,522) was raised through grants, business gifts, individual contributions, and fundraising events. There were black-tie dinners, concerts in Dublin, Limerick, Cork, and London, golf classics in world-famous Ballybunion (where Bill Clinton, then the U.S.

president, claims he shot his best round ever), raffles, tribute evenings, a calendar of Kerry writers, a tribute book to John B. Keane, and Deenihan's skilled tapping of Irish memories and pocketbooks in San Jose, New York, Boston, and Chicago.

The results are the five wonderful rooms honoring writers— Keane, MacMahon, Kennelly, Walsh, and Fitzmaurice, and a *Seanchaí* (Shan-a-key) area at the entrance of the Writers' Museum dedicated to Ireland's famous storyteller, Eamon Kelly. There is also an intimate fifteen-seat "theatre" where people can view a film of Kerry writers telling how their own place, the people, communities, and landscapes of North Kerry have inspired them. Add a new building with a 120-seat auditorium, a café, an archival library, and a reading room, carefully integrated with the old Georgian house.

And there you have it, the Writers' Museum and the Literary & Cultural Centre. A monumental concept brought down to earth and made real by the "we can" good people of Listowel.

Mizen Peninsula—Schull street scene

On the Mizen—tidal lake near Crookhaven

Sheep's Head Peninsula—
WARNING!

Sheep's Head—press on

Mountain top at the end of Sheep's Head

Priory ruin on Sheep's Head   Priory graveyard

Castletownbere sixth graders

Writers' Museum—shy singer in Keane's Pub

Bryan MacMahon—schoolmaster

John B. Keane—publican

Eamon Kelly—storyteller

Brendan Kennelly—poet

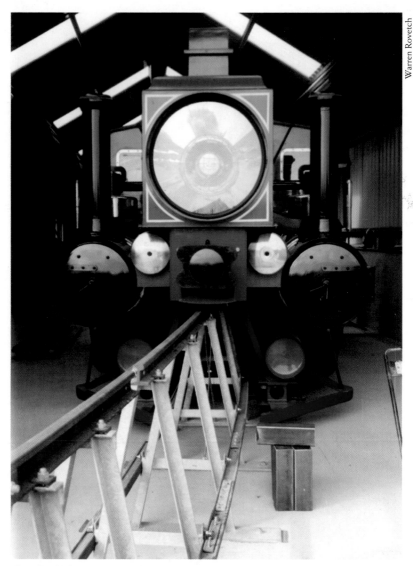

One Rail Train—Listowel & Ballybunion Railroad

Listowel—Maid of Erin

Listowel—live at the Harp & Lion

G in a procession of arches   Quin Abbey

Cloister of Quin Abbey

CHAPTER TWENTY-TWO

SO WHO ARE THESE WRITERS?

I FOUND IT IMPOSSIBLE to leave the Writers' Museum without thinking of the five writers and wanting to know more about them and their work. You may be interested in what I learned.

JOHN B. KEANE: 1928–2002

I WONDERED WHY in conversations with any number of people—shopkeepers, publicans, farmers, whoever—John B. seemed to creep in. He was universally known and loved. A local newspaper wrote of his funeral and the thousands of ordinary men, women, and children who came to say farewell: "Even in death John B. was reaching out to plain people, his people, and they responded with full hearts." When I came home to Boulder I read several things of John B.'s—two novels, *The Bodhran Makers* and *Durango*, a book of short stories, *Innocent Bystanders*, and *Letters of a Matchmaker*. First of all, he is a damn good storyteller with a genius for language that makes his characters real and unforgettable. He takes on their causes, and to hell with who is at the other end.

His work included international stage and screen successes such as *The Field*. It had a Broadway run in 1982 and in 1990 was made into a film in which Richard Harris starred as the lead, Bull McCabe. This was one of those plays, wrote *The Irish Times* (May 23, 2002) which "had an uncomfortable reality at a time in Ireland when the raw side of rural life was frequently ignored for the more acceptable . . . vision of happy maidens and cozy homesteads. Loneliness, greed, and sexual repression were themes he explored with considerable skill and courage."

The son of a schoolmaster, John B. left St. Michael's secondary school in 1946. He was embittered at a teacher's hostility to his creative imagination and encounters with brutal schoolroom discipline. He went to work as a chemist apprentice, stuck with it for five years, and then in 1951 went to England to seek his fortune. After several jobs, including that of a furnace operator, he returned to Listowel in 1955, married Mary O'Connor, put his meager savings into a pub, and began the off-duty job of writing, he said, "about people I knew and I'd grown up with." He, Mary, and their four children lived above their public house on William Street in Listowel. John B. was never far from the men and women who were the subjects of his stories.

Keane was a prodigious writer—nineteen plays, eight novels and books of short stories, two books of poetry, ten books in his letters series, and seven other publications, including *Is the Holy Ghost Really a Kerryman?* He explained his style of writing: "I listen rather than speak but I would never write down what they say to me. I'd leave it fester for a while first, and the longer it sits there, the better it turns out. In writing at least, a good memory is better than a bad pencil." On his lifestyle, he said, "I've always been a great man for the booze, and I have hundreds of friends, so the minute I go into a pub I'm established there for the night."

Brendan Kennelly described Keane as "a poetic playwright." Others were less complimentary. John Dunne, an editor who reviewed Keane's manuscript of *Durango*, said it was "Full of the . . . oul' guff' . . . should have been edited with a chainsaw." Keane took his book to another publisher, and it did very well, guff and all. In his eulogy to Keane, old friend Danny Hannon said John B. was a restless, opinionated, ambitious, approachable genius who had "run his fingers over the texture of Irish life and revealed to an astonished world the taste and authentic sound of a unique people who battled on the margins of life." Hannon ended his eulogy with the final verse of a Ray McAnally poem:

> *An awful thought has struck me,*
> *Almighty Da Serene—*
> *Is the Holy Ghost a Kerryman*
> *Or is He John B. Keane?*

MAURICE WALSH: 1879–1964

Shawn Kelvin, a blithe young lad of 20, went to the States to seek his fortune. And 15 years thereafter he returned to his native Kerry, his blitheness sobered and his youth dried to the core, and whether he had made his fortune or whether he had not no one could be knowing for certain. For he was a quiet man *not given to talking about himself and the things he had done. A quiet man, under middle size, with strong shoulders and deep-set blue eyes below brows darker than his dark hair—that was Shawn Kelvin.*

> —Maurice Walsh, "The Quiet Man,"
> *Saturday Evening Post,* February 11, 1922

ANYONE WHO HASN'T seen the cult film *The Quiet Man* must be living on a different planet. At least once a month on cable television, John Wayne (Shawn Kelvin) slugs it out with bully Victor McLaughlin (Red Will Danaher) over miles of lush, Irish countryside across hills, through a haystack, and into a stream. The quiet man has been goaded into fighting for the dowry due his feisty, red-haired wife, Maureen O'Hara (Mary Kate Danaher), who is Red Will's sister. Barry Fitzgerald (Ogie Flynn), matchmaker and bookmaker, takes bets on the outcome. You guessed it. The quiet man wins.

Movie director John Ford bought the film rights to *The Quiet Man* in 1936 for ten dollars. By the time the "epic, romantic, rich, beautifully textured" Academy Award winner premiered May 1952, Walsh had received all of an additional $6,250 for his "cooperation." When asked what he thought of the movie, Walsh said he found the Technicolor "extraordinarily fine."

Walsh, one of a family of ten, came from Ballydonoghue. He finished formal schooling at St. Michael's College in Listowel and in 1901 went into the British civil service, where he worked as a customs and excise officer in the Highlands of Scotland. When the Irish Free State came into being in 1922, Walsh returned to Ireland to help the new state create its own excise and custom service. He lived out his life in Dublin.

It seemed to me less than likely that any number of years in customs and excise departments, British or Irish, would provide the creative sustenance Walsh needed to write a flock of short stories and sixteen best-selling novels over nearly forty years, starting in 1923 when Walsh at forty-four was fresh back to Ireland. One building block was his secondary education at St. Michael's College. A classical education was the rule there, and, contrary to Keane's experience, Walsh's writing was encouraged. Equally important, Walsh's father, a farmer, had a vast library of classics. Walsh sucked these up and identified with the hero in each and every story. He said that reading all these novels gave him a feeling for romantic fiction and wonder that carried him through a lifetime.

Romantic fiction is certainly apparent in *The Key Above the Door,* the novel of romance in the Highlands of Scotland that made Walsh's name as a popular writer. In this passage, hero Tom King speaks to heroine Agnes de Burc:

> It is because we are men . . . and men in the raw too, for things have come to that pass where you are no longer to be wooed, but only to be won. . . .You have proclaimed your very splendid ideals . . . but the ultimate and savage in us has no use for these things. We are going to fight for you . . . and you will be chattel of the victor.

Walsh was Ireland's most popular writer of the 1930s. A superb storyteller in a country of storytellers, he wrote of strong, adventurous heroes, beautiful golden-haired heroines, and nasty villains. What set his writing apart from pulp fiction was the value he placed on rural and community living, the importance of belonging, and keeping a sense of place.

Walsh was a bit amused by his best-selling popularity. "I dunno why my books ever sold. They are just yarns. That's all. Just yarns."

GEORGE FITZMAURICE: 1877–1963

GEORGE FITZMAURICE has in recent years become one of the most remembered "forgotten" Irish playwrights of modern times. The George Fitzmaurice Society was launched recently in Listowel with Danny Hannon at its helm. Fitzmaurice's plays are being revived in his native Kerry and all over Ireland. A monument has been placed on his previously unmarked grave in Dublin and a library, and museum dedicated to the playwright has opened in Duagh, where Fitzmaurice grew up.

And a new hotel in Dublin, the Stephen's Green, was required to make Number three Harcourt Place a part of its design (another Deenihan effort) because that was where, in a second-floor room, Fitzmaurice, ever more withdrawn, lived out the last years of his life. In a contrary twist that would please any playwright, the Stephen's Green named two of its most bustling public rooms after the titles of plays by the reclusive Fitzmaurice—*The Pie Dish* Restaurant and *The Magic Glass* Bar.

The Writers' Museum hosts a recreation of Fitzmaurice's room at Number three Harcourt Place. There Fitzmaurice stands, pensive, looking out of a small window at a Dublin scene. What I find interesting is that Fitzmaurice was able to write so well of a society he had withdrawn from. Or was it that in his writing he moved into a fantasy world? In *The Magic Glasses*, the principal character escapes into a world of "seas and mountains and cities, grand horses and carriages, and all the wild animals of the earth" only to crash to ground and fatally collapse. In *The Ointment Blue*, the principal character is given the ointment blue (which makes him champion at all sports) and is crowned as King of Bara. And then, although he loses the crown, he wins a wife "who is not only royal but rich on her own account."

Recent commentators have written high praise of Fitzmaurice: "The most imaginative Irish writer of the twentieth century." "A remarkable writer, one of the great originals among folk dramatists." Keane said Fitzmaurice wrote with an "authentic voice" that has the "lyricism and nuances" of North Kerry as it was spoken in the kitchen of the Fitzmaurice family farm. Terms and tales associated with Fitzmaurice's writing include peasant realism, escape, supernatural folk tales and fantasy, and overly imaginative characters bent on fulfilling eccentric ideals.

Fitzmaurice was the third son and tenth of twelve children of a Church of Ireland (Protestant) parson who married a Catholic maid in the family home, Bedford House. As was the practice at the time, the sons were brought up in the faith of their father and the daughters in the faith of their mother, offering young George early experience in tolerance and a complex family life. Parson Fitzmaurice farmed family land and preached at St. John's, now the Listowel Theatre & Arts Centre. When George was four, his father died, and the family was forced to move to a farmhouse near Duagh. It was there, in the farmhouse kitchen and out in the field, that George was exposed to rural traditions, colorful characters, and the exotic language of Irish locals learning to speak English. This was rich material for "Master George," the budding playwright frequently seen scribbling away out in the woods or in the top field of the farm.

Fitzmaurice was another product of classics and creative writing at St. Michael's College, where the novels of Sir Walter Scott, the first novelist to offer sympathetic and realistic portrayals of peasant characters and conflict between different cultures, strongly influenced him. After St. Michael's, Fitzmaurice worked in a bank in Cork, quit, moved home, and started writing stories. In 1901 he moved to Dublin, where he held a minimum-wage job at the Congested Districts Board of the Land Commission, an agency set up to encourage agriculture and industry in impoverished areas. It also put him closer to the literary scene where Lady Isabelle Augusta Gregory and William Butler Yeats were in the process of creating the Abbey Theatre.

The Abbey opened in 1904, marking the official beginning of the Irish Literary Revival with plays by Yeats, Synge, Sean O'Casey, and Lady Gregory. Fitzmaurice joined this company of greats in 1907 with a very successful run at the Abbey of his first play, *The Country Dressmaker*. A serious comedy showing up the sordid side of country life, it is the story of a dressmaker, Julia Shea, who waited eight years for her one time love to return from America. When he does, his rich family will stop at nothing to make sure it is not Julia he marries. Two other Fitzmaurice plays followed at the Abbey, *The Pie Dish* (1908) and *The Magic Glasses* (1913). When people praised *The Magic Glasses* above plays by Yeats and Lady Gregory that were produced in the same repertoire, Yeats and Gregory took umbrage, rejected Fitzmaurice's next submission, *The Dandy Dolls*, and kept his plays out of the Abbey for the next ten years.

Between 1914 and 1957, Fitzmaurice wrote nine more plays, five of them after 1926, the year he began to be more withdrawn and eccentric. Retiring from his government job in 1942, he lived on a small pension, continued to write, and fell into the routine of visiting libraries during the day to read London and local newspapers. At night he met old cronies in a public house on Aungier Street. Fitzmaurice lived a five-minute walk from Dublin's theatres and shopping district and ten minutes from Trinity College, but nobody ever saw him near any of these places. In his later years, he even refused Radio Eireann permission to broadcast two of his plays, *Dandy Dolls* and *The Magic Glasses*. And so Fitzmaurice made his own contribution to being forgotten. As the Irish say of a recluse, "He went into himself."

In summary, Gabriel Fitzmaurice sees George Fitzmaurice in this way: "Unafraid to see the world as complex and contradictory, as perverse and wonderful in all its perversity, he was an increasingly uncomfortable figure for a society looking for a simple definition of itself."

BRENDAN KENNELLY (1936–)

BRENDAN KENNELLY SAYS that, while poetry has to be earned through hard labor, it is essentially a given thing—a gift that took him unawares, and one that he accepted.

The Gift

It came slowly.
Afraid of insufficient self-content
Or some inherent weakness in itself
Small and hesitant
Like children at the top of stairs
It came through shops, rooms, temples,
Streets, places that were badly-lit.
It was a gift that took me unawares
And I accepted it.

In another poem, Kennelly writes that to be a poet, even with the gift once accepted, learning goes on forever.

The Learning

The learning goes on forever.
A pigeon dozing in the ivy
Is sending out bulletins
I am trying to decipher.

The streets survive, offering their thoughts
At no cost. Lost

Rivers plead under our feet,
Astray in themselves
Sharing our anonymity.
With what devotion
The children of ignorance
Apply themselves to learn
The streets' wisdom, the rivers' rhythms
In the spell of the flesh
Failing through self-repeating evenings.

. . . In the learning that goes on forever

In the preface to his book *A Time for Voices,* Kennelly talks about himself and his poetry:

Everything I write is the story/ballad culture of my youth when a boy or girl had to be able to recite poetry and tell stories . . . before an audience. If a poem isn't shared it's not alive. . . . Many of my poems have a strong story element in them. We have little or no philosophical tradition in Ireland; reality is apprehended largely not through ideas but through stories . . .whatever ideas we have come from our stories.

Above all, poetry for me is connection, or the hope of connection both with One's self and with the outside world, with the living and the dead . . . It is critics who talk of an 'authentic voice'; but a poet living with uncertainties is riddled with different voices, many of them in vicious conflict. The poem is the arena where these voices engage each other in open and hidden combat and continue to do so until they are all heard. . . . The imagination, often interpreted in terms of hierarchy, insists on its own democracy.

Kennelly held the Chair of Modern Literature at Trinity College, Dublin. He recently retired. Along the way he served a pint or two in his father's pub in Ballylongford, where he was born in 1936, one of six rugged brothers. They were all top footballers including Brendan. His father's pub was, to borrow Bryan MacMahon's term, "early university" for young Brendan. While known to read Baudelaire at twelve (no biography of Kennelly fails to mention this), the real stuff was what his young poet's ear took in many a night at the pub. Farmers swapped stories, talked politics (Eamon de Valera was so crooked he could swallow a nail and produce a corkscrew.), sang North Kerry ballads, and recited poetry. In his poetry, Kennelly returns time and again to those days. In his poem "Living Ghosts," he writes fondly of those men and times:

Men in their innocence
Untroubled by right and wrong.
I close my eyes and see them
Becoming song.

Kennelly was in secondary school at a time when an Irish twelve-year-old was expected to master Latin. He won a scholarship to Trinity College, Dublin, but left after a year because of shyness and lack of confidence in himself. During his time off, he worked in his father's pub, put in a stint at the Electricity Supply Board, and was a bus conductor in London. A bit more seasoned, he reentered Trinity College, graduated in 1961, joined the English department in 1963, was made a fellow in 1967, and became an associate professor in 1969. In 1973, with two novels, two plays, and a flock of poetry to his credit, he was appointed to a newly created Chair of Modern Literature. By then, the once shy young man, in sport vernacular, was on his way to becoming a "phenom," or, if you prefer, "the franchise."

By the 1990s, hardly a day went by without some mention of Kennelly in the press. He was famous enough to be featured in a humorous television car commercial (even though he has never had a driver's license), and the rock group U2 admits to Kennelly's influence on them. They were special guests at his sixtieth birthday. Bono, leader of U2, said he had sung "it" from the Jesus side for long enough. Kennelly's best selling four-hundred-page *Book of Judas*, in which all sorts of evildoers slug it out with each other, showed Bono things from the other, darker side and led to his songs "Achtung Baby" and "Zooropa."

Kennelly, a great stand-up performer of his own work, says, "I tell my students, 'Enjoy yourself; relax, and try not to see human experience as something measurable. Just experience it, you know. Just experience it.'" Recently, the Ireland Fund of France honored Kennelly with the Wild Geese Award. President of the Fund, Pierre Joannon, said of the "incredibly talented and prolific" Kennelly, "As an educator in Trinity College for over forty years, he has brought his brand of wisdom and comedy to countless students."

As all actors know, comedy is harder.

Bryan MacMahon (1909–1998)

People in Listowel knew Bryan McMahon as the Master. He was a short story writer, poet, playwright and producer of plays, novelist, writer of children's books, lecturer, translator, and ballad-maker. He wrote radio features and television scripts, and he created historic pageants of story, song, and dance. One pageant ran for sixteen years in the castle of Knappogue, a MacNamara stronghold dating from 1467. MacMahon taught and was writer in residence at several American universities. But, most of all, deep down, MacMahon was a Listowel schoolmaster. The following quotations are from *The Master*, MacMahon's best-selling autobiography. I thought it best to let the Master speak for himself, beginning with the time he first started teaching in 1929.

> An ideal that I tried to transfer to my pupils, even in devious ways or simplified form, was that in the Ireland of the future there would be only one aristocracy: not that of privilege or

birth but that of ability.

It was a time of dreadful squalor . . . the hills I could view through the dingy school window were replete with the balladry of an outlawed people, and echoed to the sound of traditional music. . . . Odd as it now sounds, it seemed normal that [school] children should have dirty, bloody bare feet, that lice should crawl over their jackets, that flea-marks should pock their bodies, that they should be hungry and poor.

I realized that each child had a gift, and that the "leading out" of that gift was the proper goal of teaching. To me a great teacher was simply a great person teaching. . . . It became an obsession with me, this sense of deducing from small signals where each one's aptitude lay, even the most seemingly deprived among them . . . above all I had to identify what would preserve a sense of wonder.

An instrument of education, that's what I would be. I would read everything I could lay my hands on. I would establish contact with literature of other lands, while holding faith with what was worthy in my own country.

1936 was the year of his marriage to Kitty Ryan, who he met in Lisdoonvarna. Then came five sons in quick succession. MacMahon recognized, "I now had to rummage about my extramural activities to find some way to augment my salary." He opened a bookstore in Listowel and around the same time began to write for pay.

My average working day was now made up as follows. From nine to three at school, hammer and tongs, with no drawing back. From three to four I ate my dinner and slept—the nap as a result of excellent advice I received from an old schoolmaster who counseled me always to let the sediment of the school day settle in the well of the mind. From four to nine I assisted or relieved my wife in the bookshop. From nine to ten I walked about the streets with my lifelong friend Ned Sheehy. At ten on the dot I sat at a table and wrote until one in the morning. This routine I kept up for the better part of fifteen years, and lived to tell the tale.

A teacher and a writer draw sustenance from the same reservoir of energy; each as it were "prances on the front lawn of peoples brains" and seeks to do so with indelibility. In both my roles as teacher and writer, I venture to stress once again that success begins with humor.

An advance man for a circus coming to Listowel visited MacMahon one day at the school. He asked for help in promoting attendance. MacMahon learned that the circus had a baby elephant and made a deal for the mahout to show up the next day with his elephant outside the classroom door at noon on the dot.

I knew the following day's lesson referenced a magician. At five minutes to twelve, I expanded on the word "magician" and said to the boys that I was letting them in on a very special secret. "I am a magician," I said solemnly. "I don't want everybody to know, but it happens to be true."

The class shook with laughter. One boy asked, "What can you do?"

"If I repeat a certain formula of words, any wild animal will materialize here in the classroom."

"Can you get a tiger?"

"No, tigers, they are too dangerous," said another lad.

"A mouse?"

"Yes, but it's too small," I said.

"Rats?"

"Yes, but we've had enough of those already."

Someone was bound to suggest the animal I had in mind. "An elephant," one said at last.

"Certainly," I replied quickly. "I like elephants."

"Not a big one," someone suggested. "A baby one will do."

The hands of the clock stood at three minutes to twelve. Out of the corner of an eye through the window in the classroom door, I spied my accomplice leading the little elephant across the yard and entering the school through the open door.

"We're waiting. Where's your elephant sir?" came the cry of the impatient class.

Raising a hand for silence I made passes in the air with my willow rod. Again out of the corner of my eye I could see the waiting mahout, dressed in Eastern garb. "Abracadabra," I chanted. "All together now to give power to the magic." All the class chanted, in varying tones of belief and mockery. "Oscall an doras," I told the boy nearest the door. "Let in the elephant."

The boy hesitated, then opened the door. He backed away in utter disbelief as in came the trunk, the head and finally the entire baby elephant—it too was dressed for the occasion—followed by the mahout. There was a gasp of astonishment. Excitement then broke its bonds, and everyone began to cheer. The elephant looked on quietly out of its tranquil eyes; it had become used to the vagaries of circus audiences.

MacMahon's talent as a teacher and writer and his substantial fund of published works led to attractive offers from several universities in the States. It was now 1965. MacMahon was sixty-five, ten years from retirement as a Listowel schoolmaster.

The temptation continued to nag me. In three years in America I could earn as much as I could in a decade of active teaching years remaining to me at home. . . . There was also the prospect of a new, exciting life opening up for me in America where the writer is accorded high status.

But what would I do without the Irish dimension to life—without the cut and thrust of banter, the laughter and the ballads, the summer playground of the west coast, the observance of the interplay and counterplay of local politics and intrigue, the market meetings with country people, the in-for-a-chat of old friends and neighbors, the delightful discussion of books with my friend the retired librarian, the evening walks with Ned—all the minutiae of small-town living placed on the pan to balance that of material gain and superficial recognition?

When he did retire, MacMahon reflected on a world of change where "one thatched roof is left in a town where in my boyhood there were hundreds. I've seen the fire on the hearthstone replaced by the microwave cooker." More importantly, much had happened to the "Irish dimension to life," and a great deal of it was not to MacMahon's liking.

For the first eleven years of my life Ireland was part of the British Empire, with all the indignities that connoted. I then experienced the first fever of liberty; I now dread the new imperialism of materialism, its prime weapon manipulation. In my bones and brain I am convinced that nothing happens naturally any more, that everything and everyone is engineered by schemers and conditioned by image, projection, package, and presentation.

Bryan MacMahon died on Friday, February 13, 1998. In his essay "The Gift of Ink, The Legacy of Brian MacMahon," Gabriel Fitzmaurice, another gifted Kerry writer, wrote that MacMahon left an imprint on literature as a superb storyteller. "At his best he wrote brilliantly. But better, he wrote memorably . . . Bryan MacMahon had the gift of ink. He lived all his life in his native Listowel. A writer of the small town, but not a small town writer, he showed us how to take our place among the nations of the earth. The master is dead. Long live the master."

A NOTE OF THANKS

FOR THE EXCEPTIONAL and unforgettable experience of The Writers'

Museum and the opportunity to "meet" John B. Keane, Bryan MacMahon, Brendan Kennelly, Maurice Walsh, and George Fitzmaurice on their own turf, we want to thank Jimmy Deenihan for the original idea of the museum, Steve Simon for so brilliant an expression of the idea, Cara Trant for her excellent management, and the Literary Task Force and the people of Listowel who went out and got it done. Thanks a million!

A question remains with us. Why Listowel? How is it that this small town of 3,300 or so in North Kerry could produce the likes of Keane, Walsh, Kennelly, Fitzmaurice, and MacMahon? And new Listowel-area writers, poets, and playwrights—Gabriel Fitzmaurice, Rory O'Connor, Tony Guerin, Christian O'Reilly, Paddy Fitzgibbon, and Paddy Kennelly? Why does the creative tap continue to run?

CHAPTER TWENTY-THREE

It's the Water Is It?

When a Listowel man takes a drink from any tap in this lovely town
'Tis not only water that's going down, but the purified secrets of the dead
Flowing into his belly and through his head
No town here or in any land will do this for your body and mind
Inspiration flows through the graveyard sod
Turn a tap in Listowel, out flows God!

—Brendan Kennelly

I AM FAR from the first to wonder how and why little Listowel has for well more than a hundred years produced a disproportionate share of Ireland's first-rate writers, some of them in the genius class. I don't have an answer, but let me share the bits and pieces I have collected. At best they add up to a few notions.

Tradition of Writing

BRENDAN KENNELLY can walk through The Square in Listowel, and one person will say to him, "Brendan, I just read *Poetry My Arse*. Great Book! Great poetry!" And another Kennelly fan will remember him as a talented footballer who played minor, junior, and senior football for

Kerry along with his brothers Alan, John, Paddy, Kevin, and Colm. In Listowel, you can be well-known and admired for either or both writing and footballing. A writing tradition creates writers, as a footballing tradition creates footballers and so on. Finnish musicians, Canadian hockey players, and Kenyan marathoners are each products of a tradition.

Tradition is one reason Listowel is tops in producing both great writers and great football players. Building and sustaining a tradition, be it writing or football, requires fans, an audience, people who read and go to plays. Fans provide society's support system. Being admired is one thing. Making a living at writing is another. In Ireland and especially Listowel, writing pays both admiration and income.

IN IRELAND THEY BREATHE THE STUFF

A COUPLE OF YEARS AGO, Ruth Lily, the eighty-seven-year old heir to the Eli Lily pharmaceutical fortune, bequeathed more than $100 million to the association that owns *Poetry*, a monthly journal for new poetry. Jeremy Grant of the *Financial Times* asked Joe Parisi, editor of *Poetry*, which countries seemed naturally inclined to produce the most poets, if not the most submissions to *Poetry*. He replied,

> Oh, Ireland, without a doubt. My goodness, you get into a cab, walk down the street, wait for a bus, walk through the park in Dublin, and they will quote you poetry. And not just your classic authors, they know their contemporary poets. One of the biggest things to do in Dublin is to go to a book launch and they have four or five of them a week! Oh yes. Ireland is unbelievable.

Nuala O'Faolain, a novelist and columnist for *The Irish Times*, puts this twist on language and the Irish. "The Irish are good talkers. That is part of the personality of the country. They play with language. They use words differently. They ask more of the listener. There's a

loquaciousness and a joy in language. . . . The people are gifted in living. They risk themselves all the time."

THE BUG BITES KIDS EARLY

WRITER, POET, ESSAYIST, critic, and schoolteacher Gabriel Fitzmaurice
remembers as a young boy hearing talk about a new play *Sive* that
opened in Listowel before going on to the Abbey Theatre in Dublin.
He says the village was agog with this new play. "Stories began to filter through about its author, John B. Keane: he stayed up all night
writing; he read books while eating . . . to my impressionable mind
that was high romance. I wanted that. I wanted people talking about
me like that. (I would have been about seven at the time.)" Now, some
years later, people do talk about Fitzmaurice. He is at work on his
twenty-fifth book.

Brendan Kennelly tells of being inspired as a young lad by songs,
stories, and poems of local men in the theatre that was his father's
pub. MacMahon recalls as a boy, listening to his father's friends gath-
ered in the evening at his home discussing politics, telling tales, and
singing songs—stoking his imagination and dream of becoming a storyteller.

> Pots of gold, fairy forts, the prophecies of Colm Cille, ghostly
> night riders, headless coachmen, landlords who had cursed
> their tenants as vermin and who in turn were plagued by ver-
> min on their deathbeds with servant girls using quills to wipe
> the dead faces clean of crawling insects; faction fighting; half-
> forgotten ballads, the merits of barbed and unbarbed gaffs,
> herbal cures, holy and unholy wells—these were my fare night
> after night for a score of years.

Keane, MacMahon, and other writers were part of the everyday
Listowel scene—admired, accessible, and successful. It wasn't that
much of a reach for any lad to think of becoming a writer, just like

them. Respected writers would visit classrooms and talk with students about their writing. Or you could go with your dad to Keane's pub and exchange a word or two with John B. or today his son Billy, also a writer. Or better yet, the teacher was a writer—MacMahon at Listowel Primary, or Seamus Wilmot and Patrick Given at St. Michael's. All of them readily praised and encouraged any breath of talent.

Irish kids know that those who write books and poems and plays are important. "So why not me?"

STORYTELLING AND CLASSICAL EDUCATION

JOHN B., MACMAHON, and Walsh were among the well-known writers who attended St Michael's College, a Listowel secondary school that placed emphasis on a classical education. I asked John Mulvihill, principal of St. Michael's, about Gabriel Fitzmaurice's observation, "In the Listowel area there's something to live up to, something to pit yourself against if you're a writer." Mulvihill gave me a list of 167 novels, plays, and books of poetry. All of them bore some distinction and were written by twenty-six Listowel authors in the years between 1907 and 1993. The list included twenty books by Walsh, thirty-seven by Keane, and fourteen by MacMahon. Add another half dozen or so talented authors who have come on the scene since 1993, then consider the total in relation to Listowel's population of 3,393.

Mulvihill sees the Irish gift for storytelling and the discipline of a classical education as related ingredients in the flowering of Listowel writers.

Storytelling

IN THE SIXTEENTH CENTURY, next to kings or territorial rulers, Bardic Poets filled the highest position in the social order. Their role was poet, musician, arbiter, and historian, along with a bit of cheer-leading for the boss. Their value was thought to be too great to endanger life or limb by allowing them in battle. Stories, songs, and poems of Bardic Poets were the after-dinner entertainment in the castles of kings and chieftains. Less formally trained talents carried these stories, songs, and poems into the homes of plain people, a receptive and fascinated audience. As clan life and the Bardic tradition passed, naturally gifted local tellers of tales emerged. These were the *Seanchaí* (Shan-a-key), who collected great stories and local lore, created new stories and burnished old ones, and maintained the art of storytelling through the ages, passing tales on from one generation to another. While the *Seanchaí* may have been the stars, storytelling in Kerry was a talent that many shared.

Eamon Kelly, one of Ireland's best-loved storytellers, sits on a bench in the entrance lobby of the Writers' Museum. He is leaning on his cane and telling a tale to a young schoolgirl. In his memoir, Kelly recalls natural storytellers among his mates in his early working days. They were "fellows who spoke with authority of Copernicus and Galileo, and solid men who had been in person to the very edge of a flat earth and, looking over it had seen for themselves, piled-up below, the discarded suns and moons of all the ages."

In a similar vein, in the preface to his play *The Playboy of the Western World*, Synge writes of the extraordinary stories ordinary Irish people tell. "The wildest sayings and ideas in my play are tame indeed compared with the fancies one may hear in any hillside cabin from herdsmen and fishermen along the coast from Kerry to Mayo."

Kennelly sums it up for the Irish, "Whatever ideas we have come from stories."

Classical Education

IN NORTH KERRY, side by side with the interest in storytelling was a love of education with an emphasis on the classics. There were two classical schools in Listowel before St. Michael's opened in 1879 and became responsible for post-primary (high school) education. Timothy O'Connor, a Latin and Greek scholar and a brilliant teacher, helped form young minds at St. Michael's from 1906 to 1953. It was O'Connor "who gave me a great love of language as he did to others," Mulvihill told me. People understood a classical education challenged and developed young minds. Think of high school students reading Aristotle, Plato, Thucydides, and other Greek thinkers who probed into everything, questioned everything, sought to understand everything, and were systematic in their aim at clear definition and logical consistency. Their interests were all-consuming—natural sciences, ethics, mathematics, political philosophy, metaphysics, theology, and aesthetics. They sought truths of the highest generality.

The tradition of classical learning in North Kerry reached back a long way and touched a remarkable range of people.

1672, Sir William Petty: "Despite the brutish circumstance that the majority of Irish people were reduced to living . . . the French elegance was not unknown to many of them, nor the French and Latin Tongues. The latter whereof is very frequent amongst the poorest Irish and chiefly in Kerry, most remote from Dublin."

1673, Lord Herbert, John Butler and Cadogan Barnes, Justices of the County of Kerry: "The said county aboundeth . . . with youth learning of needless Latin instead of useful trades."

1756, C. Smith: "The common people of Kerry . . . many of them speak Latin fluently."

After surveying much of the historic evidence, in his book *Listowel and Its Vicinity*, Rev. J. Anthony Gaughan wrote of the seventeenth, eighteenth, and nineteenth centuries, "the extent of classical learning in Kerry at that time was extraordinary."

LANGUAGE—A LOVE CHILD

IT IS SAID that there is a character and quality to the English used in North Kerry that has been and remains a primary assist to writers who grow up in the area.

George Fitzmaurice. "Keane takes the North Kerry dialect (the love child of Norman French and Elizabethan English mixed with the Irish that was spoken here even into the twentieth century) and transforms it into a work of art."

Bryan MacMahon. "The words may be English but the structure, rhythm and the color that transmutes the prose into poetry are pure Irish."

John B. Keane. "Our language here [in North Kerry] is a 'spirit language'. . . . It runs like a river with high water. It gurgles, it chortles, it whispers in wisps and makes all sorts of wonderful sounds—beautiful sounds of the water spilling over and lapping against the stones—all different because of the ebb and flow of the language. . . . So the language we use here is vivid, it's colorful, it's highly charged with romanticism."

Maurice Walsh. "We produce, for so small an island, more artists per square mile than any other country in the world, and that's a challenge. In drama, poetry, and the novel, we have shown we are a distinct and distinguished people. Indeed, I might say, where England lent us her language we gave her in return her literature."

I am afraid the question of how it is that Ireland in general and Listowel in particular has produced so many good writers will continue to confound. Make a choice or make a stew—tradition, national condition, early start, storytelling and love of words, classical roots, or the language itself.

Turn a tap in Listowel, out flows God!

CHAPTER TWENTY-FOUR

WINDING DOWN IN QUIN

Quin Town is twelve miles from Limerick, six from Six-mile-bridge, 4 from Rallahine Castle in the road to Galloway. It hath nothing worth the note of a Traveler but the ruines of an Abbey. There are two faires a year, which in time past were famous for quarrelling of two families of numerous offspring hereabouts, viz., the Molounys and MacNamarras, in which 8 persons, Ulster men were kill'd and buried in one hole.

The Abbey was anciently of the order of St. Francis; here are seen the ancient Vaults & Burial places of the MacNamarras & the Molounys and hither they are brought if they dye in the Kingdom to be interred with their Ancestors.

—The Journal of Thomas Dineley, 1681

WARM GOODBYE LISTOWEL: WARM HELLO QUIN

ARMEL WHYTE, proprietor and chef at Allo's in Listowel, demonstrated as much talent in the morning for making breakfast as he had for preparing dinner the evening before. First it was fruit, perfectly scrambled eggs, enough smoked salmon to make the New York Carnegie Deli proud, sausage, and muffins. Then Armel helped with our bags and gave us a proper send-off. On our way out of Listowel, we took a last look at the artistic plaster facades of the *Harp & Lion* and the *Maid of Erin* and then stopped at the Literary & Cultural Centre so G could get a book of Brendan Kennelly's poetry and I could get a copy of Gabriel Fitzmaurice's *Kerry On My Mind*. Kennelly was the one standing on a footbridge with the words of his poetry flowing through on a stream below. Listowel was memorable, the high point of our trip, and we were now winding down.

Heading north, we crossed the River Shannon on the car ferry from Tarbert, then drove through Ballynacally and into Ennis. The barely passable cobble streets in the center of Ennis made the narrow goat tracks of Bantry seem like major highways by comparison. We lost our way three times in Ennis and then lucked our way onto the road to Quin. That afternoon, we were to meet Michael Byrne, CEO of the Eircom Information Age Project, "a live experiment to see what would happen when an entire town [Ennis] became wired." I had been working on a computer literacy project for the Boulder library and hoped Ennis's experience at being "wired" would fill in some gaps for me. Considering the state of its streets, I wondered if Ennis might not have skipped the transportation age on its way to getting wired. Or had planners decided Ennis had the perfect system for slowing and controlling traffic? Apparently streets hadn't changed much from 1941, when Sean O'Faolain wrote in *An Irish Journey* of Ennis as having ". . . the narrowest streets of any Irish town, I know, and all winding like serpents."

But on to Ardsollus Farm where we were to spend our last two days in Ireland before heading home. I have always felt that the end of a trip needs to be planned with as much care as the beginning. Home should not be where you go to recover from a vacation. This calls for one's final days to be spent in a place that is attractive, comfortable, interesting, undemanding, and close to the airport. Quin fit the bill. It is a peaceful village of less than three hundred, only nine miles and fifteen minutes from Shannon Airport. It has a core of older stone buildings that look like they belong, well-preserved remains of a fifteenth-century abbey holding the remains of John "Fireball" MacNamara, a couple good restaurants, and great tubs of flowers set along a graceful bridge over the River Rine.

Ardsollus Farm, a fifth-generation family farm, was near perfect. Arching oaks and a well-tended pasture of stud farms lined the gently rolling road from Quin to the farm. At Ardsollus, our welcome from Loreto and Pat Hannon was personal and warm. Over tea, Pat talked about the start of his farm. His great grandfather made money on road contracts, bought this 125-acre farm, and raised cattle, sheep, and horses. He had twelve children, six boys and six girls. The oldest son took over the farm and ran it for fifteen years. At age thirty-five, he bought another farm and turned Ardsollus over to his youngest son, Patrick Hannon, who was Pat's father. Pat took over in 1975, at age thirty-five, and built his herd of thirty dairy cows into one of eighty, producing eighty thousand gallons of milk a year. In 2001, frustrated with rising costs and static prices, Pat sold his allotment of eighty dairy cows, bought a small cattle allotment, and put the rest of his money into building a B&B addition on to the old farmhouse. And there we were.

Pat took us out back to the barnyard of the three-hundred-year-old farmhouse and introduced us to the rest of the Ardsollus family—one cock, eight hens, mother and father Jack Russells, their litter of five baby pups, eyes not yet open, two three-month old pups from another litter, three calico cats, and eight hunters in their stalls. The cats sat high and disdainful on bales of hay, the pups charmed us into playing with them, and the cock strutted about in command of the whole world. Any untoward move by cock, cat, or pup brought a firm quiet word from Pat, and the errant member of the barnyard family fell right into line. The world-owning attitude of the Ardsollus cock reminded G of Cleopatra, an inappropriately named chicken we met regularly in New York's Central Park on Sunday afternoons when Cleopatra was out for a stroll with José, his Dominican companion.

THE INFORMATION AGE MAN

WE HEADED BACK into Quin, where Michael Byrne sat waiting for us in front of the fireplace at the Monks Well Inn. There was nothing small-town about Byrne in his well-cut Italian suit and his initials, MB, embroidered on his shirt cuffs. Byrne had studied for the priesthood for eight years and was then was a priest for ten years before he found a new calling. He headed back to college, got a degree in sociology and psychology, earned a master's degree in Computer Based Information Systems, and moved on to a systems job with IBM. Byrne became CEO of the Eircom Information Age Project in 1998.

Ennis, population 18,000, had won a national competition to become The Information Age Town. Eircom, a telephone/technology company that sponsored the competition, put €19 million ($22.8 million) into the project. One year's free Internet connection and computers for 4,600 Ennis homes cost €8.3 million ($9.96 million). This worked out to €1,790 ($2,148) a pop for eighty-three percent of Ennis's 5,500 households. The additional amount of €1.9 million ($2.5 million) went to computer rooms for twelve primary and secondary schools, a sum equal to €365 ($438) for each of 5,200 students. The goal was, "access for every child to a computer on a regular basis, a structured scheme of work to learn how to use a computer, and teachers recognizing that computers are an integral tool in any classroom."

It was clear from the project's glossy 2002 progress report that the "largest community technology project in the world" was a copywriter's dream. Report headings in bold type announced the project was bringing "the benefits of the Information Age to the broad mass of the [Ennis] population." It was providing "a sustainable initiative that continues to improve the quality of life for the community of Ennis." It was "unparalled in its social, educational, and economic impact." As a result of their involvement, teachers, students, and parents were "committed to exploiting the benefits of [this] unrivalled technology infrastructure."

Ah, if it were all only true. With nearly $25 million spent and Eircom's interest in the project in sharp decline, Byrne concluded, "A big budget for equipment does not produce wise usage. It was rather like putting a piano in every home and expecting the family to produce musicians and composers."

Recognizing the computer "as an integral tool in any classroom" is one thing. Accomplishing something of consequence with the tool is another. Use of computers has not raised the bar. For example, most high school students find the Internet a wonderful source when it comes to writing papers on almost any subject. With Google or Ask Jeeves, they can do their "research" and finish a paper of reasonable quality more quickly than they could by bothering with books. Students then have more time for hanging out and doing things they enjoy, things that they feel improve their quality life. What educators in Ennis and most other places haven't said is that with the power of computing and Internet access to source material, we expect end products from students of greater depth, scope, and higher standard.

We talked about Ireland past, present, and future. Byrne was a bit wistful about Ireland becoming a different place. Its traditional qualities, he said, were adaptability, flexibility, being grounded in the traditions and spirituality of the society, and shared experiences, "things we allow our heart to rest on." Byrne went on. Beyond the nature of change from an agricultural to an industrial and knowledge-based society, the high-speed rate of change was transforming the whys and ways of Irish life. In 1990, the number of people at work was nine hundred thousand. In 2002, it was 1.7 million, an eighty-eight percent increase in twelve years. Where did the new workers come from? Colleges had become accessible and were producing thousands of new age professionals. Reverse immigration was bringing back trained professionals from overseas. Foreign workers were recruited. Most of all, Irish mothers poured out of their homes, exchanging cooking and cleaning for the independence and material goods a paycheck yielded. The mother thing, according to Byrne, is what will have the greatest impact of all on Ireland. "The next generation will grow up without the guiding hand and tutelage that in Ireland has always been mother's job."

That said, Byrne bid us goodbye, explaining that he had an Information Age meeting in Ennis, presumably to continue with his contribution to the transformation of Ireland.

I thought of Byrne and his comment on the mother thing when I recently heard what Irish novelist Nuala O'Faolain had to say on the subject: "Women of my generation in Ireland—I'm amazed we came through. It's so recent that women have had jobs and money of their own that Ireland doesn't know what to do with women."

THE END OF CIVILIZATION

BYRNE MISSED ONE significant indicator of change in Irish society. While the population has been growing, the sale of Guinness has fallen. It is the first decline in the 241 years since Arthur Guinness signed a long-term lease on a Dublin brewery. In a story dated September 7, 2001, Stephen Beaumont announced this in his definitive *World of Beer:* "More proof that the end of civilization is fast approaching. Guinness Ireland just released its end-of-year results and it shows a continuation of a trend toward change in traditional Irish drinking patterns." According to the story, sales of Guinness Stout in Ireland dropped by 2.7 percent in the twelve months ending June 30, 2001. Just as shocking, over the same period, sales of Budweiser in Ireland increased by 3.0 percent.

Lorna Harrison, editor of the trade magazine *Publican*, explained that with more money, more professionals, and more women in the upscale labor force, "There has been an explosion in the choice of beers available to drinkers, particularly with premium lagers. This is accompanied by the fact that women are the big growth area and they don't want to drink stout. It all adds up to a hard time for Guinness."

Drinking is a serious activity in Ireland. In 2002, the Irish spent $8 billion on alcoholic drinks, a sum equal to $2,600 for every person age 16 or over. Ireland's annual per capita alcohol consumption is 3.75 gallons, compared with an average of 2.4 gallons in all European Union countries and a comparatively modest U.S. rate of 1.77 gallons, less than half the Irish rate. Watching activity in the bar at Monks Well Inn made the numbers believable.

After Byrne left, G and I ordered up our pints of Guinness and talked with Clara Titley, owner of the Monk's Well Inn. We talked about Fannie Corbet, a neighbor in her nineties who always wanted a helicopter ride and never had one. Clara laid out her plans to have a helicopter land (it did) in Fannie's front yard on her birthday and take her on the ride (she did) she always wanted. With trophies and photos all around the pub, we got on to the subject of Jason, Clara's famous son, a jockey who at age twenty-four had won the Aintree Grand National, "the greatest steeplechase in the world," on Royal Athlete, paying off at forty-to-one. The conversation then got away from us with talk of Jason as "a fearless and great presenter of horses" to tough fences like Beechers Brook and The Chair, top horses such as Grand Habit and How's the Boss that Jason had ridden to sweet wins, and the bones steeplechase jockeys are most likely to break when their horses fall on bad jumps. Evidently, Jason breaking his collarbone, both shoulders, and all his ribs at one time or another is considered par for the course.

We got back to known territory as G and Clara recalled posters in the London Undergound and billboards everywhere advertising Guinness—"My Goodness My Guinness," "You'll Feel Better When You've Had a Guinness," "Lovely Day for A Guinness," "Guinness For Strength," "Guinness is Good For You." G speculated on Guinness's nutritional value (yeast, vitamin B, antioxidants, etc.) and asked Clara if she thought one could live on it. Without missing a beat, "There's a lot a' fellas that do."

THE PERFECT TWO-PART DRAW

I NOTICED A ROW of partially filled glasses of Guinness lined up on the back bar. Clara explained that the stout had to settle before filling the rest of the glass and went on to explain the requirements for "the perfect pint." Start with a tulip shaped imperial pint (twenty-ounce) glass, absolutely clean, dry, and at room temperature. In no circumstances can you use a chilled glass. Next, make sure dispensing lines and taps are well-cleaned, once a week at a minimum. Kegs of Guinness are stored between thirty-eight and forty-six degrees and served between forty-two and forty-eight degrees. Guinness is dispensed by a gas mixture of seventy-five percent nitrogen and twenty-five percent carbon dioxide at a pressure of thirty pounds per square inch to produce the creamy heads.

Ready to draw a Guinness. Go! A process so precise that Guinness experts have decreed the ideal time. It should take exactly 119 seconds for the two-part draw:

> Hold the glass at a forty-five degree angle close to the spout to prevent large bubbles from forming in the head. Pull the tap fully open and fill the glass seventy-five percent full.

> Allow the stout to sit for a minute or so (on the back bar) to settle completely until the beer goes all the way black and the head forms.

> Hold the glass vertically under the tap and push the tap forward slightly until the head rises "just proud off (above) the rim." Never allow the stout to overflow or run down the side of the glass.

This artistry in a glass is presented to you. Admire it for a moment or two and then take a large mouthful. I was told do not—under any circumstances—sip, as sipping ruins the majestic nature of the stout. When the Guinness is drained, rings should remain on the inside of the empty glass. Done? Ready for another pint? Most are, and this accounts for another phenomenon, the urinal wall of the Irish pub. Unlike the two or three personal ceramic receptacles in the men's john of an American bar, the Irish pub provides a ten- or twelve-foot ceramic or tin wall with a trough at the bottom, dedicated to comforting bladders. This utilitarian design allows a whole row of them's in need to perform at the same time and get back to pints that are most probably sitting on the bar waiting for them. Another Irish/American difference—you don't find blackboards and chalk in the john of an Irish pub. In America, grown men will stop and waste time to scratch out a juvenile ditty. The blackboard is there to keep them from writing on the wall. The Irish have better things to do.

We were told on good authority that ten or twelve pints of an evening are no big deal for serious drinking and up to twenty pints is not unknown. These are men not overburdened with an interest in sobriety.

THE RUSSIAN WHO IS ALSO AN AMERICAN

THIS WAS OUR last full day in Ireland. In the morning, I visited the Quin primary school. Before class started, Tomas O Siochain, who had taught in this school for thirty-three years, asked me where the name Rovetch came from. I told him my parents were born in Russia. O Siochain then sat me down next to him in a place of authority at his desk and introduced me to his class as a "Russian who is also an American." The class, thirteen boys and girls, looked puzzled. Together we counted up their relatives in the States. Among them they had thirty-seven. I asked, do you think of them as Irish who are also American? No, they said firmly. They saw them as Irish who live in the States, confirming the view that the U.S. is really just another part of Ireland.

All thirteen of the lads expected to go to college. None saw any benefit or relevance to their daily classes in Gaelic. None of their parents spoke it. Career choices of students included banking, accounting, film studio, archeology, health, veterinary medicine, being a chef, and hairdressing. Ten of the students lived in Quin and three on farms in the area. To their teacher's dismay, none thought that when they grew up they would live in Quin. Seven of their mothers worked full-time, fitting right in with the national pattern. Eight of the thirteen students had computers at home, but only two admitted to playing computer games. I didn't believe a word of this.

I had now talked with sixth-grade students in Fanore, Lispole, Castletownbere, and Quin. The "lads" were remarkably alike. Their eyes were on new opportunities in a changing world, a very different world than the one that shaped their parents and teachers.

QUIN ABBEY: A SUCCESSION OF SCENES

THE CENTERPIECE OF Quin Village is the majestic ruin of Quin Abbey. Our visit to the abbey provided a grand finale to our Irish adventure and all the more dramatic because its wonders that day were ours alone.

Bishop Richard Pococke, whose writings in the 1700s of travels to Egypt, Mesopotamia, and Syria brought him fame as an observer of architectural and antiquarian glories, said of Quin Abbey, "It is one of the finest and most entire monasteries that I have seen in Ireland." A Mr. Trotter who visited the abbey in 1817 wrote, "Quin Abbey is one of the most perfect ruins in Ireland and of wonderful beauty. . . . There we saw an incredible quantity of bones and skulls, long blanched by Time's resistless hand—they were piled in great quantities in the abbey." (This reminded me of Capela dos Ossos [Chapel of the Bones], a memorial to the mortality of man, in the Church of Sao Francisco in Evora, Portugal. Artfully arranged skulls and tibias of more than five thousand monks cover the walls and pillars of Capela dos Ossos. The inscription over the door reads, *"Nos ossos que aqui estamos. Pelos vossos esperamos."* ("Our bones here are waiting for your bones.")

When G and I explored Quin Abbey, the bones of Franciscan monks were long gone, but the "perfect ruin of wonderful beauty" remained. I have wondered why the abbey left so strong an image. All too often memory's picture is blurred. Not so with the abbey. In my mind's eye, I see a gracefully curved walk leading up a gentle slope to a stone arch framing the entrance to the abbey and a softly moving stream next to the walk. On the south side of the church, a graveyard dense with moss-covered crosses and headstones. At the entrance to the abbey, you walk up three well-worn stone steps to a scene that stretches more than a hundred feet down the nave to the altar—first the perfectly preserved fourteenth-century arched entrance to the abbey, then a high narrow arch, and beyond this a stone altar beneath three long and narrow east-facing windows that fill the Friary church with afternoon light. There was poetry to the design with a new statement at each stage—entrance, a procession of arches, altar, windows, and brilliant east light.

The abbey is a place of great drama. Off to the right, a sweeping arch opens to the Lady Chapel with four altars, a gothic figure of a saint in relief, and a monument to the MacNamaras of Rance, founders of the abbey. To the left are the Cloister, with couplets of pillars and ornamental buttresses, all beautifully proportioned, the whole creating a feeling of contemplation and peace. Off the Cloister are apartments, the refectory, a dormitory, and other rooms. A narrow stair winds up the tower and opens onto a sweeping view that reaches far beyond Quin. At the northeast corner of the Cloister wall lies the tombstone of the Rev. John Hogan, "who departed this life Anno Domini 1820 aged 80 years." Hogan's death marked the last link of Franciscan Friars to Quin Abbey.

QUIN ABBEY: FIVE CENTURIES OF DRAMA

The drama of Quin Abbey extended over five centuries:

1280. The Normans build Quin Castle to subdue the McNamara clan. (Irish form, MacConmara, "Hounds of the Sea.")

1286. MacNamaras burn Quin Castle and slay defenders to avenge the killing of clan chief O'Liddy.

1286–1402. Castle ruins sit amoldering.

1402–1430. On the foundation of castle ruins and using remaining walls, Sioda Cam MacConmara begins the building of Quin Abbey, "that it should be a burial place for himself and his sept." Mahon MacNamara continues the work, including Lady Chapel and the Bell Tower. In 1430, work is completed and Franciscan Friars establish their friary at Quin Abbey. (No fewer

QUIN ABBEY: FIVE CENTURIES OF DRAMA *(continued)*

than fifty-seven abbeys, castles, monasteries, and fortresses are attributed to the MacNamaras.)

1541.   Early Reformation. Henry VIII as supreme head of Church of Ireland attempts to impose Protestantism. The Catholic abbey is "officially suppressed," but the friars continue to live there.

1547.   Quin Abbey is granted to clan chief Conor O'Brien after he pledges allegiance to the crown. The abbey serves as a barracks for English soldiers. The "property" described in this classified ad of the times: "One acre, in which are one great church, now ruinous, covered with slate, and a steeple greatly decayed, a churchyard and cloister, one great hall, four chambers, two cellars, and a ruinous dormitory."

1580.   The MacNamaras burn the abbey. All English soldiers killed.

1604.   MacNamara family repairs abbey and friars allowed back. The friars open a college at the abbey, and by 1641 it had grown to eight hundred students.

1651.   Oliver Cromwell occupies Ireland, and the Abbey desecrated. Most monks are shot and killed.

1670.   The Restoration. Charles II back on throne. Cromwellians out. A few friars return to the abbey.

1690.   Penal laws bar Catholics from teaching or running schools "to prevent the further growth of popery," but some friars stay on in the decaying abbey.

1760.   Friars expelled from abbey again but maintain contact from a hideout in Drim. One friar, Fr John Hogan, continues to live in the abbey ruins until he dies and is buried there in 1820. The end.

John "Fireball" MacNamara (1750–1808)

Behold yon gray moss-covered stone
Where Thomond's maids shed drops of sorrow
There Sleeps Sean Budh—cold, low, lone,
The great and glorious MacNamara
The heart and nerve that never shook
The hand that left no mark unstruck

THE STORY OF QUIN ABBEY would not be complete without mention of Sean Buidh Mac ConMara, best known as John "Fireball" MacNamara. Fireball was the last of the many MacNamaras laid there to rest in the abbey. People remember him for his seeming invincibility, daring exploits, and flair for the dramatic, which began very early when Fireball received his first morsel of food from the point of a sword. He was commissioned in the French army in his twenties, killed two fellow officers who had teased him about his Irish ancestry, and fled south, where he served in the Spanish army.

MacNamara was a Protestant who won the love of the masses as a fierce supporter of Catholic emancipation. He expanded his reputation as an expert swordsman and lethal pistol shot, racking up a total of fifty-seven duels, many of them fatal to his opponents. He named his dueling pistols *Bas gan Sagart* (death without a priest). In the Irish Rebellion of 1798, he was wounded in the Battle of Vinegar Hill. Fireball's next stop was England, where he became a favorite of highborn and wealthy young ladies. The end came with his arrest for highway robbery. Despite pleas from ten of his lady admirers and two European ambassadors, the Queen refused a pardon, and John "Fireball" MacNamara was convicted and hanged. He is remembered now by his tomb that lies among those of other MacNamaras in Lady Chapel.

Goodbye Quin

G AND I FELT Thomas Dineley short-changed Quin when he wrote, "It hath nothing worth the note of a traveler but the ruines of an

Abbey." The ruins offered a great deal. But more than that, Quin was a fine place to end a good trip. We concluded our Ireland excursion with a salmon dinner at the Monks Well Inn, a perfect pint or two, an evening walk along the River Rine, goodbye to our barnyard friends at Ardsollus Farm, a comfortable night, a fine Irish breakfast, wishes for a good trip home from our fine hosts Pat and Loreto, and a fifteen-minute drive to Shannon.

CHAPTER TWENTY-FIVE

THE MAGIC BAG AND MEMORIES

AT SHANNON WE LEFT the Ford Focus at the curb in front of the terminal, dropped the keys at the Hertz counter just inside the door, and checked in at the nearby Air Canada counter. We were booked for flight AC 894, Shannon-Toronto, 1:05 P.M. to 3:05 P.M. with a 5:20 P.M. connection to Denver. More than adequate time, I thought.

Then we were ready for our usual pre-flight going home ritual. First, we spent loose change, including Euro coins the bank back home in Boulder wouldn't want to convert to dollars. G loaded up on Cadbury chocolate bars with hazelnuts that for some reason are not easy to get in the States, and we both chose reading matter for the flight. Next came a cup of coffee. I was looking forward to this, because at Shannon we would be able to get Irish coffee perfectly made with a healthy tot of Jamesons and whipped double cream in the Joe Sheridan Bar. Shannon is where Joe Sheridan invented Irish coffee, his great and lasting contribution to civilization.

THE STORY OF IRISH COFFEE

WHY AND HOW Irish coffee was created deserves to be shared. Sixty-five or so years ago, a full load of thirty-six overnight passengers

crossing the Atlantic in eighteen hours in the Boeing 314 flying boat
(183 mph cruising speed at thirteen thousand feet, unpressurized cab-
ins, private bedrooms, dining room) would arrive cold and grouchy at
Foynes, the flying boat base on the River Shannon. Passengers were
then bused to Shannon for ongoing flights. To warm and cheer them
with a comforting drink, Joe Sheridan, bartender at Shannon Airport,
invented and perfected Irish coffee. These are his instructions:

> Combine hot coffee (*strong as a friendly hand*) with a measure of
> Irish whiskey (*smooth as the wit of the land*) to within an inch of the
> brim.
>
> Mix in a tablespoon of brown sugar (*sweet as the tongue of a rogue*)
> to make the mix denser.
>
> Pour in slightly whipped double cream (*rich as an Irish brogue*),
> over the back of teaspoon to keep the cream from mixing.
>
> Do not stir. Drink the coffee/whiskey through the cream.

The Joe Sheridan Bar at Shannon Airport still makes a mean Irish
coffee.

THE MAGIC BAG

FORTIFIED WITH Mr. Sheridan's concoction, we found the flight to
Toronto painless. Wheelchairs awaited at the international terminal
arrival gate in Toronto, and off we went to collect our bags for transfer to the domestic terminal. While the bags are being transferred,
passengers take a shuttle bus from the international to the domestic
terminal.

At the baggage carousel, G's bag came in with the first batch. We
waited for mine. And we waited. And we waited. The leisurely two
hour and fifteen minute connection time eroded. The last bag from

AC-894 came in, and the carousel shut down. Forty-five minutes were gone. Off we rolled in search of the "lost bag" lady. Another half-hour passed. The wheelchair pushers remained loyal to their task, each competing to tell G more of their lives and problems. I completed the lost bag form. We had one hour to flight time. We raced to the shuttle bus. Off we went. At the domestic terminal, the sympathetic agent at the Air Canada connections desk was sweet but not optimistic about us connecting. "We will do our best, sir, but first you must collect your bag." We went to the transfer carousel. There was G's bag. And snuggled next to G's J.C. Penny Special was my well-worn Travel Pro. Magically, it had gotten there all on its own.

Showing remarkable initiative, the Air Canada agent recruited a copilot and stewardess as wheelchair pushers. Both were in superb condition, and off we raced to AC-585 Toronto-Denver. I was the shouter. "Out of the way please!" "Make way!" "Watch yourself, mister!" It was a fun time for all. We crossed the finish line and hit the gate at 5:15 P.M., with five minutes to spare.

POP-UPS, MEMORIES, AND RERUNS

WE BOARDED THE FLIGHT, went through the usual announcements, and collected ourselves after this unexpectedly exciting departure. We were no sooner in the air than scenes of Ireland began to pass through my mind, a bit like pop-ups in a children's book:

> G, to her amazement, stroking Willie Daly's cheek on his doorstep as he says to her, "You are a lovely woman."

> *Mano-a-mano* showdown at Dingle pass, grill-to-grill, car versus bus.

> In the garden at Diseart with Sister Dorothy Costello, her warmth and love and concern for all.

Another bench, this one next to the Kenmare River visiting with the Music Makers of Kenmare.

Tea at the nose of Sheep's Head.

Misty, romantic twilight walks—Kenmare Bay, Crookhaven, Lake Lien.

The Writers' Museum, Keane with a beer at his bar, MacMahon in his classroom, Kennelly on a footbridge, Fitzmaurice in his dingy Dublin bed-sit, Walsh, elegant in his Scottish writing shed.

Ireland's new wealth, the Celtic Tiger showing through in the crowd at the *Harp & Lion*.

Quin Abbey speaking to me through centuries past.

The "lads" in Fanore, Lispole, Castletownbere, and Quin classrooms.

As I revisit these and other Irish scenes, I realize the wonderful thing about memories of travel is that they last forever. And with G, together, we can savor the reruns.

And there on our arrival in Denver was our daughter Jennifer to greet us. There's no place like home.

PART II

ON BEING A TRAVELER

Last year I went around the world.
This year I think I'll go someplace else.
—Tourist A to Tourist B

THERE IS NO LACK of checklists detailing all the things one needs to do to prepare for a trip. (Example: *www.freetraveltips.com.*) Checklists of thirty-two or more categories range from "decide destination" to "unplug appliances." But a checklist is like a recipe. Even with a list of ingredients, one still needs a creative cook to make a tasty dish.

Creaky you may be, but remember, you have the advantage of years of experiences to draw on to plan a satisfying and manageable journey. As your own travel planner, you double your pleasure—daydreaming and anticipating (like a gardener planning next summer's blooms), and then the reality of your journey.

My goal is to help you become a "chef de journey," a master at defining for yourself the ingredients and the mix that add up to personally rewarding journeys. This will involve creating your own Traveler's Self-Profile (TSP) and a test, "How Creaky Am I?" But, first, let me offer some traveler's observations and words of wisdom. Eric Newby collected those beginning with Prince Herman Puckler-Nuskau in *A Book of Travelers Tales.*

OBSERVATIONS AND WISDOM OF WISE TRAVELERS

Rovetch. A tourist tastes. A traveler savors. Independent travelers find rewards in both the journey and the destination. Your imagination dances. You leave the familiar behind and bring a new self to the adventure.

Emerson. Though we travel the world over to find the beautiful, we must carry it with us or we find it not.

Calvin Trillin, 1989, Making Good Time. Many people travel as if someone was chasing them. . . . We concentrated on making time as if we were trying to beat a rival expedition to the Pole. . . . Our friend had driven non-stop northern Spain to Paris the way any red-blooded American boy would drive from northern Spain to Paris: he made good time.

Prince Herman Puckler-Muskau (1785–1871), Rules for a Young Traveler. In Rome be natural; in Austria don't talk politics; in France give yourself no airs; in Germany a great many; and in England don't spit.

W. B. Lord and Thomas Baines (1876), When Dying of Thirst in the Desert. In cases of extreme necessity, and when preservation of human life depends on obtainment of water, the supply found in the stomach of the camel should not be overlooked or forgotten. (The average per camel is about 15 pints.)

Frank Tatchell (1923), On Being Attacked. Should you be attacked by a mob in the East, hunt out one of the crowd and hurt him quickly. The others will gather chattering round the injured man and you will be able to slip away.

Royal Geographical Society (1854), On Reckoning Distances in Equatoria. In Equatoria it is almost impossible to find out how far it is to anywhere.

The answer is always in hours . . . The method is to look at your informant's legs: if they are long an hour means 4 miles; however short they are it is never less than two and a half.

John Hatt (1978), Travel Now. So pack your bags and go on your travels before it is too late. . . . And don't let the feeble excuse of work keep you back; remember the Haitian proverb: If work is such a good thing, how come the rich haven't grabbed it all for themselves?

TRAVELER'S SELF-PROFILE (TSP)

THE PLACES YOU want to put on your "hope to go to" travel list, the kinds of guest houses, hotels or B&Bs you want to stay in, the types of things you want to see and do, and experiences that will indulge your senses are among the questions you can begin to answer in your TSP. A genuine self-profile is based on the axiom "different strokes for different folks."

For example, when planning my trip to Ireland, had I been a devoted fly fisherman, my daydreams would have put me on a stream, landing the biggest brown trout ever. That evening at dinner, someone would have announced the size of this prize catch to the other envious fishermen staying at the inn. Or, if I were a hill walker or climber, I would see myself surveying a glorious vista from the heights of Sheep's Head trail. As it was, G and I were doing exactly what we had daydreamed about—quietly and casually inhaling the raw and penetrating natural beauty of southwest Ireland as we meandered about, listening to lots of good music, staying at small, comfortable, distinctive B&Bs, and leaving enough time for lovely and unexpected things to happen to us. If museums, concerts, swish hotels, and the club scene had been our thing, we would have traveled to Dublin.

So begin your own TSP now. Change it and add to it as you travel more. If you travel with a partner, merging interests and profiles becomes more complicated. You have a choice: think on it together, or one thinks for two. Profile questions I would ask myself are listed below. As you go along, add and answer your own questions. For some of the questions, before you answer, sit back, close your eyes, and picture yourself acting out your answer. If a warm glow comes on, you are in business. Also, as you go along, keep notes. When done, write your profile as if you were describing your TSP to someone else.

1. What was the best trip I ever took? What made it so good? What particular experiences on the "best trip" are especially memorable? On other trips? (Think of the things you tell other people when recalling a trip.) What experiences do I remember because they were less than satisfactory or just plain bad?

2. What are the most pleasurable scenes I can daydream myself into? An isolated beach at sunset? Good talk and good music in a lively pub? A real find in a dusty corner of an antique shop off the beaten track?

3. Am I afflicted with "traveler's remorse," anxiety from having missed something on my must-see or must-do list? If I am somewhere I really like, am I willing to stay with it and skip something else?

4. What are my physical limitations—driving, walking, climbing? How easily do I tire? If I overexert, am I out of action the next day? What time do I usually go to bed and get up? How deeply am I committed to this schedule?

5. What areas of interest turn me on—art, history, geology, geography, politics, botany/gardens, archeology, opera, wildlife, traditional music?

6. Given the choice, would I prefer an evening in a pub, eating pub food (much of it frozen and deep fried these days), and talking with locals, or would I prefer having an excellent five-course dinner at a superior restaurant? Or would I choose both?

7. Do I prefer hectic days with every minute planned, or am I comfortable leaving things open? Do I wait to see how I feel in the morning before deciding how to start that day, or do I forge ahead no matter what? What if it's raining hard?

8. Do I need social interaction? Do I like to share experiences and ideas with other people? Do I prefer to stay at a guesthouse or a small hotel where guests mingle? Have breakfast and dinner together? Am I a good party person, or am I at the other end of the string and happy to keep my own company?

9. How do I respond to physical environment? Does it make a real difference if my bedroom has good natural light and is well and cleanly furnished versus a little dark and on the dingy side? Is a view essential, or can I live without one? Do I insist on a bathroom with my room, or is one down the hall okay? Am I willing to spend time to search out somewhere special to stay, or am I more concerned with what I do during the day than where I lay my head at night?

10. How do I indulge my senses? A walk in a field of wildflowers, or losing my way in a maze of back streets in an ancient city? Or, either at different times, in different places? What really gets to me, deeply and memorably?

11. Do I crave adventure, or does safety come first? Do I feel easily threatened?

12. How much time can I devote to travel that takes me far from home? Is this once a year or more often?

13. How much can I afford to spend? Would I choose going for a longer time and staying in less-expensive places, renting a smaller car, or eating less-expensive meals? Or would I choose to live it up a bit for a shorter time?

Now, review your notes and write them up, and you'll have your personal TSP. Read it over next time you start thinking about a trip.

How Creaky Am I? A Test

AT THE END of a trip, you should not have to come home to recover. You may reach a limit on your capacity to absorb new experiences, but you should not arrive home creakier and more tired than when you left. When planning your journey and your destinations, be realistic on just how creaky you are and what you can manage. Here are some questions to ask yourself and blanks for you to enter your ratings on a one-to-five. One is best and equals not much or easy, and five is worst and equals lots or hard.

Creaky Test   Rate 1–5

1. How long can I be on my feet and walking around until I really need to sit down? 90 minutes = 1; 15 minutes = 5. _____
2. How many city blocks can I walk at a time?
   1 block = 5; 5 blocks = 1
   • With a cane _____
   • Without a cane _____
3. Can I tie my shoes bending over with my feet on the floor, or do I have to raise each foot on a curb or a chair to tie them? (If you wear only slip-ons to avoid tying laces, it's a 5). _____
4. Do I feel dizzy when I bend over or get up quickly? _____
5. When I climb or descend stairs, do I need to use a handrail? _____
6. How easy or hard is it for me to walk up/down a slope or small hill? _____
7. Can I lift a suitcase into the airplane luggage bin and get it down? _____
8. Can I put my pants (or skirt) on while standing up without having to hold onto something for support? _____
9. Do my joints and/or back ache? Never? Sometimes? Always? _____
                                                  TOTAL _____

If you scored 50, get back into bed. Otherwise, start planning your trip.

SIX BASIC PRINCIPLES OF TRAVEL

ONE WELL-KNOWN guidebook outlines two "Highlights of Ireland" circle tours. One for the east and south of Ireland, including Dublin, is five days and covers 996 miles. The other tour for the west and north of Ireland is six to seven days and covers 756 miles. Compare these circle tours with the thirty days G and I spent covering about three hundred miles, down and back in southwest Ireland. It is easy to see how in five days, covering 996 miles, even if you are making good time, one day merges into another, experiences lose identity, and there is little time to stop and inhale the wonder of a particular spot that catches your fancy.

I suggest these six principles for travelers.

Nourish your soul. Quiet times, periods of solitude in places of breath-taking beauty.

Feed your mind. Learning something of times past and present in places you visit.

Rest your body. Stay in comfortable quarters where calm and quiet are assured. Nap when the body calls.

Leave time for happenings. It is often the case that the unexpected is the most memorable. Follow Shakespeare's advice: "Keep all in readiness." When chance presents an opportunity, grab it.

Cut your losses. Move on when something is not working out. In Dingle, the weather was bad, the B&B was a disappointment, and the tourist mass was crushing. We left a day early and added one to Kenmare.

Less is more. In-depth experience is more rewarding than surface skimming. It's like true love versus a bunch of quick flings.

CHOOSING PLACES AT WHICH TO STOP AND STAY

HAVING DECIDED ON the southwest of Ireland because of its variety and natural beauty, we found that the pattern of our journey fell into place fairly easily. Co Clare and the Burren because the limestone terraces were unique and were a geological feature we had never seen before. I also wanted to investigate a matchmaking tradition in Co Clare and the victory of plain people to preserve the environment. Then the four peninsulas, going south, one after the other in Co Kerry and West Cork—Dingle, Beara, Sheep's Head, and Mizen— offered a certain logic. Kenmare was a place in between. Headed back north, Listowel made for an "urban" contrast with a literary tradition, horse racing, and other activity. The loop back was to end in Co Clare in a quiet place near the Shannon airport.

We are always looking for more than a bed because where we stay is an essential part of our whole experience. We look for several things—distinctive character, personality of the proprietor, reputation for a good breakfast, a nice view from the dining room and bedroom (for example, the view of Castletownbere Harbor out the bedroom bay window), location in relation to things we want to see and do, number of rooms (small places please), and of course, price. So choosing where we stay becomes a big part of our planning effort. Our scorecard on this trip was pretty good. Six of eight choices were excellent, one of these by chance. Two choices were mistakes.

First, I assembled my working tools. I started with a map of Ireland at a scale of one inch to seven miles. Later, when we knew more clearly the territory we were going to cover, I got Ordnance Survey of Ireland maps at a scale of one and a quarter inch to one mile. These show all back roads and detail, down to lighthouses and picnic tables. I got other publications covering B&Bs, guesthouses, and hotels that included details on the number of rooms with and without bathrooms, special features, prices, credit cards accepted, photos, and promo copy. Add to these a couple of guidebooks that offered frank opinions on places to stay. Of increasing importance is familiarity with websites that relate to areas of interest, villages, and places to stay.

With working tools in hand, it was "mess around time." I went back and forth between the most scenic, least traveled areas and wrote a preliminary month-long itinerary with lists of four or five of the most desirable-sounding places to stay at each potential stop. I then faxed or e-mailed a letter to each potential choice asking about availability for specific dates and rates (which can vary up and down from published information). I also requested a brochure and other material about their area. I find it useful to read what people say about their place and how they present themselves. Based on what I receive or what is available on websites, I make preliminary choices. Then I phone the proprietor at each place with questions about the weather at the time of year we will be there, what their rooms are like, if the rooms get a lot of natural daylight (very important to G), and so on.

If the proprietor doesn't sound particularly warm and welcoming, or something else is out of whack, I move on to the next choice. By the time we make a reservation, we have not only chosen the place we will stay and frequently the room we will have, but we also have some idea of the personality of the proprietor. We agree with Sherlock Holmes who says in *A Case of Identity*, "It has been an axiom of mine that the little things are infinitely the most important."

Having dealt with the essentials, I can then settle down to serious daydreaming and finding out more about the territory we plan to travel—unique sights, restaurants, pubs with traditional music sessions, a bit of history, and anything special that will be happening when we're there.

Here is my B&B box score.

Fanore, Rockyview Farmhouse, the Burren. Excellent. Great beginning for the journey. Warm, friendly, helpful proprietor. Comfortable room, pleasant breakfast conservatory, good food. Good Burren location.

Lispole, the Old Farmhouse, Dingle Peninsula. Mistake. Used single source (Sawday) and bought exciting sounding proprietor bio. Reality— minimal accommodations, cool treatment, unexciting breakfast, little view. Left a day early.

Kenmare, Sallyport House. Pure luxury. Good views, breakfast conservatory looking to garden and bay, good food with good choice, efficient proprietor, lovely nearby walks.

Castletownbere, The Old Presbytery, Beara Peninsula. Excellent. Sensational harbor view from comfortable room, pleasant conservatory breakfast room, good food, helpful, overworked proprietor who is also a nurse.

Schull, Grove House, Mizen Head Peninsula. Mistake. Fell in love with notion of staying where George Bernard Shaw slept and wrote. Ignored warning signs of not especially warm or accommodating proprietor. Room good, food okay. Since our stay, the management has changed.

Killarney, Carriglea House, Co Kerry. Excellent. Choice by chance. Great view across garden to lake from comfortable room. Friendly family management, okay food, great walks nearby.

Listowel, Allo's Bar, Bistro & Townhouse, Co Kerry. Excellent, Unique. Accommodating, thoughtful, responsive. Comfortable, well-furnished room, castle-sized bathroom, chef-quality food, perfect location for town activity.

Quin, Ardsollus Farm, Co Clare. Excellent. Warm, friendly, helpful in every regard. Well-furnished, modern room. Enough smoked salmon at breakfast to open a deli. Perfect place near Shannon airport to begin or end a trip.

CREATING A TRIP JOURNAL

I FIND A TRIP JOURNAL to be a necessary tool. Mine, kept in a spiral notebook, includes all essential travel details—reservation locator number (the code airlines use to track reservations), flight numbers, seat numbers, departure and arrival times, and airline telephone numbers in the U.S. and overseas. I note the same range of information for the car rental and take the e-mailed reservation confirmation that includes dates, requested car model, and rates. Then I have a separate page for each place we will stop—dates, addresses, proprietor names, telephone and fax numbers, e-mail addresses. I also include what we might want to see or do in the area—visiting waterfalls, lighthouses, or pubs with Celtic music sessions, special views, and so on. Essential correspondence, reservation confirmations, and "take with" material are in a few separate files.

REMEMBER THE FUNDAMENTALS

Here are a few of the basics every creaky traveler should remember.

- Most of all *ask, ask, ask* and *tell, tell, tell.* Let people know of any special needs you have. Airlines in particular say their greatest problem is people reticent about telling them of special needs in advance because they don't want to make a fuss. I am always astounded at the number of people who won't ask to have their table changed in a restaurant if they have been seated at a terrible one. Declan Halpin, the excellent British Airways station manager in Denver, told me about older and other people collapsing on the long walk from their planes to customs, simply because they didn't want to be a bother and ask for a wheelchair, and how much easier it is for an airline to provide a wheelchair than emergency medical services.

- If you don't have a cane, get one. It will help you walk and will encourage other people to be considerate of your needs. Folding canes fit in a tote bag.

- Always request a wheelchair to and from planes. Make this request at the time you make your reservation, repeat it at check-in, and mention it again to a steward or stewardess on the flight. You do not have to be disabled to have a wheelchair, only needful. Airport walking distances can be incredible at any time, particularly at the end of an international flight when going from arrival gate to customs and baggage collection.

- Choose an airplane seat that meets your needs—an aisle seat if you drink as much water as you should and use the lavatory more often than younger folk. Buying tickets earlier will give you a better shot at good seats. Some airlines hold the most forward seats for wheelchair passengers.

- Always check to make sure your hotel room is on a floor you can manage if there isn't an elevator. Remember, in Europe the floor count starts with ground floor and then one, two, three, et cetera. So the European third floor is the American fourth floor.

- Don't hesitate to reconfirm airline, B&B, and other reservations.

- Take a miracle spot remover with you.

- Nikes or Reeboks are tourist giveaways. If you really want to make sure locals can spot you, add a water bottle, baseball cap, and sunglasses.

- Almost everything will cost more than you planned.

- Leave time each day for the unexpected.

- If you read in bed, the first thing to do when you get to your room is to check to see if there is a bedside lamp and if the light bulb wattage is adequate. No lamp, ask for one. Low wattage, ask for a better bulb. When making your reservation, mention you are a bed reader, though more often than not this is forgotten.

- Walking somewhere may be easy, but getting back can be a trial. Plan ahead. For museums, find out if there is a coffee shop where you can take a break. In Venice, I always chose restaurants for dinner that were near Vaporetto (water bus) stops. Strolling to dinner was always lovely, but after dinner we wanted an easy way home.

- Take it really slow the first few days after moving through five or more time zones. There are a zillion "how to help your body make the change" plans. The essential of any of them is to ease into your trip. Don't do much the first day especially. I am also a believer in sleeping pills to help sleep at least a few hours on the brief overnight flight to Europe and to get to sleep the first few nights after you arrive. At first, 11:00 P.M. is still 4:00 P.M. for your body. Check with your doctor. There are sleeping pills that don't leave a hangover.

- Pub etiquette: (1) Sit at the bar and join the locals in their *craic* (banter). You will be ignored if you sit at a table. (2) Expect to be *slaged* (teased). Give it back. (3) Never say "B'Gorra."

- "*Asolare*," an Italian term meaning doing next to nothing and enjoying it, is an essential rule of travel—an afternoon with a book in a café, lolling by a stream tossing sticks in the water to see where they drift.

AUTO RENTAL ESSENTIALS

IN IRELAND, you will drive on the wrong side of the road, many roads will be remarkably narrow and something of a challenge, and short distances will more often than not seem much longer. So it is best that you rent a car you can manage reasonably well.

Criteria for size. Choose a car large and heavy enough to limit road noise and vibration, and reduce your sense of vulnerability when trucks and cars head toward you down narrow lanes. Small enough so those trucks ands cars can squeeze by you, and a boxy body design for ease of getting in and out of without bumping your head. Look for an erect driver's seat set that's high enough to ensure good road vision. I found the Ford Focus best met my criteria. Different rental companies have their own classifications. The same model can show up as economy, compact, or standard. Avoid station wagons if you can. They don't have trunk that hide luggage, and their longer wheelbase makes parking and turning around on narrow roads much harder.

Automatic transmission vs. stick shift. Automatics rent for about forty percent more than stick shifts and are less fuel efficient, a factor to consider at seven dollars a gallon for gas. With a five-speed stick shift and a right hand drive, your left shoulder will get a workout that it is not used to.

Rental rates vary significantly from company to company, so check everyone's rate for the same model. Also, even after you have made your reservation, check rates from time to time. They do change. Remember, AAA, AARP, and other discounts apply.

Color and music. You are going to look at your car frequently, so you may as well try for a color you like. Stay away from white if you can. It is the hardest color for oncoming cars to see at dusk. Ask for the color you want when you make your reservation and again at check-in. For self-preservation, always drive with your headlights on. With a tape or CD deck, you can listen to the music of the country as you travel through it.

Collision loss damage insurance. U.S. insurance coverage does not ordinarily extend to overseas rental. Some credit cards provide loss damage coverage on rentals charged to that card. Such coverage varies. Number of days may be limited. Countries may be excluded. For example, American Express coverage does not extend to car rentals in

Ireland, Italy, or Israel. Collision loss damage coverage as part of a Hertz rental in Ireland will add ten to fifteen percent to a monthly charge. Loss damage coverage included in a travel insurance policy will cost around $9.00 per day.

Age restrictions. In Ireland, Hertz will rent to drivers up to age seventy-five and from seventy-six to seventy-nine with a letter from a doctor attesting to good health plus a clean driving record. Limits for Avis and Alamo are age seventy-four, with no possible extension for any reason.

CELL PHONES AND PHONE CARDS

GIVEN THE ADDICTION many people have to their cell phones, the question may not be, do you need one traveling in Ireland, but can you live without one?

Most U.S. cell phones will not work in Ireland or elsewhere in Europe. Cell phones operate on different standards and frequencies, much like AM and FM with radios. Most U.S. cell phones operate on code division multiple access (CDMA), and most of Europe and the rest of the world (more than two hundred countries) are on global system for mobile communication (GSM). You can rent a cell phone for use in Ireland for around thirty dollars a week and charges for local calls of around $.90 a minute and $1.39 to the U.S. (Example: *www.travelcell.com.*) Incoming calls are free.

Or, you can buy a GSM phone for $100 on up. (Example: *www.telestial.com.*) With the GSM phone, you purchase a SIM card at newsstands. A SIM card is a thumbnail-sized device that you pop into the phone and that gives you a phone number and local calling rates. The phone needs to be "unlocked," meaning it will accept a variety of SIM cards and can be used in any country operating on GSM.

The cheapest way to make calls within Ireland or to the U.S. or elsewhere from Ireland is to purchase a prepaid phone card. You can buy these in advance or once you get there. Ask Google.

Before Your Trip: Home, Health, Credit Cards, and Other

Home. These are largely matters of security. (1) Complete post office form number 8076, "Authorization to Hold Mail," telling the post office to hold your mail beginning on a specific date. (2) Schedule stop and restart dates for newspaper delivery. (3) If you will be away during the growing season, enlist someone to cut your lawn and water flowers to keep up appearances. (4) Set up an automatic on/off system for lights and radio. (5) Let neighbors and police know you will be away and if someone will be house sitting or stopping by to check your house periodically. (6) The day you leave, disconnect all small appliances and set the thermostat at fifty-five to sixty degrees. (5) Give a house key to a friend or neighbor for emergencies, which could include you losing your key.

Documents, records, and cameras. (1) If you don't have a passport, apply for one. If you do have one, check for the expiration date. Issuance of a new passport can take up to twelve weeks (ordinarily less time, though) and can be done at most larger post offices. You can have your passport picture taken at some post offices. (2) Make sure your credit cards won't expire while you are on your trip. Credit card companies will advance renewal dates if needed. Also advise credit card companies of your trip so they don't suspect identity theft and block card use. (3) Photocopy your passport cover page, driver's license, and credit cards in case of loss or theft. Make a note of credit card company phone number(s) in case of card loss. Also record your flight schedule, flight numbers, and itinerary and related phone numbers along the way. Give a copy of all this information to a friend or relative and take a copy with you. (4) Cameras. Check batteries. Get film or cards for digital cameras. Battery chargers require outlet converters.

Credit cards, currency, and insurance. Make sure you know your credit card and debit card PIN (personal information number) for ATM use. Also, if you don't have a debit card, get one. Debit cards make more sense than credit cards for ATM cash withdrawals. If you use a credit card for ATM cash, high interest rate charges begin from the date of withdrawal. With debit cards, you pay only a transaction fee. The best plan is to obtain the equivalent of a hundred dollars or so in the currency of the country that will be your first stop. Most large banks in the U.S. can provide foreign currency. The rates won't be that good, but the convenience is worth it. Then use ATM machines or banks that honor credit cards when you get overseas. There will be a transaction charge for each withdrawal. Never use hotels or exchange bureaus. They always have poorer exchange rates.

Credit cards are fine to use for hotel bills, restaurants, and other purchases. These charges show up in the normal way on your next credit card statement. Keep receipts and always check for overcharges. Also, before traveling, check on credit card transaction fees for conversion of charges in foreign currency to dollars. Fees may vary from card to card. At last report, American Express was two percent, and Visa and MasterCard were three percent. The reason credit and debit cards make sense is that in using them, your purchases are bundled with those of thousands of other people and converted to dollars at the wholesale million-dollar rate. In the simplest terms, MasterCard can buy dollars cheaper than you can. Check out all possible benefits. For example, some cards have "global assist," which can include medical evacuation.

Health. (1) If you have a medical condition or are on long-term medication, check with your doctor to see if you need to take any precautions while flying or traveling. Advise the airline when making your reservation if there is anything they need to know about your condition. For example, asthma or emphysema might require oxygen in flight.

(2) Check with your doctor about medication, including, if you think you need either, sleeping pills or anti-inflammatory pills. Certain destinations may require vaccinations. Also, obtain a prescription or note saying you need your cane with you for medical reasons, just in case airport security classifies canes as a weapon. I checked with airport security in advance and was told we would need cane "prescriptions." We got them and have never been asked for them. But you never know.

(3) Get copies of all prescriptions by generic name to take with you in case you lose your medication and need prescriptions refilled overseas. In some countries, it may be simpler to have a new supply shipped to you in one or two days via UPS or FedEx.

(4) Keep medication in the original containers pharmacists supply—a caution because of concerns over illegal drugs.

(5) If you wear glasses or contacts, make sure you have an extra pair/set.

(6) On your flight, use saline nasal spray to keep mucous membrane moist and in germ-fighting form. Use antibacterial wipes on your hands to keep them germ-free. There is a whole array of new products that promise to keep you healthy on flights—carry-on filters, personal seat covers, personal air purifier, pure-ion travel pillow. Bottom line: like your mother said, wash your hands.

Travel insurance. Some companies issue single travel policies that cover nearly everything—trip cancellation, lost or late luggage, travel accidents, travel medical problems, and medical evacuation. And then there are policies for any one of these items. (Examples: *www.accessamerica.com* and *www.travelguard.com.*) Buying travel insurance is a personal decision. I don't ordinarily buy coverage, but others would never think of going without it. Many Medigap and other health insurance policies will pay for overseas medical costs. Just keep your receipts. Also, Great Britain and some other countries with national health services provide emergency services without charge.

Security and money. This is really a question of where you will be traveling. With ATMs nearly everywhere, there is no need to carry a lot of money with you at any time. Traveler's checks are almost a thing of the past. The items you need to protect are your passport, which you don't need to carry with you at all times, and credit cards that you probably will have with you all the time. I once had a pair of "travel trousers" with hidden pockets and zipper pockets, but they were more trouble than they were worth. There are a few basic rules to follow. Men, keep your wallets thin and carry them in side pockets, never in hip pockets. I keep a small, thin "wallet" for credit cards and my driver's license in one side pocket and my cash in a money clip in the other side pocket. Women, do not hang handbags at your hips. Thieves can easily grab them. Do not wear gold neck chains. If someone spills mustard on you, apologizes, and starts to help clean it off, stop that person. It's an old pickpocket ploy. He helps you, an accomplice picks you, and the third member of the team stands by for the hand-off. So, be wary but not paranoid in airports and other crowded places. And never hang a camera or a handbag over the back of your chair in a café or put anything under your chair.

Toting books. All books get heavier and heavier as a trip goes on. If I have travel information I want to take along that goes beyond what I have noted in my trip journal, I copy the few pages that interest me. If I want a whole chapter, I will tear it out of the book and staple it together. Book lovers may see this as uncaring. Knowing travelers see it as a necessity. As to general reading, G and I agree on two paperbacks each and trade when we finish. We tend to read less than we think we will because there is so much else to do. Many guesthouses and B&Bs have large collections of paperbacks that previous guests have left and are happy to have you trade a book in their collection for one of yours.

Suitcases and Packing Options— Fold or Roll?

No matter what I say, you will take too much. I take too much, G takes too much. Try as we might, using carry-on sized cases for a month of travel, we come home saying the same thing. We took too much. For what it's worth, here is advice from a packer with a qualified track record.

- Travel with a maximum of one roll-aboard (carry-on with wheels), even if you plan to check the bag, plus one carry-on tote bag. My tote bag is a small backpack with wheels. G's is a small tote that she can hook onto her suitcase. All roll-aboards should have a hook or other means of attaching the tote bag. There will be times when you are on your own and have to get your case from here to there. Curb to check-in counter, car to guest house, and so on. Stay away from expensive suitcases. They identify you as a worthy target for thieves, and you will be pained if the expensive suitcase gets damaged. I have a Travel Pro case with a lifetime guarantee that I bought ten years earlier. The guarantee actually came in handy when the handle broke last year. I could replace the case today for under seventy dollars. I think G paid thirty-nine dollars for her J.C. Penny case many years before. Be sure to tie colorful yarn or another easy to recognize identifier on your suitcase handle. Many suitcases look alike. Your personal identifier will help you spot your bag coming at you on the baggage conveyor and prevent someone else from mistaking yours for theirs. For "just in case," put your name, home address, and the address and telephone number of where you will be the first night inside your suitcase.

- In the tote bag, pack all of your medication and eye supplies; reading material (you may not like what the plane has); a sweater, in case the plane gets too cool at night; a small, refillable water bottle (some airlines distribute bottled water, others don't); moisturizer, because airplane air dries you out; and, if you plan to check your bag and are a worrier, a change of underwear and socks in case your checked bag is delayed or lost.

- These are the guidelines for what to take. (1) Clothes: layers for climate variation, colors that don't show dirt and are also coordinated for mixing and matching, wash and wear material that dries reasonably quickly. In humid Great Britain, a wash and wear oxford cloth shirt is unlikely to dry overnight, while a broadcloth shirt has a reasonable chance of doing so. The safety-first washing rules are to wash your clothes on the first night of a two-night stay in case they need extra drying time. Take extra plastic bags for packing wet and dirty clothes. Europeans believe Americans are obsessive about cleanliness, and we probably are. As a traveler, try wearing clothes a little longer than you would at home. Also, most of the world has gone casual, not sloppy, such as sweaters where only a jacket used to do. Take posh only if you plan to stay posh where, for example, the correct thing is to dress for dinner. Even then, for men posh can mean a sport jacket but no tie. (2) Comfortable walking shoes or boots. (3) Put all creams and liquids in plastic containers and the containers in plastic bags for double protection against spills. (4) Bring a basic kit—compact umbrella, travel alarm, sewing kit, spot remover, small flashlight, wash cloth in a plastic bag (many places don't provide washcloths), sunscreen (for the hopeful), vitamins, soap, small packages of Kleenex, and a first aid kit with band-aids, antiseptic cream, aspirin, diarrhea tablets, a few prunes, and extra plastic bags for who knows what. (5) Pack or carry a raincoat or rain jacket.

- And then there is the old "how to pack" argument between the "folders" and the "rollers." Take your choice. Rollers argue that when you roll up shirts, jeans, et cetera, you get more in and no creasing. Folders argue that with reasonable care and underwear or plastic bags in folds, everything comes out neatly. Also, folded clothes make it easier to see what you have and to live out of your suitcase. Whether you roll, fold, or do some of both, remember there is room in your shoes and corners of your suitcase. Arrange clothes so your case is full and things won't jumble when baggage handlers start throwing your case around. G and I are folders, and we unpack as little as possible. When we check in, we ask for suitcase stands or put our cases on top of chests of drawers. One very important reminder: pack no later than the day before you leave home on a trip, or else at the last minute you will start throwing things in for fear of forgetting something.

CHOOSING FLIGHTS AND SEATS

I have been reading *John Adams* by David McCullough and marveling at Adams's month-long crossing of the Atlantic in a sailing ship in the late 1700s as he went to take up a European post. What a sense of time and distance thirty days at sea must have offered. I was reminded of my own journeys to England between 1946 and the early fifties on the SS *Brazil*, the *Mauritania*, and the *Queen Mary* that lasted from eight to fourteen days. You knew you were going somewhere, and your mind and body were able to make an accommodating transition during these days at sea. Today, you and two or three hundred other closely packed souls hurtle through the air and land jetlagged at an airport that differs only in some small degree from the one you left eight hours or so before. No wonder you need to take pains to make this part of your travel experience manageable, especially if, like most people, you are traveling coach. So here are a few considerations and suggestions. The serious traveler—creaky and other—looks for a balance between cost, airline, schedule, and seating.

Schedule. There are daytime flights to Europe from several East Coast cities. If you can manage any of these flights, great. The flight is seven hours, with a five-hour change in time. You leave around 9:00 A.M., get in around 9:00 P.M., have a light bite, stroll around a bit, and go off to bed. Your flight is more likely to be overnight. Suggestions: (1) Maximize air time/sleep time. If you leave for Europe from an East Coast airport, you have no choice. With a flight of seven hours, between dinner and breakfast you will be lucky to have three hours for a nap. If you fly nonstop from the West Coast, you have ten to eleven hours in the air, allowing for a reasonable amount of time for sleep. The trick is to choose a flight or get routed for maximum sleep time. For example, from Denver to London or Frankfurt, you have choices—United with a Chicago or Washington change of plane or British Airways and Lufthansa nonstop with about nine hours in the air. (2) Leave late. If you fly into London, Paris, or anywhere else in the early morning and are staying in the city that day, you may well have a problem getting into your hotel room until hours later. I can remember once sitting around in the lobby of the Basil Street Hotel in London for five hours waiting for a room. So, leaving for your ocean hop as late as possible in the evening and getting in later in the morning is a good idea.

Seats. Coach seats are no joy in the best of situations, so try to make the best of it with the right seat on the right plane.

1. *Improving your odds.* Different airlines configure seats on the same type of aircraft in different ways. For example, on Boeing 777s, both United Airlines and British Airways seat nine across, but United does it 2-5-2—two seats at one window, five in the middle, and two at the other window—while British Airways planes does 3-3-3. Lufthansa flies the Airbus 340 Denver to Frankfurt with 2-4-2 seating. Sitting on the aisle of a two-seat row is my choice. G goes for the window. Ticket early for the best choice of seats. Check which day of the week the flight you want has the lightest loads, because even with three across, the middle seat could be empty. For aircraft seating configurations, see *www.seatguru.com*.

2. *Aisle or window?* If you want the freedom to get up and move around the plane or go to the john any time, without disturbing anyone, go for an aisle seat. But remember, other people have to crawl over you, or you have to get up to let them out. At the window, you have the pleasure of a view and no one crawls over you, but you have to ask whenever you want out. One other advantage

of a window seat is that when the stewardess asks for shades down to convert the airplane into a movie theatre, you don't have to. But, if you can't bear to disturb other people, do not sit at the window.

FLYING HEALTHY: BEFORE, DURING, AFTER

HERE IS WHERE you have to take control to survive the assault of flying on mind and body. You face three problems. First, the airplane is not a healthy environment. It is at best surface-clean, and at least a few passengers will be passing around the odd germ. Second, even if the correct proportion of fresh air is brought in and circulated (instead of stale air being recirculated, which uses less fuel), air is still dry and a cause of dehydration. Your third problem is circadian dyschronism, more commonly known as "jet leg." Somehow, most of us survive all these problems and go on to have a good time. Here are a few suggestions to help boost your odds for flying healthy.

Before Your Flight. (1) Get a good night's sleep to ready for the battle. (2) Make sure your tote bag has what you need—all your medication, moisturizer, antibacterial wipes, eyeshade, ear plugs, water bottle, a sweater if the plane gets chilly, and reading material or puzzles to help your mind move toward sleep. Some airlines like British Airways provide coach passengers with a kit containing an eyeshade, booties, a toothbrush, and toothpaste. Others, like United, do not provide a kit, so check. (3) Eat lightly the evening before and day of your flight. (4) Wear loose-fitting, comfortable clothing. (5) Get to the airport early and don't carry any heavy bags.

On your flight. When you check in, make sure any special requests have been noted in your computer record—wheelchair at all take off and arrival points, special meals if you have ordered them, and the seats that you reserved. Seat assignments have a strange way of changing on occasion. On the flight, follow these healthy flying rules:

- Figure out how your seat and footrest work. As a technology-disadvantaged person, I find seat mechanics a challenge. Make sure you can keep your legs elevated, because even a little elevation is important to circulation. Ensure that you have a pillow and a blanket.

- Take your shoes off, or at a minimum loosen the laces. It is a fact that low pressure and high altitude will cause your feet to swell during the flight. Give your feet lots of room.

- Drink moderate amounts of alcohol or drinks with caffeine, or better yet, none at all. Do drink lots of water. The recommended dosage is one eight-ounce glass for every hour of flight. This is to compensate for dehydration the dry air causes.

- Do simple exercises with your shoulder, back, arms, legs, ankles, and buttocks in your seat, tensing each muscle in turn and holding for five seconds. Move your feet a lot. Don't cross your legs for long or keep your hands clasped behind your head. Both limit circulation. More importantly, get out of your seat and walk up and down the aisle. You get to look at the amazing array of passengers, get a little exercise, and most importantly, move your blood around to limit any chance of deep vein thrombosis (DVT), sometimes called "economy class syndrome."

- Women, don't wear makeup other than lipstick, because makeup will contribute to drying out your skin. Do use moisturizer during and at the end of the flight. Men, you too.

- When the feeling hits you, don't hesitate to nap. More importantly, sleep at least a few hours in the night. If your doctor approves, use sleeping pills. Some people swear by melatonin, which is available without a prescription. It is still worth a check with your doctor because of potential interaction with medication you may be taking.

- If you have requested a wheelchair at the end of the flight, mention this to cabin staff. They will make sure it is at the plane door for you. If you have an hour or more for connections, most airlines have what they call a "serenity room" for wheelchair passengers. You can be dropped off and picked up again before your flight. Don't hesitate to use it. Try to remember that the airlines are happy for you not to become a problem.

- When landing, to keep your ears from blocking, use the diver's nose hold. Hold your nose and blow. This works best if you do it every five minutes or so starting about half an hour before landing.

After your flight. I am always surprised at the number of people who come home sick after traveling. They usually have a cold or some stomach complaint. These people have not listened to their bodies. Problems begin with trying to ignore jet lag, the symptoms of which include decreased concentration, irritability, and aching joints. The excitement and adrenal rush of starting a trip in a new place can blur the problem but not eliminate it. Many businesses and government agencies have rules against their people doing any business the first day after a trip that involves three or more hours of time change.

Your first day. For the sake of your whole journey, ease into the beginning. Some younger folk manage to get off the plane and through the day, eating and sleeping on the local time. If G and I are staying in the city in which we have landed, we try to nap for an hour or so before setting out. Then it's a stroll for mild exercise and exposure to daylight to give our circadian rhythm a signal to start adjusting to a new reality. At bedtime, try a warm shower, sleeping pill (we know someone who uses Nyquil), and an unexciting read, and you will be gone. With luck, the next thing you'll hear is a call to breakfast.

But please, move into high gear over a couple of days (although G and I seldom get beyond second gear), and never, never drive very far the first day you have landed.

Bon voyage, travelers!

APPENDIX I

PLACES, SITES, AND SOURCES

PLACES WE STAYED AND PEOPLE TO CONTACT

Ita and Noel Walsh
Rockyview Farmhouse
Coast Road, Fanore
Ballyvaghan, Co Clare
353-65-707-6103
www.rockyviewfarmhouse.com
info@rockyviewfarmhouse.com

Marie Beazley and Family
Carriglea House
Muckross Road (N71)
Killarney, Co Kerry
353-64-31116
www.carrigleahouse.com
carriglea@oceanfree.net

Janie and John Arthur
Sallyport House
Kenmare, Co Kerry
353-64-42066
www.sallyporthouse.com
port@iol.ie

Mary and David Wrigley
The Old Presbytery
Brandy Hall House
Castletownbere, Co Cork
353-27-70424
marywrigley@tinet.ie

Jill Sanderson
The Old Farmhouse
Minard West
Lispole, Co Kerry
353-66-915-7346

Allo's Bar, Bistro & Townhouse
41 Church Street
Listowel, Co Kerry
353-68-22880

Loreto and Pat Hannon
Ardsollus Farm
Quin, Co Clare
353-65-682-5601
www.ardsollusfarm.com
ardsollusfarm@ireland.com

WEBSITES

INTERNET SOURCES are growing exponentially. I recommend messing around. Often, one thing leads to another. So ask Google or Jeeves or Yahoo, and you might just strike a rich source of information. I have listed a few of the sites related to the places we traveled. You may find them of interest.

Ireland

www.ireland.ie
www.lookintoireland.com
www.irelandforvisitors.com

Co Clare and the Burren

www.tourclare.com
www.shannonregiontourism.ie
www.tireolas.com/links.htm
www.burrenpage.com (see links)
www.burrenarch.com (archeology)
www.burrenwalks.com

Dingle Peninsula

www.dingle-peninsula.ie
www.dingle-peninsula.ie/history.html
www.iol.ie
www.diseart.ie (Diseart Institute of Education and Celtic Culture)

Kenmare and Killarney National Park

www.kenmare.com
www.killarneyonline.com/killarney-np.html
www.killarney-insight.com/np.html

Beara Peninsula

www.bearatourism.com
www.bearainfo.com

www.cork-guide.ie/beara (Castletownbere)
www.anamcararetreat.com

Mizen Peninsula

www.mizenhead.net/goolen.html
www.crookhaven.ie
www.schull.ie
www.cork-guide.ie/mizen.htm

Sheep's Head Peninsula

www.cork-guide.ie/sheepshead
www.bantry.ie/bvg/bvg_roaddrives.htm
www.geocities.com/middleian/beara.html

Listowel

www.listowel.ie
www.heritagetowns.com/listowel.html
www.kerryguide.com/listowel

Quin

www.12travel.ie/ie/shannon/index.html

Hard Copy Sources and Guidebooks

Irish Tourist Board
345 Park Avenue
New York, N.Y 10154
1-800-223-6470

Ordnance Survey Maps

Phoenix Park
Dublin 8, Ireland
353-1-802-5300
www.osi.ie
mapsales@osi.ie

GUIDEBOOKS WITH USEFUL MATERIAL AND GOOD WRITING

The Rough Guide to Ireland
Insight Guide: Ireland
Passport Books: Ireland—The Emerald Isle and Its People
Cadogan Guides: Southwest Ireland

IRISH GAELIC PRONUNCIATION

THE IRISH LANGUAGE is not designed for use with the Latin alphabet. It is a code system imposed upon an essentially oral language. But with just a little attention to pronunciation, you can unlock the sounds of the Middle Ages if not those of the Bronze Age. There are three dialects in Irish: Ulster, Munster, and Conaught.

VOWELS

A, E, I, O, U may be short or long.

Short

- a-cat (cat) like the letter O in the English "cot, "lot"
- e-abhaile (home) like the letter E in the English "met," "let"
- i-litir (letter) like the letter I in the English "fit," "sit"
- o-gol (crying) like the letter U in the English smut. smug u = dul (going), like the letter U in the English "pull"

Long

- a-cá (where?) like the letter A in the English "call"

- e-cé (who?) like the letter A in the English "came, "same"
- i-cailín (girl) like the letters EE in the English "see"
- o-ól (drinking) as the letter O in the English "so"
- u = úilll (apple) as the letters OO in the English "too"

Vowels may be broad = a-o-u = á ó ú, or slender = e-i or é-í

CONSONANTS

THERE ARE THIRTEEN consonants in Gaelic: B, C, D, F, G, H, L, M, N, P, R, S, and T.

They may be either broad or slender.

- Consonants are broad (have a velar quality) when a broad vowel (A, O, U) precedes or follows them.
- Consonants are slender (with a palatal quality) when a slender vowel (E, I) follows them.

  bo = cow is broad B, like in the English "big"

  beo = alive is slender b as in beau, like in the English "beautiful"

1. If a consonant AE, AO, or UI follow a consonant, insert a fleeting W sound, like in the French word *bois*:
   - buidèal - bottle or Gael - Irishman

2. When each, eag, eann, eat, eo, or iu, follows a consonant, insert a fleeting Y sound, like the English "beautiful" as in
   - beo - alive or ceol - music.

ASPIRATION

SOMETIMES CONSONANTS are aspirated. That is, they suffer an alteration of sound indicated by adding the letter H after the aspirated letter.

Aspirable consonants are: B, C, D, F, G, M, P, S, and T.

- B - bh (slender) = v as in an bhean - the woman
  bh (broad) = w as in sa bhád - in the boat
- C - ch (slender) = k as in sa chistin - in the kitchen
  ch (broad) = ca as in sa charr - in the car
- D - dh (slender) = Y as in ni dherna me - I didn't do
  dh (broad) = wah as in a dhaidi
- f - fh (slender) as in don fhear - to the man
- g - gh (slender) = Y as in an ghealach - (the moon)
- m - mh (slender) as in ca mhéad = (how much)
  mh (broad) "W" mo mahc (my son)
- P - ph "F" mo phíopa (my pi pe)
- S - sh (slender) "H+Y" shiúil mé (I walked)
  sh (broad) "H" mo shac (my sack)
- T - th "H" thuas (up)

Note: bh and mh, as well as dh and gh, have the same sound when aspirated.

ECLIPSIS

ANOTHER CHANGE THAT may occur is eclipsis. When eclipsis occurs, it results in the suppression of certain consonants by other consonants that are written in front of the eclipsed consonant.

- B becomes *mb* and is pronounced M like in *i mbád* ("in a boat")
- C becomes *gc* and is pronounced G like *i gcarr* ("in a car")
- D becomes *nd* and is pronounced N like *i ndán* ("in a poem")
- F becomes *bhf* and is pronounced V like *i bhféar* ("in grass")
- W as in *an bhfuil me* ("am I")
- G becomes *ng* and is pronounced G like *i ngrá* ("in love")
- P becomes *bp* and is pronounced B like *bpl ata* ("their plate")
- T becomes *dt* and is pronounced D like *dtram* ("in a tram")

Appendix III

Pronunciation of the Irish Words in the Text

Chapter 1

Burren	Burr-in
Lispole	Lis-pole
Mizen	Miz-in
Minard	Men-ard
Mullaghmore	Mull-ak-more
Gaeltacht	Gale-tact
Diseart	Dye-shirt
Allihies	All-e-his
Beara	Bare-a
Anam Cara	Ann-am Car-a
Schull	Skull
Listowel	Lios-toe-el
Kilorohane	Kill-o-row-han
Dunmanus	Done-man-us
Knocknamaddree	Knock-na-mad-ree
Knockaphuca	Knock-a-fuka

CHAPTER 2

Fanore   Fan-oar
Lisdoonvarna   Lios-doon-varna
Sliabh Eibhe;   Sleave-aive

CHAPTER 4

Bhoireann   Vore-een

CHAPTER 6

Cullenagh   Cull-in-ack
Craic   Crack

CHAPTER 7

Moher   Mo-her
An Bord Pleanala   On Board Plan-all-a
An Taisce   On Task-a

CHAPTER 8

Slogadh   Slug-ah

CHAPTER 11

Scoil Eoin Baiste   Skull-Owen-Bosh-ta

CHAPTER 12

Diarmuid O Dalaigh	Dear-mud O Dall-ig
Pedraig O' Fiannachta	Paw-drig O Feen-ack-ta
Imblog	Imm-blog
Bealltaine	Beawl-ton-a
Lunasa	Loon-a-saw
Samhain	Sow-in
An Biobla Naofa	On Beeb-la Naof-a
Choisdealbha	Khus-dal-va

CHAPTER 13

Cruacha Dubna	Crook-a Duv-na
An Sliabh Corca	On Sleave Cork-a

CHAPTER 14

Allihies	All-e-his
Eyeries	Eye-rees
Coulagh	Cul-ack
An Cailleach Beara	On Call-ack Bare-a

CHAPTER 15

Foilnamuck	File-na-muck
Cappaghnacallee	Cap-a-na-call-a
Ballycummisk	Bally-come-isk

Chapter 16

Kilcrohane	Kill-crow-han
Ahakista	A-ha-kiss-taa
Fianna Ossin	Fen-a Osh-in

Chapter 17

Ilnacullin	Ill-na-cul-in
An Cheacfha	On Quaw-fa
Loch Uacharach	Lock- Uck-a-rock
Na Cruacha Dubha	Naw Crook-a Duv-a
Lough Mhucrois	Lock Muck-rosh

Chapter 20

Tinceir	Tin-care

NOTES

INTRODUCTION

xvii " . . . as elusive as the fairy gold": *Insight Guides: Ireland,* APA
Publications (1990), "The Irish Character," Brian Bell, p. 16

xvii " . . . In spite of all its old ways . . .": Joseph Harris, "Ireland
Unleashed," Smithsonian (March 2005)

CHAPTER 1

5   " . . . polite and lush . . .": *The Rough Guide to Ireland,* Penguin
Putnam USA (2001), p. 313

6   " . . . remote finger of land . . .": Rough Guide (see above) p. 306

CHAPTER 4

21   " First of all, there was a sense . . .": *The Book of the Burren,* Tir
Eolas (2001), "Ordinary People and the Mountain," Lelia
Doolan, p. 239

CHAPTER 5

28–29 Quotations from the introduction and various letters in *Letters of a Matchmaker,* John B. Keane, Mercier Press (1975)

30 " . . . a brogue soft enough . . .": *The Craic,* Phoenix (1999), Mark McCrum, p. 190

37 " . . . online dating, rather than being impersonal . . .": David Brooks, "Love, Internet Style," New York Times (November 8, 2003)

CHAPTER 6

42 "Would result in overdevelopment . . .": Gordon Deegan, "Euro 13 Million Cliffs of Moher Complex," Clare Champion (January 2, 2002)

46 An Instructive Example: data supplied by Denver International Airport

CHAPTER 8

60 "All the contestants have to be virgins": *www.holidayhound.com*

62 Official Lurcher & Staghound website: *www.users.daelnet.co.uk/lurchers*

CHAPTER 9

71 The Dolphin Academy: *www.curacao-tourism.com*

CHAPTER 10

80   "A Gaelic speaker will never say . . ." Conny van den Bor, "Revival of Irish Language," Radio Netherlands (December 27, 2001) *www.rnw.n1*

CHAPTER 12

96   " . . . its inhabitants moved elsewhere . . .": Kenmare Home Page, *www.neiden.net*

97   "Kenmare Kestrels Have Taken the Lead": *www.livejournal .com/communityhogwarts*

97–100 Background on Tidy Town movement and Kennelly poem from "A Report on Bord Failte's Tidy Towns Competition 1958–1982," an An/CoBord Failte Research Project

CHAPTER 13

105   Butte, Montana—Ireland's Fifth Province: *www.butteamerica .com/birish.htm*

108   " . . . one of the first great bowlers . . ." and background on road bowling: *Road Bowling in Ireland,* Brian Toal (1996)

116   "With their bag of spare clothes . . .": Riobard O'Dwyer, *www.rootsweb.com*

CHAPTER 15

135   " . . . rolling patchworks of green fields . . .": Kieran O'Reilly, New York Times (June 1, 1977)

135   " . . .wild fuchsia hedges . . .", Patrick Whitehurst, *www .finetravel.com*

CHAPTER 16

142   "An oasis in a desert . . .": Irish Tourist Board, St. Martins Press (2001), p. 358
143   " . . .climbed out of their carriages . . .": Irish Tourist Board (see above), p. 225
143   " . . . a handsome appendage . . .": *Ladies in Waiting,* St. Martins Press (1976), Dulcie Ashdown, p. 173
146–47 "Lake of Learning": *www.killarney.ac/innisfallentour,html*
147   " . . . [Annalists] admitted nothing . . .": *www.alia.ie/tirnanog/ sochis/xhtml*

CHAPTER 17

151   " . . . the work of Pat McAuliffe . . .": *Listowel and Its Vicinity (*1973), Rev. J. Anthony Gaughan, p. 505
155   " . . . three elements which largely constitute . . .": *Kerry on My Mind: Of Poets, Pedagogues and Place,* Salmon Publishing (1999), Gabriel Fitzmaurice, p. 49
156   "We spoke of many things . . . ": *Innocent Bystanders,* Mercier Press (1994), "Waiting for Tuesday," John B. Keane, p. 78
156   "Robert Emmet, a failed reformer . . .": *www.ireland-informa-tion.com/articles/robertemmet.htm*
158   "Emphasizes skill and tactics . . .": *The Oxford Companion to Irish History,* Oxford University Press (1999), p. 212
160   " . . .the boys and girls . . .": *Kerry on My Mind* (see above), p. 67

160   "At the Ball Game": *Kerry on My Mind* (see above), p. 72

CHAPTER 18

164   1901 data: *www.rootsweb.com~irlker/cenlist.html*
165   " . . . vivid recollection of The Market . . ." *The Master,*
        Poolbeg Enterprises (1993), Bryan MacMahon, p. 5
166–67 "The Singular Achievement of John B. Keane": *Kerry on My
        Mind.* (see above), p. 15
167   " . . . Jeremy-Diddler-kind of hotel . . . ": *www.biblomania.com*

CHAPTER 20

182   " . . . the workings of the Lartigue . . ." *Transport in Ireland
        1889–1910,* Flanigan, p. 178
183   "As its appearance . . .": *Listowel and Its Vicinity* (see above),
        p. 267
184   "Mons. Lartigue conceived the idea . . .": The Listowel and
        Ballybunion Railway, Oakwood Press, (1989), Michael
        Foster, pp. 20–22

CHAPTER 22

198   "He explained his style . . .": Shirley Kelly, "Books Ireland,"
        April 1994, pp. 73–74
200   " . . . feeling for romantic fiction . . .": Michael O'Reagan,
        Irish Times, August 1, 1995
200   "It is because we are men . . .": *The Key Above the Door,*
        Penguin (1958), Maurice Walsh, pp. 170–71

201   "Walsh was a bit amused. . .": *www.pgil-eirdata.org*

203   "Unafraid to see the world . . .": "The Magic Glasses of George Fitzmaurice," in *The Listowel Literary Phenomenon: North Kerry Writers,* Gabriel Fitzmaurice ed., pp. 13–25

204–7   Kennelly talks about himself in *A Time for Voices,* Bloodaxe Books, pp. 11–12

207   "Just experience it": *www.cnn.com/2000/fyi/teachers.tools*

CHAPTER 23

214   "Oh, Ireland, without a doubt . . .": "Money for Art's Sake," Jeremy Grant, Financial Times, July 26, 2003

214   "The Irish are good talkers . . .": "Irish Writer O'Faolain Brings Eloquent Anger to Aspen Fest," *Denver Post,* May 31, 2005

215   " . . . stories began to filter through . . .'; *Kerry on My Mind,* (see above) pp. 12–14

215   "Pots of gold, fairy forts . . .": *The Master,* (see above) p. 24

CHAPTER 25

235–36   "Irish Coffee": *www.bbc.co.uk/history*

INDEX

Maps and photographs are denoted by an *m* and *p*, respectively.

About the Author

Born in Detroit in 1926, Warren Rovetch completed his undergraduate studies at Wayne University in Detroit, and graduate studies at Oxford (Balliol College), where he was a Sir Robert Mayer Fellow and Fulbright Scholar, receiving his M. Phil. in economics in 1950.

Rovetch has been a government economist, an industrial engineer, a regional director for the Foreign Policy Association, and a consultant to colleges and universities. The first of his many entrepreneurial enterprises was Education Research Associates, where he created a Denver center for dropouts, and directed a study of post secondary education for the Colorado Legislature. His next step was Campus Facilities Associates, with a focus on campus planning and studies of institutional priorities. Foundations for Learning—the next company he started—published textbooks and trained teachers to achieve a new paradigm of teaching and learning, and was acquired by Simon & Schuster.

Rovetch then went on to establish Columbia River Properties and developed an environmentally based education and tour center on the Lewis and Clark Water Trail of the Lower Columbia River.

His travels began in 1946, his pre-creaky days, with a yearlong adventure through six countries of war-torn Europe. In England, he spent nearly six months giving current-events talks for the United States Information Agency and lectures on American history for a British army officers training program. Over the rest of the 20th century and into the 21st, Rovetch and his wife of 50 years made 25 extended trips to Europe and effected the transition from traveler to Creaky Traveler.

Sentient Publications, LLC publishes books on cultural creativity, experimental education, transformative spirituality, holistic health, new science, ecology, and other topics, approached from an integral viewpoint. Our authors are intensely interested in exploring the nature of life from fresh perspectives, addressing life's great questions, and fostering the full expression of the human potential. Sentient Publications' books arise from the spirit of inquiry and the richness of the inherent dialogue between writer and reader.

Our Culture Tools series is designed to give social catalyzers and cultural entrepreneurs the essential information, technology, and inspiration to forge a sustainable, creative, and compassionate world.

We are very interested in hearing from our readers. To direct suggestions or comments to us, or to be added to our mailing list, please contact:

SENTIENT PUBLICATIONS, LLC
1113 Spruce Street
Boulder, CO 80302
303-443-2188
contact@sentientpublications.com
www.sentientpublications.com

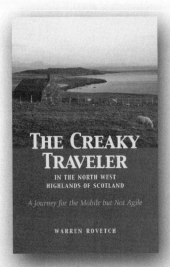

THE CREAKY
TRAVELER

IN THE NORTH WEST
HIGHLANDS OF SCOTLAND

A Journey for the Mobile but Not Agile

WARREN ROVETCH

The Creaky Traveler in the Northwest Highlands of Scotland explores the hidden places of Britain's last wilderness along the rugged coast of NW Scotland. Part travel story and part guidebook, but all charm and wit, this book transports us to another culture. On the way it details the planning and navigation tips essential for travelers who are "mobile but not agile" as well as for their younger counterparts.

Recommended on NPR's *Morning Edition*

"If the rest of this series is half as good as this first volume, we had best keep our bags packed."
—Donald Laing, *American Book Review*

"I have never met a travel book with so much love in it—for nature, for the oddities encountered, for good food, and for the privilege of living on this planet. The book is deliciously readable and reveals a breadth of curiosity that is enticing."
—Anthony Smith, *Explorers of the Amazon*

"This well researched, detailed and evocative book reminded us of why we moved to this most beautiful part of the world. The attention to detail, while not losing sight of the broader canvas, is reminiscent of Bill Bryson and Paul Theroux."
—Kevin Crowe & Simon Long,
Loch Croispol Bookshop and Restaurant, Durness

Available wherever books are sold and directly from the publisher via phone, mail, or web.

SENTIENT PUBLICATIONS
1113 Spruce St
Boulder, CO 80302
sentientpublications.com
(866) 588-9846 (toll-free)